EQUAL IS NOT ENOUGH

Discriminatierecht in theorie en praktijk / Discrimination law in theory and practice

Editors
Stefan Sottiaux en Jogchum Vrielink

EQUAL IS NOT ENOUGH

Edited by
Daniel CUYPERS
Jogchum VRIELINK

intersentia
Cambridge – Antwerp – Portland

Intersentia Ltd
Sheraton House | Castle Park
Cambridge | CB3 0AX | United Kingdom
Tel.: +44 1223 370 170 | Fax: +44 1223 370 169
Email: mail@intersentia.co.uk
www.intersentia.com | www.intersentia.co.uk

Distribution for the UK and Ireland:
NBN International
Airport Business Centre, 10 Thornbury Road
Plymouth, PL6 7 PP
United Kingdom
Tel.: +44 1752 202 301 | Fax: +44 1752 202 331
Email: orders@nbninternational.com

Distribution for Europe and all other countries:
Intersentia Publishing nv
Groenstraat 31
2640 Mortsel
Belgium
Tel.: +32 3 680 15 50 | Fax: +32 3 658 71 21
Email: mail@intersentia.be

Distribution for the USA and Canada:
International Specialized Book Services
920 NE 58th Ave. Suite 300
Portland, OR 97213
USA
Tel.: +1 800 944 6190 (toll free) | Fax: +1 503 280 8832
Email: info@isbs.com

ISBN 978-1-78068-406-2
D/2016/7849/116
NUR 823

British Library Cataloguing in Publication Data. A catalogue record for this book is available from the British Library.

CONTENTS

ABOUT THE AUTHORS

David Barrett (PhD) is a lecturer in law at Nottingham Law School (Nottingham Trent University). He holds a PhD in law from the University of Bristol. His PhD thesis examined how equality and human rights law could be utilised to address socio-economic inequality in England, particularly in the context of education. This combined doctrinal, theoretical, historical, inter-disciplinary and empirical methods. His research interests are focused upon issues of socio-economic inequality, the enforcement of equality law and human rights (particularly via regulators), and schools as sites of research for the implementation of law.

Daniël Cuypers is full professor at the Law Faculty of the University of Antwerp, teaching labour law and European discrimination law. After several years as a practising lawyer, he served many years as the academic secretary, vice-dean, member of the Research Council and now as a member of the Educational Council of the University. He is member of several editorial boards of law reviews and has published nearly 200 books and articles. He was the supervisor and a board member (2002–2016) of the (Flemish) *Policy Research Centre for Equal Opportunities*. He was the convenor of several international conferences in Antwerp (e.g. Equal is not Enough II (2010) and III (2015)).

Sarah Ganty is a researcher (PhD candidate) in law at the Institute for European Studies and the Perelman Centre for Legal Philosophy (Faculty of Law) of the *Université libre de Bruxelles*, since October 2013. Previously, she was a lawyer at the bar of Brussels and teaching assistant at the *Université catholique de Louvain*. Her research deals with civic integration policies for migrants in Europe and is conducted in the framework of an interdisciplinary research project *Action de recherche concertée*. Her fields of interest are migrant law (refugee law, immigration law and integration law), discrimination law and fundamental and human rights law. Sarah is part of Belgian non-profit organisations for migrants' rights and participates in the organisation of the *Université libre de Bruxelles* Equality Law Clinic. She is also affiliated with the research network 'The Global Challenge of Human Rights Integration: Towards a Users' Perspective'.

Erica Howard (PhD) is Associate Professor of Law at Middlesex University, London. She holds a PhD in European discrimination law. Her research areas include racial discrimination, religious discrimination, the right to freedom of religion and its intersection with other rights, including freedom of expression and the right not to be discriminated against on the ground of sexual orientation, and multiple discrimination. She has published two books and a number of articles on these subjects. Her website is: www.mdx.ac.uk/about-us/our-people/staff-directory/howard-erica.

Roberta Medda-Windischer (LLM, PhD), Senior Researcher and Group Leader for National Minorities, Migration and Cultural Diversity at the Institute for Minority Rights of the European Academy of Bolzano/Bozen, Italy (EURAC), is an international lawyer specialising in human rights and minority protection. Dr Medda-Windischer's research focuses on the protection of minorities in international law and on new minorities stemming from migration, on which she has authored and edited monographs and multi-authored volumes, and published numerous articles and chapters in edited volumes both in Italy and abroad.

Päivi Johanna Neuvonen was a post-doctoral research fellow at the Policy Research Centre on Equality Policies at KU Leuven until December 2015. She is currently a visiting fellow at the Centre for European Law and Internationalisation at the University of Leicester. She completed her doctorate in EU Law at the University of Oxford in 2014 and her first monograph *Equal Citizenship and Its Limits in EU Law: We the Burden?* was published by Hart Publishing (2016). Her research interests include EU law, anti-discrimination law, and European human rights law.

Sébastien van Damme holds a master's degree in law. Until recently, he worked as a PhD researcher and teaching assistant at the University of Antwerp (Research Group Social Competition and Law). He was also a member of the Policy Research Centre on Equality Policies. His research focuses on the intersection of European/international discrimination law and Belgian labour law, in particular the right to work of people with disabilities. Since October 2015 Sébastien van Damme has worked as a lawyer at the Antwerp Bar. He still publishes regularly in the field of labour law.

Jogchum Vrielink (PhD) is the coordinator of the Centre for Discrimination Law at the University of Leuven). He holds a PhD in law, and also studied public administration and anthropology. His PhD thesis concerned the topic of racist and anti-religious hate speech and Holocaust denial, and combined legal and socio-legal research. His research topics include discrimination law, fundamental and human rights (freedom of expression and freedom of religion in particular) and legal anthropology. Jogchum Vrielink has published widely in national and international journals and books on these issues. His website is: www.discriminationlaw.be

INTRODUCTION

Daniel Cuypers and Jogchum Vrielink

In February 2015 the University of Antwerp hosted the third *Equal is not Enough* conference. The conference was organised by the Flemish Policy Research Centre on Equality Policies (a consortium of the universities of Antwerp, Brussels, Ghent, Hasselt and Leuven).

The *Equal is not Enough* conferences have aimed, over the years, to generate a better understanding of what shapes and reshapes inequalities by inviting and promoting multi-disciplinary insights and reflection. In the third edition the conveners focused on the causes, consequences and the dynamics of inequality along socio-demographic lines in contemporary societies, and on policies to combat these inequalities.

One of the conference's sections focused on discrimination law. Discrimination law aims to lead, *inter alia*, to a more participatory society with respect for minority rights, and to a meritocratic labour market. The ethical and political aims of discrimination law are high, as is evidenced for instance by the relevant EU directives:

> 'Employment and occupation are key elements in guaranteeing equal opportunities for all and contribute strongly to the full participation of citizens in economic, cultural and social life and to realizing their potential' (consideration 9 FD 2000/78).

Discrimination law is, therefore, not (merely) an aim in itself; it is also considered instrumental to social policy and social justice.

The conveners (including the editors of this volume) welcomed papers on the relationship between social policy and discrimination law (or closely related human rights issues), which investigated the tensions and (in)compatibilities between the respective aims and tools of social policy and discrimination law. They were particularly interested in papers that transcend legal technicalities and reflect on the function of discrimination law as part of a wider social policy in the European Union and its member states. Likewise, multi- and interdisciplinary approaches were especially welcomed.

The call for papers, widely distributed in the summer of 2014, yielded 29 abstracts. Of those abstracts only 17 finally made it to the conference. The strict critical selection left substantial time for lively and academically satisfying discussion among participants and speakers, after the presentations in the workshops.

1. FROM CONFERENCE TO PROCEEDINGS

The authors of the best papers were asked to publish their text in the conference proceedings. The selection was made by the presidents of the workshops and the editors. Criteria for selection were: readability, documentation, critical analysis and relevance to social policy behind and within discrimination law. The contributors first rewrote their texts based on the comments they received in the workshop (internal peer review). Subsequently, the papers were submitted to a double-blind external peer-review process, following which the authors again revised their texts.

The choice was made to publish in the Intersentia book series *Discrimination Law in Theory and Practice* (series editors Stefan Sottiaux and Jogchum Vrielink), which aims to publish topical scholarship from within the field of discrimination law, *sensu lato*. The series is aimed at both academics and policy makers.

In short, within this volume the reader will find a high-quality selection of interesting papers presented at the Equal is not Enough conference. Below, the reader is provided with a preview of the texts, and why these make for such a thought-provoking read.

2. OVERVIEW

The first paper, by David Barrett, focuses on the issue of socio-economic inequality. Barrett shows how successive British governments have sought to address socio-economic inequality by means of a range of policies that have proved to have limited impact. The paper argues that different legal mechanisms being utilised in other countries (i.e. socio-economic rights and prohibiting discrimination on grounds of social condition) are more capable of addressing socio-economic inequality and thus should be adopted.

Subsequently, Roberta Medda-Windischer's paper addresses the question of housing rights and inclusion of Roma and Travellers. The paper tackles a highly controversial problem in the discrimination and human rights debate: how far can a State's duty to fulfil its positive obligations in order to respect the fundamental rights and freedoms under the ECHR be extended? Does the necessity of 'special consideration' also imply that the State should take into account the traditional lifestyle of minority groups? In light of recent and innovative rulings of the Strasbourg Court *vis-à-vis* Roma and Travellers' rights in the field of housing, the paper analyses whether, and if so in what circumstances, positive actions can be imposed on Member States in this context.

In the third paper Sébastien Van Damme analyses the concept of reasonable accommodation in disability case law. The very concept of reasonable accommodation is at the centre of the social model of disability and has, in many cases, proved to be an effective lever for disabled persons especially in the working context. Because the notion should be tailored to fit the various forms of disability, the proportionality test leaves a substantial margin of appreciation for the judge. The paper attempts, therefore, to elucidate the abstract right to reasonable accommodation in relation to the right to work.

Erica Howard likewise focuses on the duty of reasonable accommodation, but rather in the field of religion. She argues that there is no reason why the duty to make reasonable accommodation for people with disabilities, within EU law, could not be extended to include religious people and people with other characteristics which attract protection under anti-discrimination law. Even if this duty is *not* extended, Howard suggests that something which comes close to such a duty is already part of the concept of indirect discrimination.

In the fifth paper, Sarah Ganty focuses on integration policies for migrants, utilised as a prerequisite for obtaining certain rights or a specific legal status (so-called 'civic requirements'). In her paper, Ganty argues that civic integration requirements amount to differences in treatment on the basis of the socio-economic status of migrants: socio-economically underprivileged migrants are particularly disadvantaged. Focusing mainly on the Dutch and Belgian contexts, the paper analyses whether European and international anti-discrimination clauses – especially the ground of social condition – can be employed in order to protect migrants that are treated differently on the basis of their socio-economic situation within civic integration policies.

Jogchum Vrielink questions whether discrimination law really makes a difference, in practice, for (potential) victims. The paper firstly addresses research concerning the way in which victims make use of the legislation or – as is often the case – fail to do so: the issue of the so-called 'dark number'. Afterwards, several intended and unintended empirical effects that discrimination law may have are discussed. The picture that emerges from this is a complicated one. Although discrimination law has a number of unequivocally positive effects, there seems reason for caution too, as other research suggests that the legislation serves merely to shift or mask the phenomenon it purports to address, and it may even lead to counterproductive effects.

In the last paper Päivi Johanna Neuvonen tackles one of the cornerstones of discrimination law: the comparability test. She points out that this test may easily lead to a narrow view of what constitutes relevant subjectivity in discrimination law, and thereby result in an easy dismissal of discrimination claims. Her paper, as such, seeks to consider alternatives to the comparability analysis in discrimination law. Neuvonen proposes that discrimination law should move from a 'relative' to a more 'relational' ideal of equality, arguing that this would better reconcile the legal framework for combating discrimination with wider objectives of distributive social justice.

THE IMPORTANCE OF EQUALITY LAW AND HUMAN RIGHTS IN ADDRESSING SOCIO-ECONOMIC INEQUALITY

David BARRETT

1. INTRODUCTION

Socio-economic inequality is a major issue in the twenty-first century. This can be seen in the rapid rise of the Occupy movement which aims to mobilise the poorest 99% of the population to fight against socio-economic inequality and the political system that has allowed itself to be monopolised by the richest 1% to further their interests at the expense of the 99%. This resulted in protests in over 500 cities across the world.[1]

This brought the issue of socio-economic inequality starkly on to the political agenda and thus led to governments across the developed world introducing a range of measures aimed at improving this persistent form of inequality. This is particularly true of successive British governments who have sought to address socio-economic inequality primarily via the Child Poverty Act 2010 and various different policies (such as the Child Poverty Strategy and Social Mobility policies). At the same time, at the European level, action has been taken in the form of the Open Method of Coordination on Social Exclusion. This chapter argues that for a variety of reasons these have had limited impact. However there are various legal mechanisms currently being utilised in other countries (that is socio-economic rights and prohibiting discrimination on grounds of social condition). It will be argued that these are more capable of addressing socio-economic inequality and thus should be adopted. The chapter will begin by outlining what constitutes socio-economic inequality and illustrating to what extent it is a problem within the UK. It will then go on to assess the current mechanisms introduced to address it, before illustrating how socio-economic rights and extending equality law to cover social condition would be more able to fully address socio-economic inequality.

1 See: Occupy Movement, www.occupytogether.org (accessed 15 June 2014).

2. SOCIO-ECONOMIC INEQUALITY

Socio-economic inequality consists of three interlinked concepts: economic inequality, class and poverty. All aspects need to be addressed if socio-economic inequality is to be successfully tackled.

2.1. ECONOMIC INEQUALITY

Economic inequality concerns the difference in economic resources between individuals (particularly differences in individual salaries and holdings of capital). In the UK the top 1% of earners receive 15% of income.[2] This is high internationally, with only the USA having higher income inequality.[3] Although income inequality is high, these inequalities 'seem mild, moderate, and almost reasonable' compared to inequalities with respect to capital.[4] Capital is a bigger component of wealth by a factor of between five and six. Crucially it is also more unequally concentrated compared to income, with the top one per cent in the UK holding between 25–30% of capital and the top ten per cent holding around 70%.[5] A stabilising growth rate, higher returns on capital and a lowering demographic rate mean that economic inequality is only likely to increase in the future, to the extent that 'inequalities of wealth that had supposedly disappeared are close to regaining or even surpassing their historical highs'.[6]

High (and increasing) levels of economic inequality are significant because countries with higher economic inequality, such as the UK, have increased social problems such as lower levels of trust, higher levels of mental illness and drug use, reduced health and life expectancy, worse educational attainment, higher teenage birth rates, increased violence and higher prison populations.[7] Importantly these problems do not just affect the poorest but all members of society regardless of whether they are rich or poor.[8] For example the lowest income bracket in Sweden (one of the countries with the lowest levels of inequality) has a lower death rate than the highest social class in England and Wales.[9] Consequently, it is important to adopt measures to address rising economic inequality.

---

2 T. Piketty, *Capital in the Twenty-First Century* (Belknap Press 2014) 316.
3 Ibid. 317.
4 Ibid. 244.
5 Ibid. 346.
6 Ibid. 471.
7 R. Wilkonson & K. Pickett, *The Spirit Level: Why Greater Equality Makes Societies Stronger* (Bloomsbury 2009) 53, 66, 70, 87, 105, 122, 135, 145.
8 Ibid. 176.
9 Ibid. 178.

2.2. CLASS

However just addressing economic inequality is insufficient as even if some of the wealth of the rich was redistributed to the poor this does not mean that the poor would be able to effectively utilise this wealth as there are many barriers that exist in society which make it easier for some individuals to utilise assets than others. For example in 2014 70% of job offers at elite firms went to graduates who had been educated at selective state or fee-paying schools, compared to 4% and 7% of the population as a whole, with working class applicants needing higher qualifications to be appointed.[10] As a result there also needs to be an emphasis on class and removing barriers that prevent lower classes from achieving their potential.

Historically class scholarship has focused upon structural definitions of class through Marx (an individual's relationship to the means of production)[11] and Weber (an individual's market situation).[12] More recently these more economic conceptions of class have been challenged by Pierre Bourdieu's more social conception. Bourdieu argues that individuals possess various types of capital: economic, cultural (e.g. education and interests), social (e.g. connections) and symbolic (e.g. prestige). Individuals can exchange one sort of capital for another (for example exchange economic capital in the form of payment of university tuition fees into cultural capital in the form of a degree). Individuals utilise their capital to advance their position and thus a person's class is determined by how an individual's capital holdings compare to those of other individuals.[13]

This would not be particularly problematic if every individual had similar levels of capital (which economic inequality and poverty illustrate they do not) and equal opportunities to utilise them to do the things they value. However structures exist which make it easier for middle class individuals to accumulate certain types of capital and thus achieve success than working class individuals. In many cases this is actually encouraged and legitimised by the state. For example the education system favours middle class cultural capital (visiting historic sites, theatre, classical music and so on) over working class cultural capital (football, cinema, pop music and so on). Schools assume pupils will have undertaken these middle class activities with their parents prior and during a child's school years and base the curriculum and assessments upon

10 L. Ashley & others, 'A Qualitative Evaluation of Non-Educational Barriers to the Elite Professions' (Social Mobility and Child Poverty Commission 2015).

11 A. Giddens, *The Class Structure of the Advanced Societies* (2nd edn, Hutchinson 1981) 28.

12 H.H. Gerth & C. Wright Mils, *From Max Weber: Essays in Sociology* (Routledge and Kegan Paul 1948) 182.

13 P. Bourdieu, 'The Forms of Capital' in J.G. Richardson (ed.), *Handbook of Theory and Research for the Sociology of Education* (Greenwood Press 1986).

them.[14] However, most working class children have not undertaken these activities and as a result they struggle in school and consequently go on to achieve fewer qualifications than their middle class counterparts. Thus children receiving free school meals (the poorest children in the UK) 'are almost twice as likely to not meet expected standards in reading, writing and maths' and 62 per cent do not obtain at least five A*-C grades at GCSE (the uniform standard expected of all pupils).[15] Action to address socio-economic inequality thus needs to focus on dismantling structures that favour the middle classes over the working classes.

2.3. POVERTY

As with economic inequality, removing class structures is insufficient on its own to fully address socio-economic inequality; there also needs to be a focus on poverty. Focusing on technical concepts of economic inequality and class can overlook the desperate everyday existence of the poorest individuals in society and ignore the urgency of their situation. A focus on poverty ensures that this situation is at the forefront of efforts to address socio-economic inequality.

Poverty can be defined in various ways: economically (how far below a consumption/income line individuals fall – for example the UK and EU focus on individuals who have less than 60% of the median income of citizens), utilising the capability approach (that is a failure to achieve certain minimal or basic capabilities such as receiving an adequate education), or as social exclusion (the exclusion of individuals from full participation in society).[16] However one defines poverty, the UK has high levels of it. For example in 2012/13 around 13 million people were in economic poverty (their net yearly income was less than 60% of the median) with 6.6 million of these being in a family where someone worked.[17] Utilising the capability approach, poverty can be argued to be a problem within the UK as a significant number of children and young adults are not attaining the basic capabilities within education (in 2013 39 per cent of 16 year olds did not obtain at least five A*-C grades

---

14 P. Bourdieu, 'Cultural Reproduction and Social Reproduction' in J. Karabel & A.H. Halsey (eds.), *Power and Ideology in Education* (Oxford University Press 1977).

15 T. Macinnes & others, *Monitoring Poverty and Social Exclusion 2014* (Joseph Rowntree Foundation 2014) 126–128; Department for education, 'GCSE and Equivalent Results in England 2012/13 (Revised)' (SFR 01/2014, DfE 23 January 2014).

16 C. Ruggeri Laderchi, R. Saith & F. Stewart, 'Does it Matter that we do not Agree on the Definition of Poverty? A Comparison of Four Approaches' (2003) 31(3) Oxford Development Studies 243.

17 T. Macinnes & others, *Monitoring Poverty and Social Exclusion 2014* (Joseph Rowntree Foundation 2014) 26.

(including English and Maths) at GCSE).[18] Finally, in terms of social exclusion, 52,000 households were accepted as homeless in 2013/14,[19] and 2.24 million people were unemployed.[20]

Action to address socio-economic inequality thus needs to reduce economic inequality, remove barriers that favour middle class individuals over working class individuals and to take individuals out of poverty. Various measures have been introduced to attempt to achieve this. The next section will outline these and assess their success in reducing socio-economic inequality.

3. CURRENT MECHANISMS TO ADDRESS SOCIO-ECONOMIC INEQUALITY

The UK has introduced a wide range of measures in an attempt to address socio-economic inequality. These include the Child Poverty Act 2010 and child poverty and social mobility policies. Current equality law has also often been claimed as a way of addressing socio-economic inequality. At the European Level, the Social Exclusion Open Method of Coordination was introduced in an attempt to address socio-economic inequality across Europe. These will be discussed in turn and their success in addressing socio-economic inequality will be assessed.

3.1. THE CHILD POVERTY ACT 2010

The Child Poverty Act places a duty on the Secretary of States for Work and Pensions and Education to meet four targets by 1st April 2020.[21] These are that less than 10% of children in the UK live in households where the net income is less than 60% of the UK median income at the time (the relative low income target);[22] less than 5% of children live in households where the net income is less than 70% of the median income and they are experiencing material deprivation – that is they lack the basic goods and services that they need (the combined low income and material deprivation target);[23] less than 5% of children live in households where the net income is less than 60% of the adjusted base amount (i.e. the 2020 equivalent of the median income in 2010) (the absolute low

18 Department for education, 'GCSE and Equivalent Results in England 2012/13 (Revised)' (SFR 01/2014, DfE 23 January 2014).
19 T. Macinnes & others, *Monitoring Poverty and Social Exclusion 2014* (Joseph Rowntree Foundation 2014) 54.
20 Office for national statistics, 'Labour Market Statistics, April 2014' (Office for National Statistics 2014).
21 Child Poverty Act 2010, s 2.
22 Ibid. s 3.
23 Ibid. s 4.

income target);[24] and that under a specified percentage of children (7% has been proposed)[25] have lived in households where the median income is less than 60% for at least three years (the persistent poverty target).[26] The Act requires a strategy to be produced by the government that outlines the approaches that will be taken to meet these targets.[27] These include improving the employment situation of parents (i.e. creating more and better jobs), reducing the cost of living and increasing the quality of education.[28] The Act also requires local authorities and partner authorities to make arrangements to cooperate 'with a view to reducing, and mitigating the effects of, child poverty in the responsible local authority's area' and this must include producing a local child poverty needs assessment.[29]

The Act does not provide for any specific legal mechanisms to challenge failure to meet the targets or failure to comply with the terms. Despite this the Child Poverty Action Group did bring successful judicial review proceedings to challenge the first child poverty strategy that was produced on the basis that the Act required that the Secretary of State requested the advice of the Child Poverty Commission and have regard to this advice when producing the strategy.[30] As the Commission had not yet been established by the time the Secretary produced the strategy, the Court declared that producing the strategy without seeking their advice was a breach of the Act.[31] Consequently it is likely that legal actions could also be brought if the Secretary of State fails to comply with the procedural requirements of producing the strategy[32] or fails to consult with bodies listed within the Act.[33] Proceedings could also probably be brought against local authorities that do not make arrangements to promote cooperation and do not publish a local child poverty needs assessment.[34] Given that the statutory targets are likely to be missed by a 'considerable margin'[35] it is unclear whether, after the target year (the 2020 financial year), proceedings can be brought against the Secretary of State for failure of their duty to ensure the targets are met.[36] Even if this is possible (which is unlikely) any remedy

24 Ibid. s 5.

25 Secretary of State for Work and Pensions, *Consultation on setting the 2020 persistent child poverty target* (Cmd 8875, 2014) para 20.

26 Child Poverty Act 2010, s 6.

27 Ibid. s 9.

28 HM Government, 'Child Poverty Strategy 2014–17' (HMSO 2014).

29 Ibid. ss 21–22.

30 This requirement has since been repealed.

31 *R. (on the application of Child Poverty Action Group)* v *Secretary of State for Work and Pensions, Secretary of State for Education* [2012] EWHC 2579.

32 Child Poverty Act 2010, s 9.

33 Ibid. s 10.

34 Ibid. ss 21–22.

35 Social mobility and child poverty commission, *Response to the consultation on the Child Poverty Strategy 2014 to 2017* (Social Mobility and Child Poverty Commission 2014) para 32.

36 Child Poverty Act 2010, s 2.

would be limited as the court is unlikely to award a mandatory order to require the Secretary of State to meet the targets. Additionally having to wait until 2020 to bring legal proceedings can also be criticised as this is likely to lead to increasing socio-economic inequality. As a result mechanisms to challenge socio-economic inequality via the Child Poverty Act can be argued to be extremely limited, being confined solely to failure to comply with procedural requirements and even if successful they are unlikely to have a significant impact on eradicating child poverty.

3.2. GOVERNMENT POLICIES

In contrast to legal mechanisms, historically UK governments have attempted to address socio-economic inequality via various policy initiatives. In this regard the Coalition Government adopted Child Poverty[37] and Social Mobility Policies.[38] Both place significant emphasis on schools, with education being 'one of the main routes out of poverty' and aiming for schools to 'be engines of social mobility'.[39] One of the main measures for achieving this is the Pupil Premium where schools are given additional funding (in 2014/15 this was £1,300 for primary pupils and £935 for secondary pupils) for every poor child (any child who has been eligible for free school meals in the last six years).[40] The school is responsible for utilising this funding to produce 'an excellent and individually tailored education for these children'.[41]

Although these policies have advantages, and can contribute to improving socio-economic inequality, leaving responses solely to policy can be criticised on a number of grounds. Firstly, policies lack permanency. Thus the previous Labour Government also had a social mobility policy that focused on modernising and rebuilding school buildings and introducing flexibility into the curriculum so it would be relevant and engaging for all.[42] Yet when the Coalition were elected they stopped the Building Schools for the Future Scheme[43] and produced a 'very

37 Secretary of State for Work and Pensions, *Child Poverty Strategy 2014–17* (Department for Work and Pensions 2014).

38 HM Government, *Opening Doors, Breaking Barriers: A Strategy for Social Mobility* (Cabinet Office 2011).

39 Secretary of State for Work and Pensions, *Child Poverty Strategy 2014–17* (Department for Work and Pensions 2014) 36; HM Government, *Opening Doors, Breaking Barriers: A Strategy for Social Mobility* (Cabinet Office 2011) 36.

40 Secretary of State for Work and Pensions, *Child Poverty Strategy 2014–17* (Department for Work and Pensions 2014) 38.

41 HM Government, *Opening Doors, Breaking Barriers: A Strategy for Social Mobility* (Cabinet Office 2011) 38.

42 HM Government, *New Opportunities: Fair Chances for the Future* (Cmd 7533, 2009) paras 4.3 and 4.18.

43 H. Richardson, 'School buildings scheme scrapped' (BBC, 5 July 2010).

heavily prescribed' national curriculum.[44] Thus there is nothing preventing a different government undoing the Coalition initiatives in the future. This is problematic because, as the Coalition Government correctly recognised, achieving socio-economic equality is 'a long-term undertaking … [t]here is no magic wand we can wave to see immediate effects'.[45] The consequences of using a solely policy-led approach is that any measures likely to improve socio-economic inequality are not in place long enough to have a significant impact and where improvements are made these can be undone by new policy initiatives of future governments.

Secondly, as policies tend to be less prescribed than laws, there is more potential for them to conflict and counter other policies. For example, in addition to introducing the pupil premium, the Coalition later introduced free school meals for all 4–6 year olds.[46] This has resulted in a significant decline in students receiving the pupil premium as it is reliant on the poorest parents completing forms to ensure their children receive free school meals but as meals are now free for all 4–6 year olds there is no incentive for parents of these children to complete these forms. This means that it is often difficult for schools to help these children and thus by the time the forms are completed and they are eligible for additional funding (at aged 7) they are already significantly far behind other children.

Thirdly, recent policies have been very focused upon poverty. Whilst important, this neglects issues of class and economic inequality which means that policies tend to be built upon middle class values. For example part of the Child Poverty strategy is to provide parenting classes to help parents to 'parent well'. Parenting well involves 'helping their child in learning activities (e.g. teaching songs and nursery rhymes, playing with letters and numbers and visiting the library)'.[47] This is problematic as it assumes a middle class model of parenting (i.e. that parents should be co-educators).[48] This differs from the role working class parents have traditionally seen for themselves, being supportive rather than compensatory and interventionist.[49] Although different, neither approach has a greater impact on the educational outcomes of children,

---

44 R. Garner, '100 academies savage Education Secretary Michael Gove for 'conveyor-belt curriculum' for schools, *The Independent* (London, 19 March 2013).

45 HM Government, *Opening Doors, Breaking Barriers: A Strategy for Social Mobility* (Cabinet Office 2011) 3.

46 Education Act 1996, s 512ZB.

47 Secretary of State for Work and Pensions, *Child Poverty Strategy 2014–17* (Department for Work and Pensions 2014) 42.

48 S.J. Ball, 'New class inequalities in education: Why education policy may be looking in the wrong place! Education policy, civil society and social class' (2010) 30(3/4) International Journal of Sociology and Social Policy 155, 163.

49 D. Reay, 'Education and Cultural Capital: The Implications of Changing Trends in Education Policies' (2004) 13(2) 50 Cultural Trends 73, 77.

with it being parental class that makes the difference.[50] Despite this, working-class parents are 'blamed for the under-attainment of their children … [and characterised] as providing limited support to their children's learning, having deficient parenting skills, being socially isolated and lacking in self-confidence and self-esteem'.[51] Additionally, it assumes working class parents do not help with their child's learning either because they do not want to or they lack the ability to and thus need to be educated how to do so. In reality they may be unable to do this as they are expected to both work their way out of poverty at the same time as educating their children, a requirement that middle class parents do not face.[52]

Finally there is no necessity to act. Whilst there may be political impetus to act and political accountability for failed attempts to act, there is no requirement to take particular actions or for policies to address socio-economic inequality to be given a high priority. This is recognised by the Social Mobility and Child Poverty Commission in their response to the Child Poverty Strategy consultation. Whilst supportive of many aspects of the strategy, they were critical that the strategy had not been reconciled with government action to reduce the deficit which could result in many of the initiatives being undone by reduction measures elsewhere. As a result the Commission recommended giving the Office of Budget Responsibility a role in independently assessing the social mobility and child poverty impact of budgets and carrying out cumulative impact assessments of future cuts.[53] However this recommendation was not adopted by the Government in their Child Poverty Strategy suggesting that eradicating child poverty is not as a high a priority as they claim.

3.3. CURRENT EQUALITY LAW

Although equality law was not purposefully intended to improve socio-economic inequality, some scholars have recognised that it can indirectly have this effect.[54] British equality law currently covers a range of protected characteristics including age, disability, race, sex and sexual orientation. Successful claims can have a redistributive dimension.[55] This is illustrated by equal pay provisions which allow women to claim equality of pay with male workers in like work,

50 D. Hartas, 'Parenting for social mobility? Home learning, parental warmth, class and educational outcomes' (2015) 30(1) Journal of Education Policy 21.

51 S. Gewirtz, 'Cloning the Blairs: New Labour's programme for the re-socialization of working-class parents' (2001) 16(4) Journal of Education Policy 365, 375.

52 Ibid. 374.

53 Social Mobility and Child Poverty Commission, *Response to the consultation on the Child Poverty Strategy 2014 to 2017* (Social Mobility and Child Poverty Commission 2014) para 75.

54 H. Collins, 'Discrimination, Equality and Social Inclusion' (2003) 66(1) Modern Law Review 16.

55 S. Fredman, *Discrimination Law* (2nd edn, Oxford University Press 2011) 26.

work rated as equivalent or work of equal value. Thus in *Abdulla*[56] 170 women employed by Birmingham City Council were successful in equal pay claims which meant that they were, for the first time, able to afford things that many people take for granted, such as a new kitchen or a deposit for their grandchild to buy a house.[57] In addition, indirect discrimination allows individuals to challenge provisions, criteria or practices that put people of a protected characteristic at a particular disadvantage. Thus policies and practices which prevented part-time workers from access to pensions, protection against unfair dismissal and equal hourly pay were held to indirectly discriminate against women (as they are more likely to undertake part-time work).[58] Finally, the public sector equality duty requires public sector bodies to integrate equality thinking into their decision making and thus consider how decisions will impact protected groups. Where this is not clearly followed, decisions and policies can be challenged via judicial review. This can be seen in *Bracking* where the decision to close the Independent Living Fund (a non-departmental public body which provides funding to over 19,000 disabled people to allow them to live independently) was quashed for a failure to clearly and transparently consider how this decision would impact on disabled individuals.[59]

Groups sharing 'protected characteristics' (as defined in section 1 of the Equality Act 2010) are more likely to be in poverty or earn less. Thus 27% of female employees are paid below the living wage (cf 15% of men) and the gender pay gap is 19.7%; 24% of families with a member who is disabled are in poverty (cf 20% of families with no disabled members); and only 7% of working age white individuals are unemployed (cf 15.5% Black and 17.3% mixed ethnicity).[60] As a result current equality law can be utilised strategically in order to address socio-economic inequality. For example 43% of Black Caribbean pupils do not get 5 A*-C grades at GCSE. If there was a provision, criteria or practice that caused this it could be argued to be indirectly discriminatory and, if proved, could indirectly pressure for its removal. Although this would primarily advance the position of Black Caribbean pupils it could also be advantageous to white working class pupils (with 68% of white British pupils receiving free school meals failing to obtain 5 A*-C grades) and thus be an indirect mechanism for

---

56 *Birmingham City Council* v *Abdulla and others* [2012] UKSC 47.

57 C. Davies, 'Equal pay: the women who won case against Birmingham city council' *The Guardian* (London, 11 April 2014).

58 Case 1007/84 *Bilka-Kaufhaus* [1986] ECR 1607; *R* v *Secretary of State for Employment, ex parte Equal Opportunities Commission* [1994] IRLR 176.

59 *R. (on the application of Bracking)* v *Secretary of State for Work and Pensions* [2013] EWCA Civ 1345.

60 T. Macinnes & others, *Monitoring Poverty and Social Exclusion 2013* (Joseph Rowntree Foundation 2013) 28 and 44; D. Bovill, 'Patterns of Pay: Results from the Annual Survey of Hours and Earnings, 1997 to 2012' (ONS 2013); Institute of Race Relations, 'Poverty, Inequality, Employment and Health' www.irr.org.uk.

improving socio-economic inequality.[61] This can also be seen with the Public Sector Equality Duty where non-compliance can be challenged by judicial review and thus decisions to stop school building projects[62] and to reduce welfare rights and advice services were quashed for failing to comply with the duty in relation to disability, race and sex.[63] Although these decisions were advantageous to disabled individuals, ethnic minorities and women, they were also advantageous for a wide range of other groups suffering from socio-economic inequality (i.e. they too would benefit from new schools and access to a comprehensive welfare rights and advice service).

Despite these advantages, relying on current equality law to address socio-economic inequality would ultimately be limited. Many of the most useful provisions are capable of justification (e.g. equal pay and indirect discrimination). This could allow economic considerations to trump social ones. For example in *Seymour-Smith,* the House of Lords accepted that a two-year qualifying period for employees to be able to claim unfair dismissal which indirectly discriminated against women (which increased the precarious nature of many women's work and thus their likelihood of experiencing poverty) was justifiable as it encouraged employers to recruit more individuals.[64] Additionally, it would only be an ad hoc solution, as although in some situations cases could be utilised to advance the situation of a significant number of disadvantaged people, often they will just be of benefit to the claimant (thus having little or no impact on structural barriers of class), or individuals with a particular characteristic (such as the disabled).[65] Furthermore, an action that benefits a wide range of individuals may be challenged by individuals with a specific characteristic. This can be seen in *Kaur* where a decision to prioritise groups which provided services to all women experiencing violence was successfully challenged by black and ethnic minority women for failing to take due regard of their interests.[66] Equality law also often benefits the 'creamy layer' of a disadvantaged group rather than the group as a whole thus it is likely that decisions are more likely to favour the wealthy.[67] This is furthered by the fact that legal action is often very expensive and thus in most cases the people that will most benefit from an action will be unable to bring them. Finally, even if a claim is successful it does not mean that the overall result will be positive. This is illustrated in *Bracking* where although the claimant

61 T. Macinnes & others *Monitoring Poverty and Social Exclusion 2014* (Joseph Rowntree Foundation 2014) 128–129.

62 *R. (on the application of Luton BC and others)* v *Secretary of State for Education* [2011] EWHC 217; *R. (on the application of Essex CC)* v *Secretary of State for Education* [2012] EWHC 1460.

63 *R. (on the application of Meany and others)* v *Harlow DC* [2009] EWHC 559.

64 R. v *Secretary of State for Employment, ex parte Seymour-Smith* (No. 2) [2000] 1 WLR 435.

65 *R. (on the application of Bracking)* v *Secretary of State for Work and Pensions* [2013] EWCA Civ 1345.

66 *R. (on the application of Kaur and another)* v *London Borough of Ealing* [2008] EWHC 2062.

67 K. Sankaran, Towards Inclusion and Diversity: India's Experience with Affirmative Action' in O. Dupper & C. Garbers (eds), *Equality in the Workplace* (Juta 2010).

was successful in quashing the decision to close the Independent Living Fund the decision was simply taken again, this time with full compliance with the procedural requirements of the Public Sector Equality Duty.[68] Thus, although existing equality law can contribute to improving socio-economic inequality, it is partial and ad hoc and not able to offer a comprehensive approach.

3.4. OPEN METHOD OF COORDINATION

The Open Method of Coordination (OMC) is a soft law mechanism introduced by the EU. It involves 'fixing guidelines for the Union combined with specific timetables for achieving the goals which they set in the short, medium and long terms; establishing, where appropriate, quantitative and qualitative indicators and benchmarks against the best in the world and tailored to the needs of different Member States and sectors as a means of comparing best practice; translating these European guidelines into national and regional policies by setting specific targets and adopting measures, taking into account national and regional differences; periodic monitoring, evaluation and peer review organised as mutual learning processes.'[69] This allows 'the Commission, Member States and other actors to have a constructive exchange about shared policy objectives, good practice and good governance, all the while respecting subsidiarity.'[70]

There are various streams of the OMC but the ones that are most relevant to socio-economic inequality are the employment, social inclusion and reform of pensions streams. The principal advantages of the OMC are 'that it provides the means to move towards common solutions to common problems without demanding the sort of harmonisation that would be anathema to many governments, and that it can be implemented by governments without recourse to major and potentially contested legislative change'.[71] Additionally the OMC has contributed to cognitive shifts (by exposing policy makers to new approaches and encouraging them to challenge long-established policies); political shifts (by placing new issues on the domestic political agenda); and programmatic shifts (by contributing to changes in specific national policies).[72]

In addition to these advantages, the OMC has numerous other benefits that could potentially contribute to the achievement of socio-economic equality. It

68 'Disability Living Fund closure to go ahead – minister', BBC, 6 March 2014.

69 Lisbon European Council 23 and 24 March 2000, Presidency Conclusions, Conclusion 37.

70 European Commission, 'Working together, working better: A new framework for the open coordination of social protection and inclusion policies in the European Union' (Communication) COM (2005) 706 final, 2.

71 B. Ardy & I. Begg, 'The European Employment Strategy: Policy Integration by the Back Door?' South Bank European Papers, No 4/2001, South Bank University European Institute, 11.

72 J. Zeitlin, 'Is the Open Method of Coordination Alternative to the Community Method?' in R. Dehousse (ed.), *The Community Method: Obstinate or Obsolete?* (Palgrave Macmillan 2011) 135, 142.

contributes to better horizontal coordination and cross sectorial integration of interdependent policy areas.[73] This is important as the causes of disadvantage are interlinked so there needs to be a coordinated effort in various different policy areas (e.g. schools working with health services to improve the health of socio-economically disadvantaged children).[74] It also enhances vertical coordination between national, regional and local governments.[75] This is particularly important in the UK with separate governments for Scotland, Wales and Northern Ireland and a north/south divide in England between a rich south and a significantly poorer north. It increases the involvement of non-state actors such as charities and non-governmental organisations.[76] Additionally, it helps identify blind spots where more information is needed on a particular situation.[77] Finally, it is much more likely than hard law to affect deep-seated values and attitudes and thus lead to real change.[78]

Despite these advantages the OMC is often criticised. Some oppose its 'weak' nature compared with the hard Community Method (the usual method of decision-making which results in binding laws being adopted) and argue that it lacks the legitimacy of the Community Method as it has a vastly decreased role for the Court, the Parliament and the European Council/Council of Ministers.[79] However, these criticisms can be countered by the fact that evidence suggests that the OMC is used alongside the Community Method rather than as an alternative to it.[80] The process can also be very bureaucratic in places (for example the way the guidelines and targets are formulated) but also very soft-touch in others (such as the short process of peer review).[81] There is also no definition of what constitutes good practice and little existence of innovative approaches, thus there is little to guide member states.[82] Finally, it has had little

73 Ibid 143.

74 HM Government, 'New Opportunities: Fair Changes for the Future' (The Stationary Office 2009).

75 J. Zeitlin, 'Is the Open Method of Coordination Alternative to the Community Method?' in R. Dehousse (ed.), *The Community Method: Obstinate or Obsolete?* (Palgrave Macmillan 2011) 135, 143.

76 Ibid.

77 M. Ferrera, M. Matsaganis & S. Sacchi, 'Open coordination against poverty: the new EU 'social inclusion process'' (2002) 12(3) Journal of European Social Policy 227, 236.

78 D. Trubek & L. Trubek, 'Hard and Soft Law in the Construction of Social Europe: the Role of the Open Method of Co-ordination' (2005) 11(3) European Law Journal 343.

79 J. Zeitlin, 'Is the Open Method of Coordination Alternative to the Community Method?' in R. Dehousse (ed.), *The Community Method: Obstinate or Obsolete?* (Palgrave Macmillan 2011) 135, 137.

80 Ibid.

81 T. Sakellaropoulos 'The open method of coordination: A sound instrument for the modernisation of the European Social Model' in T. Sakellaropoulos & J. Berghman (eds.), *Connecting Welfare Diversity within the European Social Model* (Intersentia 2004) 55.

82 M. Daly, 'Whither EU Social Policy? An Account and Assessment of Developments in the Lisbon Social Inclusion Process' (2007) 37(1) Journal of Social Policy 1, 12; T. Sakellaropoulos, 'The open method of coordination: A sound instrument for the modernisation of the

practical impact. This is because it has been presented as a discretionary policy.[83] This has meant that actors have been reluctant to engage with the OMC[84] and even where they have engaged, the involvement of non-state actors and interest groups has been limited, especially in the UK.[85] For example, rather than national action plans driving domestic priorities as they are supposed to, the UK plan has simply reflected its existing priorities.[86] As a result, although the OMC could contribute to improving socio-economic inequality in theory, in practice it is currently having very little impact.

4. ALTERNATE MECHANISMS TO ADDRESS SOCIO-ECONOMIC INEQUALITY

In order to address socio-economic inequality a number of states have adopted more wide-ranging legal mechanisms, such as incorporating socio-economic rights into domestic law, and prohibiting discrimination on the basis of social condition. This section will examine these provisions in more depth and examine how they are being utilised to address socio-economic inequality.

4.1. SOCIO-ECONOMIC RIGHTS

The UK has signed and ratified numerous human rights treaties, however as a largely dualist legal system they are not justiciable within UK courts unless they are incorporated by an Act of Parliament.[87] For example the European Convention on Human Rights was not justiciable until it was incorporated by the Human Rights Act 1998. There are a variety of treaty regimes that the UK are members of that contain economic and social rights: the Universal Declaration of Human Rights, the International Covenant on Economic, Social and Cultural Rights (ICESCR), the International Covenant on Civil and Political Rights (ICCPR), the European Social Charter (ESC) and the Conventions and Recommendations of the International Labour Organization (ILO). These

---

European Social Model' in T. Sakellaropoulos & J. Berghman (eds.), *Connecting Welfare Diversity within the European Social Model* (Intersentia 2004) 55.

83 S. Fredman, *Human Rights Transformed: Positive Rights and Positive Duties* (Oxford University Press 2008) 162.

84 D. Ashiagbor, *The European Employment Strategy: Labour Market Regulation and New Governance* (Oxford University Press 2005) 225.

85 Ibid 225, 229.

86 E. Macphail, 'Examining the impact of the Open Method of Coordination on sub-state employment and social inclusion policies: evidence from the UK' (2010) 20(4) Journal of European Social Policy 364, 368.

87 D. Feldman, 'The Internationalization of Public Law and its Impact on the UK' in J. Jowell & D. Oliver (eds.), *The Changing Constitution* (7th edn, Oxford University Press 2011).

contain rights such as the right to social security, the right to just and favourable working conditions, the right to an adequate standard of living, the right to education and the right to the enjoyment of the highest attainable standard of physical and mental health. However these treaties have not been incorporated into domestic law so they are not justiciable within UK courts.

In contrast to the UK, the Bill of Rights within the South African Constitution specifically includes a wide range of justiciable socio-economic rights.[88] These were included to tackle the great inequalities that existed between black and white South Africans under apartheid.[89] The state is required to respect, protect, promote and fulfil these rights[90] and courts are required to interpret them to promote human dignity, equality and freedom.[91] As a result the courts have been able to address many issues of socio-economic inequality. Under section 10, the right to dignity, the courts required national authorities to allow asylum seekers to work where this is their only means of subsistence as 'dignity has no nationality. It is inherent in all people – citizens and non-citizens alike – simply because they are human'.[92] Under section 26, the right of access to adequate housing, the courts have required the state to devise and implement a coherent co-ordinated programme that provides relief to those desperately in need of housing[93] and that the courts should supervise eviction to ensure individuals are not evicted for trifling debt.[94] Under section 27, the right of access to health care services, sufficient food and water and social security, the courts have held that restrictions on access to anti-HIV drugs that prevent mother to child infection should be removed and that the drug should be made available at clinics and hospitals and that social security provisions should be read as including non-citizens who are permanently resident as well as citizens.[95]

A significant criticism of socio-economic rights is that they are too indeterminate to be utilised by courts and thus that, at most, they should be seen as aspirational principles to be aspired to by politicians.[96] However they

---

88 Constitution of the Republic of South Africa, 1996.

89 E.C. Christiansen, 'Adjudicating Non-Justiciable Rights: Socio-Economic Rights and the South African Constitutional Court' (2007) 38 Columbia Human Rights Law Review 321, 325.

90 The obligations to respect, to protect and fulfil are also recognised at the international level in relation to the ICESCR via the Limburg Principles.

91 Constitution of the Republic of South Africa, 1996, ss 7(2) and 39(1).

92 *The Minster of Home Affairs* v *Watchenuka* [2003] ZASCA 142, para 25.

93 *The Government of the Republic of South Africa v Grootboom* [2000] ZACC 14; *City of Johannesburg Metropolitan Municipality v Blue Moonlight Properties 39 (PTY) LTD* 2012 (2) SA 104 (CC).

94 *Jaftha v Schoeman, Van Rooyen v Stoltz* 2005 (2) SA 140 (CC).

95 *Minister of Health v Treatment Action Campaign (No 2)* 2002 (5) SA 721 (CC); *Khosa v The Minister of Social Development, Mahlaule v The Minister of Social Development* 2004 (6) SQ 505 (CC).

96 C. Gearty & V. Mantouvalou, *Debating Social Rights* (Hart Publishing 2011) 1, 8.

have been operationalised by the courts in South Africa to arrive at determinate standards which can be utilised to assess government compliance. The socio-economic rights contained within the South African constitution require reasonable legislative and other measures.[97] By adopting such measures the rights acquire content and that content is subject to the constitutional standard of reasonableness.[98] The South African Constitutional Court has recognised that this is not an 'impossible standard of perfection', a wide range of responses could be said to be reasonable and that the standard is applicable to implementation measures as well as legislative measures.[99] Reasonableness requires the government 'to explain the choices it has made ... [and] provide the information it has considered and the process it has followed to determine its policy'.[100] It must also show 'that the policy is being reconsidered consistent with the obligation to "progressively realise" social and economic rights'.[101] A number of open-ended, non-exhaustive indicators of reasonableness have been adopted[102] including reasonable formulation and implementation of programmes;[103] transparency;[104] non-discrimination against groups in their access to relevant programmes;[105] the impact of the deprivation on other rights such as life, dignity and equality;[106] meaningful engagement with affected groups; and the availability of resources.[107]

Utilising the reasonableness standard the courts have adopted a role for themselves that balances the need to guard the constitution against the need to work alongside the democratically elected government to consolidate the transition from apartheid to democracy.[108] Under this role they simply 'make suggestions for possible policy alternatives that in general only constrain the government's options within a certain range, rather than directing any one particular outcome'.[109] Thus in *Soobramoney* the Constitutional Court

---

97 *The Government of the Republic of South Africa v Grootboom* [2000] ZACC 14, para 28.

98 *Mazibuko v City of Johannesburg* 2010 (4) SA 1 (CC), para 66.

99 Ibid. para 161; *The Government of the Republic of South Africa v Grootboom* [2000] ZACC 14, paras 41–42.

100 *Mazibuko v City of Johannesburg* 2010 (4) SA 1 (CC), para 71.

101 Ibid. para 162.

102 *Khosa v The Minister of Social Development, Mahlaule v The Minister of Social Development* 2004 (6) SA 505 (CC), para 44; G. Quinot & S. Liebenberg, 'Narrowing the Band: Reasonableness Review in Administrative Justice and Socio-Economic Rights Jurisprudence in South Africa' (2011) 3 Stellenbosch Law Review 639, 656.

103 *The Government of the Republic of South Africa v Grootboom* [2000] ZACC 14, paras 40–43.

104 *Minister of Health v Treatment Action Campaign (No 2)* 2002 (5) SA 721 (CC), para 123.

105 *Khosa v The Minister of Social Development, Mahlaule v The Minister of Social Development* 2004 (6) SA 505 (CC), para 44.

106 Ibid.

107 *The Government of the Republic of South Africa v Grootboom* [2000] ZACC 14, para 46.

108 T. Roux, 'Legitimating Transformation: Political Resource Allocation in the South African Constitutional Court' (2003) 10(4) Democratization 92, 101–105.

109 P. Nolette, 'Lessons Learned from the South African Constitutional Court: Toward a Third Way of Judicial Enforcement of Socio-Economic Rights' (2003) 12 Michigan State Journal of

refused to order the state to provide kidney dialysis to the appellant as these choices involve 'difficult decisions to be taken at the political level in fixing the health budget, and at the functional level in deciding upon the priorities to be met'.[110] In *Grootboom* the Court held that the state's housing programme was unreasonable as it failed to provide relief to those desperately in need of housing. They did not require any specific programme be adopted but that the state devised and implemented a comprehensive and coordinated programme that incorporated those desperately in need of housing, the details of which were left at the state's discretion.[111] Finally, in *Treatment Action Campaign*, the Court did require a specific remedy (i.e. that a HIV drug was provided country-wide on the recommendation of medical professionals to pregnant women to prevent mother to child transmission). However this was only because it was clearly shown that the cost of the drug was within the available resources of the state, there was already a policy in place (it was just restricted to specific sites) and it was only unreasonable restrictions which were preventing the availability of the drug more widely.[112]

It can be seen that the introduction of socio-economic rights in South Africa has begun to have a positive impact on socio-economic inequality, such as requiring the state to have a housing programme for individuals who are homeless and ensuring children are born free from HIV. Although the implementation of these decisions is not without criticism,[113] they have helped to alleviate the situation of many living in poverty by ensuring they have the basic capabilities to live a dignified life (i.e. basic health) and that they are not socially excluded (i.e. they have a home).[114] Consequently, socio-economic rights primarily address poverty as they focus upon providing individuals with basic necessities. However, they can also have some impact on economic inequality, as they will generally be funded from taxation which will tend to tax the wealthy more heavily. What socio-economic rights do not generally do is address class structures which means that even if individuals have the basic necessities it can be very difficult for them to utilise these to advance their social position.

International Law 91, 112.

110 *Soobramoney v Minister of Health (Kwazulu-Natal)* 1998 (1) SA 765 (CC), para 29.

111 *The Government of the Republic of South Africa v Grootboom* [2000] ZACC 14.

112 *Minister of Health v Treatment Action Campaign (No 2)* 2002 (5) SA 721 (CC); P. Nolette, 'Lessons Learned from the South African Constitutional Court: Toward a Third Way of Judicial Enforcement of Socio-Economic Rights' (2003) 12 Michigan State Journal of International Law 91, 114–115.

113 P. Joubert, 'Grootboom Dies Homeless and Penniless' *Mail & Guardian* (Online, 8 August 2008) <http://mg.co.za/article/2008-08-08-grootboom-dies-homeless-and-penniless> accessed 22 March 2015.

114 C. Rodriguez-Garavito, 'Beyond the Courtroom: The Impact of Judicial Activism on Socioeconomic Rights in Latin America' (2011) 89 Texas Law Review 1669, 1681; E. Wickeri, 'Grootboom's Legacy: Securing the Right to Access to Adequate Housing in South Africa?' (2004) Centre For Human Rights and Global Justice Working Paper 5/2004.

Consequently the prohibition of discrimination based upon social condition is also needed.

4.2. EXTENDING EQUALITY LAW TO COVER SOCIAL CONDITION/DISADVANTAGE

Social condition has been a ground of discrimination in the Canadian provinces/territories, of Québec since 1975, Northwest Territories since 2004 and New Brunswick since 2005.[115] Manitoba added social disadvantage in 2012.[116] All four jurisdictions take different approaches to defining it. Social condition is not defined in the Québécois legislation with it being left to the courts to define. The courts have identified objective and subjective components. The objective component concerns the economic rank or social standing of an individual based on factors such as income, occupation or level of education. Whereas the subjective component concerns the value attributed to an individual based upon social perceptions or stereotypes associated with factors such as income, occupation or level of education.[117] It is wider than social origin, as it refers to an individual's present situation as well as their past.[118] It should be looked at holistically, not all criteria need be present (e.g. an individual could have had a good education but now be unemployed).[119] It can also be a temporary state and need not be immutable.[120] A potential limit of the definition is that it is prima facie symmetrical (i.e. as well as poor individuals being able to challenge discriminatory treatment, rich individuals can also challenge any discriminatory treatment against them, for example having to pay a higher rate of tax, which could act to prevent government attempts to address socio-economic inequality through redistribution). However, the courts have defined social condition in a manner that recognises its purpose (i.e. to help the very poorest individuals in society challenge discriminatory treatment) and thus a doctor's level of income and being a judge were not

115 Québec Charter of Human Rights and Freedoms 1975, s 10; Northwest Territories Human Rights Act 2002, s 5(1); New Brunswick Human Rights Act 2011; W. Mackay & N. Kim, 'Adding Social Condition to the Canadian Human Rights Act' (Canadian Human Rights Commission 2009).

116 Manitoba Human Rights Code 1987, s 9(2); DAVID ADAMS, 'Social Condition in Canadian Human Rights Legislation' (British Columbia Human Rights Coalition 2013) 3.

117 *Québec (Commission des droits de la personne) v. Gauthier* (1993), 19 CHRR D/312; *Centre Hospitalier Regina Limitée v. Commission des droits de la personne du Québec et Laurin* (1985), 7 CHRR D/3359; *D'Aoust v. Vallières*, (1994) 19 CHRR D/322 (TDPQ); *Leroux et CDPQ v. J. M. Brouillette Inc.*, [1994] JTDPQ No. 16.

118 *Québec (Commission des droits de la personne) v. Gauthier* (1993), 19 CHRR D/312; *D'Aoust v. Vallières*, (1994) 19 CHRR D/322 (TDPQ).

119 *Québec (Commission des droits de la personne) v. Gauthier* (1993), 19 CHRR D/312.

120 Ibid.

found to constitute a social condition and thus they were unable to challenge discriminatory treatment on this ground.[121] The majority of claims have focused upon discrimination based on receipt of social assistance,[122] however it is also much broader, for example encompassing the type of occupation an individual has (for example refusing to rent to a freelance writer on the assumption that they will have a low level of income).[123] The Québécois Human Rights Commission also believe it extends to students (e.g. not allowing students in a shop on their lunch break) and to the homeless (e.g. requiring homeless people to pay for food in a restaurant in advance).[124]

In contrast to Québec, the Northwest Territories have provided a statutory definition of social condition which is defined as 'the condition of inclusion of the individual, other than on a temporary basis, in a socially identifiable group that suffers from social or economic disadvantage resulting from poverty, source of income, illiteracy, level of education or any other similar circumstance'.[125] This has been criticised for including the requirement of an individual being part of a socially identifiable group which has been argued to be unnecessary.[126] The Northwest Territories Supreme Court have held that social condition should be interpreted broadly, but that it is insufficient that a person has a disadvantage that impacts their ability to obtain the necessities of life. They thus laid out a four-part test requiring that an individual: (i) must be part of a socially identifiable group; (ii) other than on a temporary basis; and (iii) that group must suffer from social or economic disadvantage; and (iv) this disadvantage must result from poverty, source of income, illiteracy, low levels of education, or any other similar circumstance.[127] Thus it was held that a seasonal worker would fall under the definition of social condition as he belonged to an identifiable group (seasonal workers), he belonged to this group over a number of years and not on a temporary basis, seasonal workers suffered both economic and social disadvantage, and this disadvantage resulted from the group's low education levels and source of income.[128]

---

121 *Skelly and Quebéc Human Rights Commission* v. *O'Hashi*, [1996] JTDPQ No. 32; *Vaillancourt v. Centre communautaire juridique Laurentides-Lanaudière*, J. E. 93–1412 (C.S.).

122 *Sejko v. Gabriel Aubé inc.*, [1999] JQ No. 2858 (CQ); W. Mackay & N. Kim, 'Adding Social Condition to the Canadian Human Rights Act' (Canadian Human Rights Commission 2009) 27.

123 *Bia-Domingo et Québec (CDPDJ) v. Sinatra*, [1999] JTDPQ No. 19.

124 Commission des Droits de la Personne et des Droits de la Jeunesse, 'Social Condition' <www.cdpdj.qc.ca/en/droits-de-la-personne/motifs/Pages/condition-sociale.aspx> accessed 1 December 2014.

125 Northwest Territories Human Rights Act 2002, s 1(1).

126 Northwest Territories Legislative Assembly, 'Standing Committee of Social Programmes, Report on Bill 1, Human Rights Act' (N.W.T. Committee Report 10–14(5), 2002).

127 *Northwest Territories (Workers; Compensation Board) v. Mercer*, 2012 NWTSC 57, paras 32–50.

128 Ibid. para 45.

New Brunswick also define social condition within the legislation. Social condition is 'the condition of inclusion of the individual in a socially identifiable group that suffers from social or economic disadvantage on the basis of his or her source of income, occupation or level of education'.[129] There is no case law on social condition in New Brunswick but guidance has been provided by the Human Rights Commission. They suggest possible sources of income that would be covered include income assistance, employment insurance, retirement income, a rent subsidy and a workers compensation pension. Types of occupations that might be covered include students, freelance workers, seasonal workers and casual workers.[130] In relation to housing, as well as discrimination occurring when a landlord refuses to rent to an individual receiving benefits, they argue that the utilisation of rent/income ratios could constitute indirect discrimination and that requiring a damage deposit only from students could also constitute discrimination.[131] In relation to employment social condition discrimination would include asking potential employees in the interview if they have ever been in receipt of benefits or harassing employees who have a perceived low status.[132] There is also a specific exception to social condition discrimination where it is required or authorised by an Act of the Legislature.[133]

Finally Manitoba define social disadvantage as 'diminished social standing or social regard due to: (a) homelessness or inadequate housing; (b) low levels of education; (c) chronic low income; or (d) chronic unemployment or underemployment'.[134] This is later limited by a requirement that 'discrimination is based on a negative bias or stereotype related to that social disadvantage'.[135] Like New Brunswick, there has been no case law but the Human Rights Commission have published guidance. For low income, unemployment or underemployment to be 'chronic', it requires a pattern or lengthy period of low income or un/underemployment.[136] The Commission note that context and surrounding circumstances are important as income for a single person might not be considered low but the same income for a single parent with four children might. In addition to the other situations outlined in relation to the other jurisdictions, the Commission believe social disadvantage discrimination would prevent different rental terms being imposed on underemployed or undereducated individuals, requiring a certain level of education regardless of

---

129 New Brunswick Human Rights Act 2011, s 2.

130 New Brunswick Human Rights Commission, 'Guideline on Social Condition' (New Brunswick Human Rights Commission 2005) 4.

131 Ibid. 5.

132 Ibid. 6.

133 New Brunswick Human Rights Act 2011, s 9.

134 Manitoba Human Rights Code 1987, s 1.

135 Ibid. s 9(2.1).

136 Manitoba Human Rights Commission, 'Interpretation of Social Disadvantage' (*Manitoba Human Rights Commission*, 2012).

whether it is necessary for the job or not, and denying insurance to people with low socio-economic status.[137]

Although it is often thought that extending equality law to cover socio-economic inequality is likely to lead to a huge increase in the number of cases being brought and every government policy being subject to challenge, the experience of these four jurisdictions does not support this. There has only been a small increase in the caseload (about 3–4%) and in Québec (which has extended equality law to social condition for the longest period) the courts have been extremely wary of upholding challenges to government programmes, such as work assistance programmes or paying foreign doctors at specialised rates.[138] Although the Québécois caseload has settled at around 3%, it was originally higher due to the lack of statutory definition which is why the other jurisdictions that introduced social condition much later opted for written definitions.[139] An additional advantage of the definition is that it can be written in a way that excludes claims by rich individuals which were originally permitted by the judiciary in Québec in the absence of any legislative limits.[140] There needs to be a balance over detail though as, while 'a minimal statutory definition is desirable ... too much detail at the statutory level might be counterproductive'.[141] Although the actual application of social condition/disadvantage discrimination has been limited, the cases that have been brought show that it has been useful in challenging prejudices and stereotypes against the poor, particularly by landlords who can no longer 'rely on previous negative experiences they may have had with renters affected by the same social condition to justify a refusal to lease accommodation'.[142]

Although the prohibition of discrimination based upon social condition does have some impact on poverty it primarily addresses class structures. For example, in contrast to socio-economic rights it generally cannot be utilised to require the state to provide basic necessities (such as housing) to individuals. However it can be utilised to ensure individuals from lower socio-economic backgrounds are not excluded from areas of society (e.g. housing market, employment) or given a poorer service (e.g. education) as a result of discriminatory treatment. Given the cost and complexity of legal proceedings, it is likely to be especially effective if there is a positive mainstreaming duty that is not reliant on individual

137 Ibid.

138 W. Mackay & N. Kim, 'Adding Social Condition to the Canadian Human Rights Act' (Canadian Human Rights Commission 2009) 104; *Lambert v. Québec (Procureur général)*, [2002] JQ No. 364 (CA); *Villenuve v. Québec (Procureur général)*, [1998] AQ no 5 (CA).

139 W. Mackay & N. Kim, 'Adding Social Condition to the Canadian Human Rights Act' (Canadian Human Rights Commission 2009) 107.

140 *Guimond v. Université de Montréal*, [1985] 1985-03-29 (CS); *Droit de la famille – 1473*, (1991) RDF 691 (CS).

141 W. Mackay & N. Kim, 'Adding Social Condition to the Canadian Human Rights Act' (Canadian Human Rights Commission 2009) 127.

142 *Reeves et Québec (CDPDJ) v. Fondation Abbé Charles-Émile Gadbois*, [2001] JTDPQ No. 13.

complaints, such as section 1 of the UK Equality Act 2010 (which unfortunately was not implemented),[143] that requires actors to consider possible barriers to socio-economic inequality and explore the removal of these. For example, the Department of Health could decide to provide services outside working hours to ensure people from low socio-economic (working) backgrounds have access to health services.[144] Thus it can be seen that combined with socio-economic rights, prohibiting discrimination based upon social condition would have a significant impact on socio-economic inequality.

5. CONCLUSION

Socio-economic inequality is a major issue across the world but particularly in the UK. It is important to begin to combat it to improve the social situation of British citizens. However this chapter has argued that the current responses are inadequate as they lack permanency, often conflict, are ad hoc, focus on limited aspects of socio-economic inequality and are optional. As a result they cannot provide the comprehensive response to socio-economic inequality that is needed. In contrast, socio-economic rights combined with the prohibition of discrimination on the grounds of social condition focus upon ensuring the state does its utmost to provide individuals with basic necessities, while at the same time removing barriers that exist in society that prohibit individuals from utilising these to live the lives they wish. Consequently, if politicians are serious about reducing socio-economic inequality they should introduce socio-economic rights and prohibit social condition discrimination rather than leaving it to the whims of the political system.

---

143 This required certain public bodies 'when making decisions of a strategic nature about how to exercise its functions, [to] have due regard to the desirability of exercising them in a way that is designed to reduce the inequalities of outcome which result from socio-economic disadvantage.'

144 Explanatory Notes to the Equality Act 2010, para 27.

HOUSING RIGHTS AND THE INCLUSION OF ROMA AND TRAVELLERS

Towards Positive Action Measures from the Rulings of the European Court of Human Rights?

Roberta Medda-Windischer

1. INTRODUCTION

Among the most effective ways to protect and promote minority rights is for many the introduction of specific legislative or administrative measures imposing a duty of positive action. Yet, an obligation to adopt positive action is still controversial within the system of the European Convention on Human Rights (Convention or ECHR) as it has not yet been formulated in clear terms by the Strasbourg Court (Court, Strasbourg Court or ECtHR), although other organs of the Council of Europe, such as the European Committee of Social Rights and the CoE Parliamentary Assembly, have been much more progressive in this respect. The Court's position in this regard is rather ambiguous and half-hearted: the Convention does not compel the Member States to provide for positive actions in favour of minorities; however, it does not automatically prohibit them as long as the difference in treatment is justified in each case.

Generally, the Strasbourg Court has been reluctant to recognise minority claims and it has thus often left a wide margin of appreciation to the states, especially as long as the recognition of these claims amounts to positive actions or additional financial burdens for the Member State and not simply a negative obligation to refrain from performing certain acts or practices. The Court has taken a positive stance toward minority rights only when, under the specific circumstances of the case, a given practice or omission by the state constitutes 'a clear and disproportionate disadvantage' or an 'excessive burden' for certain groups. Otherwise, the state's margin of appreciation has been broadly recognised.[1]

In light of some recent and innovative judgments of the Strasbourg Court *vis-à-vis* Roma and Travellers'[2] rights in the field of housing, the present chapter analyses whether and in which circumstances positive actions can be expected on the part of the state. A conceptual differentiation between positive *obligations* and positive *actions* will constitute the framework and the starting point of the analysis. The second part of the chapter will examine three major decisions of the Strasbourg Court on housing and Roma and Travellers. This analysis will serve as a basis to discuss whether from these openings of the Strasbourg case law we can derive specific positive action measures or social policy prescriptions that can be imposed on Member States with special reference to Roma and Travellers.

2. STATE OBLIGATIONS IN THE STRASBOURG SYSTEM: LIMITS AND STRENGTHS OF POSITIVE OBLIGATIONS

Within the Strasbourg system, the European Court of Human Rights has increasingly recognised the existence of positive obligations flowing from the European Convention on Human Rights,[3] i.e. obligations on state authorities to *take positive steps* or measures to protect the Convention rights of individuals.[4] These

1 On this point, see, among others, ECtHR, 22 October 1981, Dudgeon v. The United Kingdom, no. 7525/76, para. 52; ECtHR, 24 November 1986, Gillow v. the United Kingdom, no. 9063/80, para. 55; ECtHR, 26 September 1996, Buckley v. The United Kingdom, no. 20348/92, para. 75; ECtHR, 19 December 1989, Mellacher and Others v. Austria, nos. 10522/83, 11011/84 and 11070/84, para. 45; ECtHR, 27 May 2004, Connors v. The United Kingdom, no. 66746/01, para. 82; ECtHR, 28 October 1998, Osman v. The United Kingdom, no. 87/1997/871/1083, para. 116.

2 The term 'Roma and Travellers', though opposed by some groups that do not recognise themselves under this term, is used in this chapter as an umbrella that includes a wide range of diverse groups of people, whether sedentary or not: on the one hand, Roma (and sub-groups), Sinti/Manush, Kale/Romanichals, Boyash/Rudari, the Eastern groups (Dom and Lom), all of whom accept a shared ethnic origin, and, on the other hand, associated groups such as Travellers, Yenish, and Balkan Egyptians (Egyptians and Ashkali), as well as the populations designated under the administrative term '*gens du voyage*' and persons who identify themselves as Gypsies.

3 In the leading *Marckx* and *Airey* cases, dated 1979, positive obligations were recognised as 'inherent' in the Convention system. The Court has justified its finding on positive obligations as being necessary to make a Convention right 'secured' – as imposed by Article 1 ECHR – and 'effective'. See, ECtHR, 13 June 1979, Marckx v. Belgium, no. 6833/74, at 31; ECtHR, 9 October 1979, Airey v. Ireland, no. 6289/73.

4 See, A. Mowbray, *The Development of Positive Obligations under the European Convention on Human Rights by the European Court of Human Rights* (Oxford: Hart Publishing, 2004). D.J. Harris, M. O'Boyle, E.P. Bates and C.M. Buckley, *Law of the European Convention on Human Rights* (Oxford: Oxford University Press, 2009), at 51; M. Pitkänen, 'Fair and Balanced Positive Obligations – Do They Exist?', (2012) 5 *EHRLR (European Human Rights*

obligations take a number of forms. The most straightforward and obvious arise where, by their very nature, Convention rights require the provision of resources. For instance, the right to free legal assistance in criminal cases under Article 6(3)(c), the right to education under Article 2 of Protocol 1 and the duty to hold elections under Article 3 of Protocol 1.[5] Positive obligations thus necessitate *action* by the government, whereas negative obligations require only that the government *abstain* from curtailing rights. However, not all rights can be classified as strictly positive or negative; some fall along the spectrum between these two extremes.[6]

The Strasbourg Court has declared several times that the object and purpose of the ECHR is that the rights which it guarantees must be practical and effective,[7] although it has explicitly declined to develop any 'general theory' of positive obligations.[8] Positive obligations have thus been created as a consequence of applying the effective and dynamic interpretation of the ECHR to protect the rights of individuals.[9] The foundation and the content of positive obligations in the Convention system – the so-called 'standard of effectiveness'[10] – lies thus in the recognition that a purely negative approach to the protection of human rights cannot guarantee their effective protection.[11]

Although Van Dijk considers that in principle practically all ECHR provisions leave room for 'implied' positive obligations,[12] some provisions in the Convention have been interpreted more often than others as implying positive obligations. As will emerge in the second part of this chapter, the provision of housing for those unable to secure their own accommodation is considered an area of potential expansion of positive obligations.[13]

Law Review), 538–550, at 539; K. Starmer, 'Positive Obligations Under the Convention', in J.L. Jowell and J. Cooper (eds.), *Understanding Human Rights Principles* (Oxford: Hart Publishing, 2001), at 104.

5 K. Starmer, *ibid.*, 104; D.J. Harris, *et al.*, *ibid.*, at 18.

6 C. Wilkie and M. Zisman Gary, 'Positive and Negative Rights under the Charter: Closing the Divide to Advance Equality', (2011) 30 *Windsor Review of Legal and Social Issue*, 38.

7 See, ECtHR, 21 June 1988, Platform 'Ärzte für das Leben' v Austria, no. 10126/82, at 31.

8 *Ibid.*

9 M. Pitkänen, *supra*, at 540.

10 D. Xenos, *The Positive Obligations of the State under the European Convention of Human Rights* (London: Routledge, 2012), at 207.

11 K. Starmer, *supra*, at 104.

12 P. Van Dijk, 'Positive Obligations implied in the European Convention on Human Rights: are the states still the 'Masters' of the Convention?', in M. Castermans-Holleman *et al* (eds.), *The Role of the Nation-State in the 21st Century: Human Rights, International Organizations and Foreign Policy. Essays in Honour of Peter Baehr* (The Hague: Kluwer Law International, 1998), at 32. Specifically on Article 14 (non-discrimination clause) states may have positive obligations under Article 14 as well as the negative obligation not to discriminate in their official acts. See, ECtHR, 23 July 1968, Case 'relating to certain aspects of the laws on the use of languages in education in Belgium' v. Belgium (merits), nos. 1474/1677/1691/62; 1769/1994/63; 216/64, para. 400. However, there is no express positive obligation under Article 14 so any obligation of this kind must be implied. D.J. Harris, *et al.*, 610.

13 See, A. Mowbray, *supra*; C. Cahn, 'Towards Realizing a Right to Positive Action for Roma in Europe: Connors v. UK', (2005) 1 *Roma Rights Quarterly*, 13–26.

If it is generally acknowledged that positive obligations are not confined to any particular kind of Convention right, it is also accepted that the *extent* of any positive obligation arising will vary according to the nature of the issue at stake.[14] It is in fact an intrinsic characteristic of positive obligations that the duties they impose are seldom absolute. What is required by the state, therefore, varies according to the importance of the right and the resources to be disbursed to meet any positive obligation. Consequently, it is acknowledged that in this domain states have a *margin of appreciation* with respect to the general and more detailed content of positive obligations.[15]

The margin of appreciation doctrine is limited by the 'fair balance test' according to which, as the Court observed, in determining the steps to be taken to ensure compliance with the Convention 'regard must be had to the fair balance that has to be struck between the competing interests of the individual and of the community as a whole.'[16]

The 'fair balance test' inherent in positive obligations is intimately linked to the limited availability of state's resources coupled with the economic disparities existing among Member States. The 'fair balance test' between state interest and the interests of individuals ensures that positive obligations will not impose unbearable or disproportionate burden on states to fulfil the obligations imposed by the Strasbourg Court.[17] Hence, the specific content of any positive obligation is determined in relation to the particular requirements of protection and the contextual differences involved. In this way, this approach satisfies the standard of effectiveness and guarantees the functioning of the Convention in the reality.[18]

Having analysed the circumstances and the limits under which positive obligations arise within the Strasbourg system, the following paragraphs will look at the differences between positive obligations and positive or affirmative action. The analysis will go beyond the Strasbourg system so as to include the EU legal mechanisms, as these are more familiar with the legal discussion on the concept of positive action.[19]

---

14 K. Starmer, *supra*, at 159.

15 D.J. Harris *et al*, *supra*, at 343; ECtHR, 18 December 1986, Johnston and Others v. Ireland, no. 9697/83. On this point, see, M.W. Janis, R.S. Kay and A.W. Bradley, *European Human Rights Law* (Oxford: Oxford University Press, 2008); A. Legg, *The Margin of Appreciation in International Human Rights Law* (Oxford: Oxford University Press, 2012); Y. Arari-Takahashi, *The Margin of Appreciation Doctrine and the Principle of Proportionality in the Jurisprudence of the ECHR* (Antwerp: Intersentia, 2002); O. Mjöll Arnardóttir, *Equality and Non-Discrimination under the European Convention on Human Rights* (The Hague: Martinus Nijhoff Publishers, 2003).

16 ECtHR, 21 February 1990, Powell and Rayner v. The United Kingdom, no. 9310/81, para. 41; ECtHR, 10 October 2006, Paulik v. Slovakia, no. 10699/05, para. 43.

17 ECtHR, Osman, *supra*, para. 116.

18 M. Pitkänen, *supra*, at 545.

19 In this context, it has to be recalled that the EU Charter of Fundamental Rights (2000) provides: 'In so far as this Charter contains rights which correspond to rights guaranteed

3. POSITIVE ACTION AND SOCIAL POLICY PRESCRIPTIONS IN THE EUROPEAN LEGAL SYSTEM

In comparison to positive obligations, which, as seen previously, require states to act rather than refrain from doing something, positive (or affirmative) action measures consist of forms of preferential and proportionate measures undertaken with the purpose of achieving full and effective equality in practice for members of groups that are socially or economically disadvantaged, or otherwise face the consequences of past or present discrimination or disadvantage.[20] In this sense, positive action measures can be considered a type of positive obligations, but more specific as to their purpose and legitimisation, i.e. to compensate for disadvantages.

For positive action measures to be lawful and permissible, they must be proportionate – weighed against the principle of equality for persons belonging to advantaged groups – whereas measures going further than the proportionality test are usually described as 'positive (or reversed) discrimination'.[21]

In the European context, the European Court of Justice (ECJ) has set out the most sophisticated and articulated jurisprudence on positive action.[22] In its case law on gender equality, the ECJ has held that measures which give absolute and unconditional priority to the under-represented sex (typically women) at

by the Convention for the Protection of Human Rights and Fundamental Freedoms, the meaning and scope of those rights shall be the same as those laid down by the said Convention.' (Art. 52(3)).

20 U. Archibong, M. Bell, L. Waddington, et al., *International Perspectives on Positive Action Measures. A Comparative Analysis in the European Union, Canada, the United States and South Africa* (Luxembourg: European Commission – Office for Official Publications of the European Communities, 2009), at 62; W. Benedek (ed.), *Understanding Human Rights* (Antwerp: Intersentia, 2012), at 439; G. Gerapetritis, *Affirmative Action Policies and Judicial Review Worldwide* (New York: Springer, 2015); J. Marko, 'Five Years After: Continuing Reflections on the Thematic Commentary on Effective Participation. The Interplay between Equality and Participation', in T.H. Malloy and U. Caruso (eds.), *Minorities, Their Rights and the Monitoring of the European Framework Convention for the Protection of National Minorities. Essays in Honour of Rainer Hofmann* (Leiden: Martinus Nijhoff Publishers, 2013), at 116–117.

21 *Ibid.*

22 For an analysis of the ECJ case law on positive action, see, among others, M. Bell and L. Waddington, 'Exploring the boundaries of positive action under EU law: A search for conceptual clarity', (2011) 48/5 *Common Market Law Review*, 1503–1526; C. O'Cinneide, 'Positive Action and the Limits of the Law', (2006) 3 *Maastricht Journal of European and Comparative Law*, 351–365; L. Charpertier, 'The European Court of Justice and the rhetoric of affirmative action' (1998) 4/2 *European Law Journal*, 167–195; S. Moore, 'Nothing positive from the Court of Justice' (1996) 21 *European Law Review* 156–161; A. Peters, 'The Many Meanings of Equality and Positive Action in Favour of Women under European Community Law – A Conceptual Analysis', (1996) 2/2 *European Law Journal*, 177–196; P. Cabral, 'A step closer to substantive equality', (1998) 23 *European Law Review*, 481–487.

the point of employment selection constitute unlawful discrimination against members of the other sex.[23]

In two leading cases, *Kalanke* and *Marschall*, the European Court of Justice has set out this principle and established its limits.[24] In *Kalanke*, the ECJ distinguished between *equal opportunities* and *equal results*, and concluded that positive action measures aiming at results are inadmissible.[25] The ECJ's argument was that an absolute preference for women goes beyond the implementation of equal opportunity, and instead establishes equality of result, which is not the aim of Community law. The ECJ has thus interpreted EU equality law so as to preclude a strict national quota without an 'escape' clause.[26] In *Marschall*, the ECJ clarified and refined the scope of *Kalanke* by considering a national quota provision accompanied by an escape clause to be compatible with Community law. Under *Marschall*, Member States' hiring and promotion quotas for women in state employment are legal as long as a statutory escape clause guarantees that male candidatures are individually and objectively assessed, so that a comprehensive balancing decision may override the statutory priority accorded to women.

In addition to the above, for the ECJ, to be justified under EU law a national measure should aim at remedying an existing situation of imbalance between men and women in a specific section or career trade.[27] This means that *evidence* should be provided of the existence of such an imbalance for the positive action measure to be legitimate. Secondly, a positive action measure should be *adequate*. The ECJ will assess whether it is likely that the scrutinised measure will achieve the aim of remedying the existing concrete situation of imbalance. Finally, for the positive action measure to be lawful it must be *proportionate* – weighed against the principle of equal treatment for persons who do not benefit from it (otherwise, as seen previously, such measures become unlawful 'positive (or reverse) discrimination'). In other words, to be lawful and legitimate, the measures must be *necessary*, *appropriate* and *not go beyond what is needed* to achieve their objective. This implies, as seen earlier, that automatic or absolute preferences can never be allowed. What is required, in short, is a case-by-case examination.

As for the temporariness of positive action measures, it is generally acknowledged that once a positive action measure has achieved its aim, and the situation of social or economic disadvantage or the consequences of past or present discrimination or disadvantage has been eliminated, the measure should be discontinued. However, this does not mean that all positive action measures should automatically be temporary in nature. Some forms of exclusion and

---

23 U. Archibong, M. Bell, L. Waddington, et al., *supra*, at 25.

24 ECJ, Case C-450/93, *Kalanke*, EU: 1995:322; Case C-409/95, *Marschall*, EU: 1997:533.

25 ECJ, *Kalanke, supra*, para. 22.

26 For Peters, the laconic holding of the ECJ is subject to criticism especially as the dichotomy 'equal opportunity – equal results' is unhelpful and overly simplistic, and the distinction is far from clear-cut and difficult to apply. See, A. Peters, *Women, Quotas and Constitutions* (The Hague – Boston: Kluwer Law International, 1999), at 236.

27 ECJ, Case C-476/99, *Lommers*, EU: C: 2002:183.

disadvantage are in fact so embedded that only long-term positive action schemes can help to correct them, and where a group-related characteristic is likely to lead to a permanent reduction in (employment and educational) opportunities, permanent positive action schemes can be proportionate and justified.[28]

The analysis conducted in the previous paragraphs of the notion of positive action measures and the limits within the EU legal system serves as a framework to look at positive actions within another European legal system, i.e. the Council of Europe, that has a specific mandate on human rights and, particularly, on the protection of minorities, including Roma and Travellers.

Specifically on Roma and positive action measures, the Parliamentary Assembly of the Council of Europe (PACE) has called upon the Member States to meet six general conditions, which are necessary for the improvement of the situation of Roma in Europe, in terms of improving their legal status and the level of equality and living conditions of Roma, including developing and implementing 'positive action and preferential treatment for the socially deprived strata, including Roma as a socially disadvantaged community, in the field of education, employment and housing'.[29]

Another monitoring body of the Council of Europe, the European Committee of Social Rights (ECSR), has also formulated a positive action obligation for the state to redress the particular situation of Roma. The ECSR affirmed that 'for the integration of an ethnic minority as Roma into mainstream society measures of positive action are needed' and held that indirect discrimination may arise by failing to take adequate steps to ensure that the rights and collective advantages that are open to all are genuinely accessible to all. Thus, government failure to undertake specific action to address the particular situation of Roma constitutes a breach of the state's obligations under the European Social Charter.[30]

Despite the positive openings of the ECJ and relevant bodies of the Council of Europe, the judges of the European Court of Human Rights have always maintained a rather cautious and ambiguous approach to positive action. In its early leading Belgian linguistic case, the Strasbourg Court stated that the European Convention on Human Rights not only does not prohibit a Member State from treating groups differently in order to correct *factual inequalities* between them, but, in certain circumstances, a failure to attempt to correct inequality through different treatment may in itself give rise to a breach of the Convention (Article 14 – non-discrimination clause).[31] However, on the issue of whether positive action measures are *required* or only *permitted* in order to correct

28 U. Archibong, M. Bell, L. Waddington, et al., *supra*, at 26.

29 PACE, Rec. 1557 (2002), *The legal situation of Roma in Europe*, para. 15(d).

30 See, European Committee of Social Rights (ECSR), 30 November 2006, *European Roma Rights Center (ERRC) v. Bulgaria*, no. 31/2005.

31 ECtHR, Case 'relating to certain aspects of the laws on the use of languages in education in Belgium' v. Belgium *supra*, para. 10; ECtHR, 8 April 2000, Thlimmenos v. Greece (Grand Chamber), no. 34369/97, para. 44.

factual inequalities, Judge Costa made a rather straightforward statement when discussing the measures to be taken to address the problem of the 'special schools' for Roma pupils. In his concurring opinion attached to the decision in the *D.H.* case, he stated: 'it seems to me that up till now this Court has refused to consider it [positive action] a State obligation.'[32] This approach is also reflected in the Preamble to Protocol No. 12 to the European Convention on Human Rights on the principle of non-discrimination that clearly affirms: 'the present Protocol does no impose any obligation to adopt such measures [positive action measures].'[33]

A more open approach to positive action on the part of the Strasbourg Court, though not yet consolidated in subsequent cases, can be found in the decision of the Grand Chamber of the Strasbourg Court in the *Oršuš v. Croatia* case again concerning the separate education of Roma children for the reason of language deficiencies.[34] In this case, the Court affirmed that 'the State … had the obligation to take appropriate positive measures to assist the applicants in acquiring the necessary language skills in the shortest time possible, notably by means of special language lessons, so that they could be quickly integrated into mixed classes'[35] as well as by means of an active and structured involvement on the part of the relevant social services in order to counteract the high drop-out rate of Roma pupils.[36]

At this point of the discussion, a remark is necessary on the distinction between positive action measures and general policies to promote social inclusion. Some initiatives are easily categorised as positive action, for example a hospital internship programme that is limited to people from a minority ethnic background. At the other end of the spectrum, there are measures which loosely benefit disadvantaged groups but which are traditional elements of national social welfare policy – such as state pensions or free education – rather than positive action.[37] Some measures, however, cannot be easily distinguished as they fall on the boundary between social policy and positive action. Is state provision of financial assistance to persons with disabilities or to persons from a particular ethnic background in order to encourage them to take up employment a form of positive action (designed to compensate for disadvantage) or is it an element of the state social assistance regime? On this point, some clarifications can be made by recognising that, in contrast to social policy prescriptions, positive action measures have some common characteristics: they are *targeted at a well-defined*

32 ECtHR, 7 February 2006 (Chamber), D.H. and Others v. The Czech Republic, no. 57325/00, Concurring opinion of Judge Costa, para. 7.

33 Explanatory report of Protocol No. 12 to the European Convention on Human Rights, 4 November 2000, para. 16.

34 ECtHR, 16 March 2010 (Grand Chamber), Oršuš and Others v. Croatia, no. 15766/03. For an analysis of the Oršuš case as a pioneering case of positive duty to take special positive measures for minorities, see, J. Marko, *supra*, at 116–117.

35 *Ibid.*, para 165.

36 *Ibid.*, para 177.

37 U. Archibong, M. Bell, L. Waddington, et al., *supra*, at 28.

group; they seek to redress disadvantages in a *specific setting*, such as housing or access to education or employment; and they are subject to *periodic review.*[38] As discussed earlier, this does not mean that positive action must be given a time limit, but it is also not automatically assumed to be indefinite.

To conclude by drawing from the analysis conducted in this section, positive action measures cover a wide range of activities, initiatives, strategies and interventions designed to achieve 'full equality in practice' or substantial equality. In more detail, positive action measures are undertaken to achieve one or more of the following goals: (1) preventing or compensating for disadvantages and discrimination, whether these arose in the past or are still ongoing; (2) promoting substantive equality by taking into account the specific situation of members of disadvantaged groups and breaking the cycle of disadvantage associated with membership of a particular group; and/or (3) redressing under-representation and promoting diversity in participation of all groups in social, economic, cultural and political life. Positive action measures achieve these goals by influencing the way in which social goods, such as employment, education, housing or healthcare, are allocated.[39]

Before analysing the Roma and Travellers cases on housing rights, it is worth looking briefly at the approach of the Strasbourg Court *vis-à-vis* social and economic rights, as housing falls largely within this category.

4. HOUSING RIGHTS AND SOCIAL AND ECONOMIC RIGHTS WITHIN THE STRASBOURG SYSTEM

The Strasbourg Court has rejected the argument that the European Convention on Human Rights is a treaty solely concerned with civil and political rights. In one of its most significant judgments, *Airey v. Ireland* (1979) the Court held: 'Whilst the Convention sets forth what are essentially civil and political rights, many of them have implications of a social or economic nature. The Court therefore considers … that the *mere fact* that an interpretation of the Convention may extend into the sphere of social and economic rights should not be a decisive factor against such an interpretation; there is no water-tight sphere from the fields covered by the Convention.'[40] It follows that the 'mere fact' that a human rights violation is capable of being articulated in the language of socio-economic rights does not of itself mean that the Strasbourg Court will reject its jurisdiction.[41]

---

38 *Ibid.*, at 28.

39 *Ibid.*, at 24.

40 ECtHR, Airey v. Ireland, *supra* (Emphasis added).

41 L. Clements and A. Simmons, 'European Court of Human Rights. Sympathetic Unease', in M. Langford (ed.), *Social Rights Jurisprudence* (Cambridge: Cambridge University Press,

As seen earlier for positive obligations, in matters of welfare or economic policy the margin of appreciation enjoyed by states is relatively wide.[42] Specifically in cases under Article 8 of the Convention (home and private/family life), this same margin becomes narrower if and when cases involve 'rights of central importance to the individual's identity, self-determination, physical and moral integrity, maintenance of relationships with others and a settled and secure place in the community.'[43]

In addition, although Article 8 of the Convention (home and private/family life) does not require states to provide a home for everyone, there are circumstances when positive obligations of the Convention will suggest this, for instance for severe disability. The Court specified that: 'although Article 8 does not guarantee the right to have one's housing problem solved by the authorities, a refusal of the authorities to provide assistance in this respect to an individual suffering from a severe disease might in certain circumstances raise an issue under Article 8 of the Convention because of the impact of such refusal on the private life of the individual'.[44]

In the context of housing, the Strasbourg Court has so far been dealing with housing rights with an attitude almost of indifference towards the other main mechanism on human rights within the Council of Europe, i.e. the European Committee on Social Rights, which has been developing important jurisprudence on state obligations in this area on a regular basis. The next section will analyse in more detail to what extent and in what circumstances the case law of the Strasbourg Court is developing along the same lines.

5. THE ECtHR CASE LAW ON HOUSING AND ROMA/TRAVELLERS' TRADITIONAL WAY OF LIFE

At the outset it is noteworthy to look at the state-of-the-art within the Strasbourg case law following an important and innovative set of leading cases on Roma and Travellers, i.e. the *Buckley*,[45] *Chapman*,[46] *Connors*,[47] *D.H.*[48] and *Oršuš*[49]

2009), at 409–410. See also, I.E. Koch, *Human Rights as Indivisible Right. The Protection of Socio-Economic Demands under the European Convention on Human Rights* (Leiden – Boston: Martinus Nijhoff Publishers, 2009).

42 ECtHR, 8 July 2003 (Decision on the admissibility), Sentges v. the Netherlands, no. 27677/02.

43 ECtHR, Connors, *supra*, para. 82.

44 See, ECtHR, 4 May 1999 (Decision on the admissibility), Marzari v. Italy, no. 36448/97, at 8.

45 ECtHR, Buckley, *supra*.

46 ECtHR, 18 January 2001 (Grand Chamber), Chapman v. The United Kingdom, no. 27238/95.

47 ECtHR, Connors, *supra*.

48 ECtHR, 13 November 2011 (Grand Chamber), D.H. and Others v. The Czech Republic, no. 57325/00.

49 ECtHR, Oršuš and Others v. Croatia, *supra*.

cases, covering a range of time between 1996 (*Buckley*) and 2010 (*Oršuš*).[50] Most cases concerning Roma/Travellers and housing (the *Buckley, Chapman* and *Connors* cases) are connected with their traditional way of life and Article 8 (home and private/family life).[51] They are generally related to situations in which the applicants wished to settle down with their caravans in areas where the authorities would not authorise their dwelling on various grounds, generally for environment protection.

In these cases – though not in *Buckley*, where only the dissenting Judge Pettiti supported a positive obligation approach – the Strasbourg Court identified the need to 'facilitate the gypsy way of life' as a 'positive obligation' of the state. In *Chapman* (2001), the Court specifically stated: 'The vulnerable position of gypsies as a minority means that some special consideration should be given to their needs and their different lifestyle both in the relevant regulatory framework and in reaching decisions in particular cases ... To this extent, there is thus a *positive obligation* imposed on the Contracting States by virtue of Article 8 to facilitate the gypsy way of life.'[52] In addition, the Court underlined that there is an emerging international consensus amongst the Member States of the Council of Europe recognising the special needs of minorities and an obligation to protect their security, identity and lifestyle, not only for the purpose of safeguarding the interests of the minorities themselves but to preserve cultural diversity that is of value to the whole community.[53]

In the *Buckley* case, according to the majority, the decision to prioritise the landscape over the accommodation needs of the Buckley family, despite the lack of suitable alternative accommodation, was not considered disproportionate and in breach of Article 8.[54] Yet, in his dissenting opinion, Judge Pettiti commented: 'The Buckley family is caught in a "vicious circle" ... In attempting to comply with the disproportionate requirements of an authority or a rule, a family runs

---

50 For an analysis of the case law of the Strasbourg Court on Roma and Travellers, see, among others, R. Sandland, 'Developing a Jurisprudence of Difference: The Protection of the Human Rights of Travelling Peoples by the European Court of Human Rights', (2008) 8/3 *Human Rights Law Review*, 475–516; R. Medda-Windischer, 'Dismantling Segregating Education and the European Court of Human Rights. D.H. and Others vs. Czech Republic: Towards an Inclusive Education?', (2007/8) 7 *European Yearbook on Minority Issues*, 19–55; H. O'Nions, 'Divide and teach: educational inequality and the Roma', (2010) 14/3 *The International Journal of Human Rights*, 464–489; C. Cahn, *supra*; L. Peroni and A. Timmer, ' Vulnerable groups: The promise of an emerging concept in European Human Rights Convention law', (2013) 11/4 *International Journal of Constitutional Law*, 1056–1085; K. Henrard, 'The Council of Europe and the Rescue of Roma as a Paradigmatic Case of Failed Integration? Abstract Principles versus Protection in Concreto', (2013) 10 *European Yearbook of Minority Issues*, 269–316; D. Farget, 'Defining Roma Identity in the European Court of Human Rights', (2012) 19/3 *International Journal on Minority and Group Rights*, 291–316.

51 On the right to housing under the European Convention on Human Rights, see I.E. Koch, *supra*, at 113–148.

52 ECtHR, Chapman, *supra*, para. 96.

53 ECtHR, Chapman, *supra*, para. 93.

54 R. Sandland, *supra*, at 486.

the risk of contravening other rules. Such unreasonable combinations are in fact only employed against gypsy families to prevent them living in certain areas.'[55]

For Sandland, in the *Buckley* case, the Strasbourg Court 'accepted a construction of "Gypsies" as *per se* being a problem for domestic authorities',[56] whereas, in *Chapman*, the Court recognised the particular problems and prejudices faced by Roma and Travellers and, equally importantly, that issues of identity, not merely land use, are at stake.[57]

In *Chapman*, however, the Court clarified this point by stating: 'It is important to recall that Article 8 does not in terms recognise a right to be provided with a home. Nor does any of the jurisprudence of the Court acknowledge such a right. While it is clearly desirable that every human being has a place where he or she can live in dignity and which he or she can call home, there are unfortunately in the Contracting States many persons who have no home. Whether the State provides funds to enable everyone to have a home is a matter for *political not judicial decision*.'[58]

As for alternative accommodation in case of eviction, the Court noted: 'if no alternative accommodation is available the interference is more serious than where such accommodation is available. The more suitable the alternative accommodation is, the less serious is the interference constituted by moving the applicant from his or her existing accommodation'.[59] In addition, for the Court there is generally a need to balance 'the particular needs of the person concerned – his or her family requirements and financial resources – and, on the other hand, the rights of the local community to environmental protection.'[60]

In the *Chapman* case, the Court noted that Chapman had entered the land unlawfully,[61] and had been given a 'full and fair opportunity' to put her case.[62] Nor was the Court persuaded, in the absence of evidence from Chapman, that there was no alternative site available to her.[63] In the view of the Court, it was legitimate for the authorities to refuse permission, particularly as the site was on a protected area (Green Belt). Hence, there was no violation of Article 8.[64]

Chapman was not a unanimous decision: seven of the 17 members of the Grand Chamber found a breach of Article 8. For the dissenting judges, the case needed to be reviewed in the light of recent developments, in particular the emerging consensus across Contracting States concerning the CoE Framework

---

55 ECtHR, Buckley, *supra*, at 28–9.
56 R. Sandland, *supra*, at 483.
57 *Ibid.*, 488–9.
58 ECtHR, Chapman, *supra*, para. 99 (Emphasis added).
59 *Ibid.*, para. 103.
60 *Ibid.*, para. 104.
61 *Ibid.*, para. 107.
62 *Ibid.*, para. 106.
63 *Ibid.*, para. 113.
64 *Ibid.*, paras. 114–6.

Convention on the Protection of National Minorities (FCNM) and Article 27 of the UN International Covenant on Civil and Political Rights (ICCPR). As will be seen in the next section, the arguments raised in *Chapman* by the dissenting judges have only since been put forward by the majority in the most recent rulings of the Strasbourg Court.

As a matter of established principle, the Court will thus take into account the specific position of the Roma and Traveller population, who as a result of their history have become a *specific type of disadvantaged and vulnerable minority* and therefore require *special protection.*[65] Moreover, the Court derives from the vulnerable position of Roma and Travellers that *special consideration* should be given to their needs and their different lifestyle both in the relevant regulatory framework and in reaching decisions in particular cases.[66]

The 'special consideration' principle is strictly linked to the Strasbourg Court's approach according to which equality does not necessarily treat all individuals in the same way.[67] The Court thus supports policies of preferential treatment in favour of minority groups that suffer widespread and structural discrimination.[68] These politics of difference, in contrast to politics of sameness,[69] may also concern housing through the mechanism of Article 8 (home and private/family life) combined with Article 14 (anti-discrimination) and Article 3 (prohibition of torture and inhuman/degrading treatment).

If politics of difference for minorities are generally acknowledged, what does it mean to 'facilitate a gypsy way of life' and to provide 'special consideration' to Roma and Travellers as a result of their 'vulnerable position'? Should government social housing policy remain colour-blind or should it instead take into consideration the 'special needs' of Roma and Travellers? Should measures and policies for Roma and Travellers be adopted as an identity-based issue or should Roma/Traveller-specific housing policies counter a housing emergency? In a set of recent case law that will be analysed in the following section, the Strasbourg Court has further elaborated the concept of 'special consideration' for the needs and lifestyle of Roma and Travellers. In this way it has developed useful arguments to answer some of the questions raised in this chapter.

---

65 ECtHR, Oršuš, *supra*, para. 147.

66 *Ibid.*, para. 148 referring to ECtHR, Chapman, *supra*, para. 96, and ECtHR, Connors, *supra*, para. 84.

67 ECtHR, 6 April 2000 (Grand Chamber), Thlimmenos v. Greece, no. 34369/97, para. 44.

68 R. Sandland, *supra*, at 496.

69 *Ibid.*, 496. On this point, see A. Tremlett, 'Making a difference without creating a difference: Super-diversity as a new direction for research on Roma minorities', (2014) 14/6 *Ethnicities*, 830–848.

6. FURTHER ECtHR CASE LAW ON HOUSING RIGHTS AND ROMA/TRAVELLERS: A VELVET REVOLUTION?

A step further in the direction of more clarity regarding the meaning to be given to the term 'special consideration' for the needs and lifestyle of Roma and Travellers has been given by the Court in a set of recent decisions. In the following sub-sections this set of cases will be presented and analysed. Comments on this case law from a comparative perspective will then be included in the subsequent section, where some concluding remarks will also be made in the broader context of the debate concerning positive action measures and social policy prescriptions on housing rights for Roma and Travellers.

6.1. ADEQUACY OF HOUSING SOLUTIONS: SEDENTARY VS. NOMADIC LIFESTYLE

The first in this set of case law is *Gabriel Louis Stenegry et Sonia Adam c. France*.[70] The facts of the case are similar to the previous *Buckley* and *Chapman* cases. Here, the applicants were Travellers who acquired a piece of land located in an agricultural area on which no buildings could be erected. Once the applicants decided to settle on their own land and took care of the formalities in order to benefit from electricity connection and water, the mayor refused the necessary authorisation on environmental grounds.[71]

Subsequently, the local representative of the government (*préfet*) suggested that the applicants seek public housing or alternatively move to the reception areas provided for Travellers leading a nomadic way of life (*gens du voyage itinérants*). These proposals were supposed to be temporary solutions until the so-called 'family sites' (*terrain familiaux*) project was finalised.

Relying on Article 8 of the Convention, the applicants complained that these proposed solutions were not consistent with their culture and their way of life as could be instead the so-called 'family sites' (*terrain familiaux*) specifically foreseen by a 2000 national law for the reception and housing of Travellers. They also noted that the option of social housing did not respect their culture, which involves living in caravans, and that the reception areas provided for Travellers with a nomadic way of life (*gens du voyage itinérants*) were not appropriate for their sedentary status.[72]

70 ECtHR, 22 May 2007 (Decision on admissibility), Gabriel Louis Stenegry et Sonia Adam c. France, no. 40987/05. Note that the text of the decision is only available in French.

71 *Ibid.*, p. 2.

72 *Ibid.*, p. 6.

In this case an important distinction was clearly made by the applicants and later in the reasoning of the Court between the solutions for Travellers with a nomadic way of life (*gens du voyage itinérants*), for whom a reception area would be adequate, and the solutions for Travellers (*gens du voyage*) who are at least partly sedentary and for whom only a specific area where they can live in caravans but without implying or being forced to move and have a nomadic way of life would be adequate.

The Court recalled, on the one hand, the positive obligation to facilitate the Gypsy lifestyle and the special attention that should be given to the needs and different way of life of the applicants due to their vulnerability and minority status. On the other hand, the Court noted that the applicants had settled on land they had acquired in full knowledge of its agricultural character, and where no buildings could thus be erected. The refusal of the authorities was accordingly based on these grounds.

The Court accepted that the proposal that the applicants could live in social housing did not meet the lifestyle of the applicants. However, it had a different approach *vis-à-vis* the option of the reception area. For the Court this solution would have been able to respect the way of life in a caravan chosen by the applicants because, although it did not match the sedentary lifestyle to which the applicants aspired, it was nevertheless a temporary solution pending the completion of appropriate 'family sites'.[73]

Accordingly, the Court considered that the decision-making process adequately took into account the lifestyle of the applicants. Therefore, it considered that the options offered were not disproportionate to the legitimate aim pursued, and, consequently, the complaint was considered manifestly ill-founded and rejected.[74]

6.2. UNLAWFUL SETTLEMENTS AND DISADVANTAGED POSITION ENTAILING SPECIAL ASSISTANCE

The second case to be analysed is *Yordanova and Others v. Bulgaria*.[75] This case is partly different from the previous case where the applicants were the owners of the land. The *Yordanova* case concerned a group of Roma who had lived for many years in the makeshift houses they or their ancestors built on state or municipal land,[76] and from which, in 2005, the Bulgarian authorities decided to remove them.[77]

---

73 *Ibid.*, p. 13.
74 *Ibid.*, p. 13.
75 ECtHR, 24 April 2012, Yordanova and Others v. Bulgaria, no. 25446/06.
76 *Ibid.*, para. 102.
77 *Ibid.*, para. 104.

For the Court the fact that the applicants unlawfully occupied the land did not mean that their houses could not be considered 'homes' under the meaning of Article 8.[78] In addition, the fact that the case concerned the expulsion of the applicants as part of a community of several hundred persons and that this measure had repercussions for the applicants' lifestyle and social and family ties, meant that the interference affected not only their 'homes' but also their 'private and family life'.[79]

The applicants alleged that the removal order did not pursue a legitimate aim but was intended to benefit a private entrepreneur and to satisfy racist demands to free the area of an unwanted Roma settlement. The Government's position was that the aim of the measure was to recover illegally occupied municipal land, realise plans for urban development and put an end to a situation involving health and safety risks that had given rise to complaints.[80]

At the outset, the Court clarified that it is legitimate for the authorities to seek to regain possession of land from persons who do not have a right to occupy it.[81] Moreover, it was undisputed that the Roma settlement comprised buildings which did not meet the relevant construction requirements and that there was a general intention on the part of the authorities to use the land occupied by the applicants for urban development.[82] The motives behind the authorities' plans to transfer the land to a private investor for development purposes were considered proper and legitimate. Improvement of the urban environment by removing unsightly and substandard buildings and replacing them with modern dwellings meeting the relevant architectural and technical requirements was, for the Court, a legitimate aim in the interests of economic well-being and the protection of the health and the rights of others.[83]

As seen previously, in spheres involving the application of social or economic policies, including those regarding housing, the margin of appreciation left to the authorities is very broad. However, this margin is narrower where the right at stake is crucial to the individual's effective enjoyment of intimate or key rights and the extent of the intrusion into the personal sphere of the applicant is significant.[84] In addition, for the Court the loss of one's home is a most extreme form of interference with the right under Article 8 to respect for one's home, and therefore the measure implying this interference must be proportionate and reasonable.[85]

Although for the Court there was no doubt that the authorities were in principle entitled to remove the applicants who occupied municipal land

78 *Ibid.*, para. 103.
79 *Ibid.*, para. 105.
80 *Ibid.*, para. 109.
81 *Ibid.*, para. 111.
82 *Ibid.*, para. 112.
83 *Ibid.*, para. 113.
84 *Ibid.*, para. 118 (b).
85 *Ibid.*, paras. 118 (d) and 118 (e).

unlawfully,[86] in a crucial part of the ruling, the Court noted that for several decades the national authorities did not move to dislodge the applicants' families or ancestors and, therefore, *de facto* tolerated the unlawful Roma settlement.[87]

Considering that a whole community and a long period were concerned, the principle of proportionality required that such a situation be treated as being entirely different from routine cases of removal of an individual from unlawfully occupied property.[88] In this specific case, however, the removal order did not mention any special circumstance, such as decades-old community life, or possible consequences, such as homelessness.[89] In other words, the municipal authorities did not give reasons other than stating that the applicants occupied land unlawfully and, moreover, expressly refused to hear arguments about proportionality and the length of time the applicants and their families had lived undisturbed in the area concerned.[90] For the Court, this approach was considered in itself problematic, amounting to a failure to comply with the principle of proportionality.[91]

In this case, moreover, a contradictory approach by the Bulgarian authorities – and not uncommon across countries in Europe – was also raised by the Court: on the one hand, the authorities supported the adoption of national and regional programmes on Roma inclusion based on the understanding that the applicants are part of an underprivileged community whose problems are specific and must be addressed accordingly; on the other hand, they maintained that so doing would amount to 'privileged' treatment and would discriminate against the majority population.[92] In sum, for the Court, the Bulgarian authorities took an incongruous approach in dealing with Roma and Travellers.

Linked to the above consideration, it is an important part of the ruling that, in this regard, differs to some extent from previous cases on Roma, at least for the clarity with which the Court has explained its reasoning. Considering the argument raised by the Bulgarian authorities that different treatment for the Roma would amount to discrimination against the majority population, the Court noted that the applicants, 'regardless of their ethnic origin', are a social group in need of assistance, an outcast community and a socially disadvantaged group.[93] For the Court this entails providing special assistance to such a social group in order to guarantee that this group is able effectively to enjoy the same rights as the majority population.[94] In other terms, a severe social disadvantage

86 *Ibid.*, para. 120.
87 *Ibid.*, para. 121.
88 *Ibid.*, para. 121.
89 *Ibid.*, para. 122.
90 *Ibid.*
91 *Ibid.*, para. 123.
92 *Ibid.*, para. 128.
93 *Ibid.*, para. 129.
94 *Ibid.*

amounts, in certain circumstances, to treating groups differently in order to correct 'factual inequalities' between them and guarantee effective and substantial – not only formal – equality. A failure to do so may indeed give rise in itself to a breach of Article 14 of the Convention (non-discrimination clause).[95]

Finally, among the circumstances considered by the Court there was the fact that the applicants were not very active in seeking an alternative solution. It appeared that they were reluctant to seek social housing at least partly because they did not want to be dispersed, found it difficult to cover the related expenses and, in general, resented the radical change in their living environment that moving into blocks of flats would have entailed.[96]

Despite the reluctance on the part of the applicants to seek alternative accommodation, for the Court, the relevant point in this case was nonetheless that the *disadvantaged position* of the social group to which the applicants belong could and should have been taken into consideration, for example in assisting them to obtain officially the status of persons in need of housing, which would make them eligible for available social housing on the same footing as others. This was recognised by the Bulgarian authorities in their national and regional programmes, but did not result in practical steps being taken in the present case.[97]

The *underprivileged status* of the applicants' group therefore had to be considered a weighty factor in considering approaches to dealing with their unlawful settlement and, if their removal was considered necessary, in deciding on its timing, the way it was done and, if possible, arrangements for alternative shelter. For the Court, this was not done in the present case.[98] The Bulgarian authorities failed to respect the proportionality principle in their removal order which, accordingly, was not 'necessary in a democratic society' as required by the European Convention on Human Rights and thus was not in line with Article 8 of the Convention.

6.3. AN EMERGING RIGHT TO ALTERNATIVE ACCOMMODATION IN CASE OF FORCED EVICTION?

The last case to be analysed is *Winterstein and Others v. France* concerning a group of Travellers (*gens du voyage*), who were established for many years (five to thirty years) in a wood; however, in 2005, they had to leave following a removal order issued on grounds of environmental protection.[99] As in the *Yordanova* case, the Court considered that the applicants maintained sufficiently close

95 *Ibid.*
96 *Ibid.*, para. 131.
97 *Ibid.*, para. 132.
98 *Ibid.*, para. 133.
99 ECtHR, 17 October 2013, Winterstein and Others v. France, no. 27013/07. At the time of writing the text of the judgment was only available in French.

and continuous links with their caravans and bungalows located in the wood that these could be considered their 'homes', regardless of the legality of the occupation under domestic law.

As for the traditional lifestyle, the Court clarified that 'living in a caravan' is an integral part of the identity of Travellers, even if they no longer live in a nomadic way, and that measures concerning caravan parking affect their ability to maintain their identity and lead a private and family life in accordance with that tradition.[100]

For the Court a crucial element in this case was that the authorities in principle had the right to evict the applicants, who were illegally occupying the municipal area. However, the same authorities had taken no action in this direction for many years and, similarly to the *Yordanova* case, had thus *de facto* tolerated this illegal occupation.[101]

The inactivity of the authorities meant that the applicants had developed close ties with the place and had built a community. The Court concluded that the *principle of proportionality* required that such situations, where a whole community and a long period of time are involved, are treated differently from common situations where an individual is expelled from a property s/he occupies illegally.[102]

Despite the similarities with the *Yordanova* case, *Winterstein* differed from *Yordanova* because here the areas occupied were not municipal areas but private land of which the applicants were mostly tenants or owners, or, in some cases, were private areas for camping and caravans on which, without an official authorisation, permanent stationing of caravans was not permitted.[103]

The main argument of the Court was that the national authorities ordered the expulsion of the applicants without analysing the proportionality of the measure: having established the non-conformity of the applicants' presence according to the land plan, the authorities gave this aspect paramount importance without balancing it with the arguments raised by the applicants.[104] The Court concluded that the applicants did not benefit, as part of the removal process, from a review of the proportionality of the interference given the length of their presence, the presence of their families and the community they formed.[105]

Most importantly, in this case the Court referred to other international treaties and documents, in particular those of the Council of Europe, the FCNM and the European Social Charter (Revised), and those of the UN Committee on Economic, Social and Cultural Rights requiring alternative accommodation

100 *Ibid.*, para. 142, referring to Chapman, *supra*, para. 73, and Connors, *supra*, para. 68.
101 *Ibid.*, para. 150.
102 *Ibid.*, para. 150.
103 *Ibid.*, para. 152.
104 *Ibid.*, para. 156.
105 *Ibid.*, paras. 159 and 158.

in case of forced eviction.[106] The Court referred specifically to the decision of the European Committee of Social Rights (ECSR) concerning the insufficient number of suitable dwellings for Roma and Travellers who have opted for a sedentary way of life.[107]

This is an important step in the direction of recognising a positive obligation and a parallel right to an alternative domicile in the event of expulsion. The Court emphasised in this regard that many international treaties and legal documents adopted within the Council of Europe stressed the need, in the case of forced evictions of Roma and Travellers, to provide alternative accommodation, except in the event of force majeure. This point is particularly relevant because, in the Strasbourg system, the principle of proportionality is measured, among others, on the consensus emerging at the international level and among contracting parties.

Another salient point emerging from this case is that the Court combined two aspects of the Roma/Travellers group, namely that it was an ethnic minority with a specific identity and culture and, at the same time, an underprivileged social group. This approach has also been strongly supported by other European bodies, in particular by the Advisory Committee of the FCNM.[108]

The Court concluded that for the families who opted freely for social housing, the authorities had paid sufficient attention to their needs.[109] On the contrary, the Court reached the opposite conclusion regarding those applicants who applied for resettlement on family sites (*terrain familiaux*).[110] The 'family sites' project was in fact abandoned by the municipality concerned, which decided to allocate the plots provided for this purpose to the reception area for Travellers leading a nomadic way of life (*gens du voyage itinerants*).[111] In this regard, the Court also emphasised that the applicants could not be blamed for not having requested or accepted social housing because, as seen in the *Stenegry et Adam* decision, the Court accepted that this type of accommodation is not adequate for their lifestyle.[112]

---

106 *Ibid.*, para. 159. See, CoE, Committee of Ministers, Rec. 2005(4), *Improving the housing conditions of Roma and Travellers in Europe*, para. 26; PACE, Res. 1740 (2010), *The situation of Roma in Europe and relevant activities of the Council of Europe*, para. 17.5; United Nations, Committee on Economic, Social and Cultural Rights, General Comment 7, *Forced evictions, and the right to adequate housing* (1997), U.N. Doc. E/1998/22, para. 17.

107 ECtHR, Winterstein and Others v. France, *ibid.*, para. 165. See, European Committee of Social Rights, 19 October 2009, *European Roma Rights Centre v. France*, no. 51/2008.

108 ECtHR, Winterstein and Others v. France, *ibid.*, para. 160. See, R. Medda-Windischer, 'The Roma and the Framework Convention for the Protection of National Minorities: a Tool to Disentangle the Dichotomy between a Socially Disadvantaged Group and a National Minority', in M. Goodwin and P. De Hert (eds), *European Roma Integration Efforts. A Snapshot* (Brussels: Brussels University Press, 2013).

109 ECtHR, Winterstein and Others v. France, *ibid.*, para. 161.

110 *Ibid.*, para. 162.

111 *Ibid.*, para. 162.

112 *Ibid.*, para. 163.

The Court concluded that Article 8 was violated in the case of all applicants as to the expulsion procedure because this was not based on a proportionate decision. Moreover, in the case of the applicants who opted for relocation to the so-called 'family sites' (*terrains familiaux*) there was equally a violation of Article 8 as the decision-making process did not sufficiently taken into account their needs.[113]

7. CONCLUDING REMARKS

Roma and Travellers are considered by the Strasbourg Court to be members of minority groups that are particularly *underprivileged* and *vulnerable* and in need of special protection as a result of their history and past and current discrimination; on this, there is a broad consensus at the international and European level. But from these general statements can we infer concrete positive obligations, or even obligations as regards positive action measures or social policy?

It is clearly acknowledged that the Strasbourg Court accepts not only negative obligations, i.e. to prevent the state from doing something, but also positive obligations requiring actions from the state. Moreover, we have seen that social and economic rights, including housing, are not absent from the Convention system. It has been noted that the richest case law on positive obligations and that with the longest heritage in the judgments of the Court concerns Article 8 and the right to respect for home and private and family life. However, the Court has also clearly held that the state's positive obligation in connection with respect for the home does not include a duty to see that each family has its own home.

As far as positive action measures are concerned – namely activities, initiatives and strategies to prevent or compensate for disadvantages and discrimination, whether these arose in the past or are still ongoing, in order to promote substantive equality and redress under-representation of certain groups – the Court is more hesitant and cautious. The position of the Court seems to be that it would accept them but not actively require them or make them obligatory. However, as seen, some progressive trends in the direction of state obligation can be inferred from recent case law on housing and Roma and Travellers.

Along the lines of this discussion it has been noted that positive actions on housing and Roma/Travellers would fall on the boundary between 'simple' positive obligations and social policy prescriptions; in this regard they could be considered to be mixed or blurred policies. However, to the extent that these measures clearly target a well-defined group, seek to redress disadvantages in a specific setting, and are subject to periodic review, then these measures can be considered to be 'positive action measures'.

113 *Ibid.*, para. 167.

Yet, it has to be recalled that from the Court's perspective, a clear principle is that in the choice and implementation of social or economic policies, including those on housing, the margin of appreciation left to states is very wide. This margin of discretion has limits when the rights at stake, such as those involved under Article 8 (home and family/private life), are of central importance to the individual's identity, self-determination, physical and moral integrity, maintenance of relationships with others and a settled and secure place in the community.

Together with the margin of appreciation, the principle of proportionality is also central and is a pivotal litmus test for the Court's assessment. It requires that situations where, for instance, a whole community and a long period in a settlement are concerned or where for several decades the national authorities did not move to dislodge the applicants and, therefore, *de facto* tolerated an unlawful Roma/Traveller settlement must be treated as being entirely different from routine cases of removal of an individual from unlawfully occupied property.

Therefore, a clear obligation on states and local authorities that can be inferred from the analysis of the Court's case law is that the requirement to give 'special consideration' to Roma and Travellers means that the national authorities must take into account factors such as decades-old community life, possible consequences such as homelessness, or the inactivity and passivity of the authorities towards serious conditions of deprivation and want incompatible with human dignity.

In the recent rulings of the Strasbourg Court an important notion emerges with regard to Roma and Travellers, housing and their traditional way of life, i.e. adequate housing alternatives compatible with their traditional lifestyle. This notion can also be found in many national legal frameworks on Roma integration elaborated by EU states at the request of the European Commission in 2011.[114]

In general, the Court acknowledges that *living in a caravan* is for Roma and Travellers an integral part of their identity, even if they no longer live in a nomadic way. In addition, the Court distinguishes between housing solutions for Roma and Travellers with a nomadic way of life (*gens du voyage itinérants*), for whom reception areas would be adequate and consistent with their traditional lifestyle, and housing solutions for Roma and Travellers (*gens du voyage*) who are, at least partly, sedentary and for whom only specific areas where they can live in caravans but without implying or being forced to move and have a nomadic way of life would be adequate (*Winterstein* case). In contrast, social housing is

114 European Commission, *An EU Framework for National Roma Integration Strategies up to 2020*, COM(2011) 173 final, 5 April 2011.

generally considered by the Court to be inconsistent with the traditional way of life of Roma and Travellers (*Yordanova* case).

Whether or not finding alternative accommodation can be considered a positive obligation or even a positive action, the Court has been, in this regard, very cautious referring in some cases only to the obligation to assist the Roma/Travellers applicants to obtain officially the status of persons in need of housing in order to make them eligible for available social housing on the same footing as others. In other words, the underprivileged status of Roma/Traveller applicants must be a weighty factor in considering approaches to dealing with their unlawful settlement and, if their removal is necessary, in deciding on its timing and the way it is done; however, as far as alternative shelters are concerned, these are foreseen as an obligation only 'if possible' (*Yordanova* case).

The Court's approach to alternative accommodation follows the same orientation of other European mechanisms, especially the European Committee on Social Rights on suitable dwellings for Roma and Travellers who have opted for a sedentary way of life. The European Committee on Social Rights has in fact expressly required, in the case of forced evictions of Roma and Travellers, alternative accommodation but only 'unless force majeure'.

The reference to force majeure is connected with the allocation of scarce resources and the prioritisation of competing policy concerns that the allocation of housing and alternative accommodation, in the case of forced eviction, involves. The problem of the allocation of limited resources poses a significant obstacle in the attempt to impose positive obligations or positive action measures on government. In this context, there is a tension between the conflicting needs of the state, which aims to control expenditure, and equality-seeking groups who seek to impose positive obligations on government.[115] Positive action measures could thus be justified and required as necessary and appropriate only when there is evidence that the previous distribution method disproportionately disadvantaged members of certain groups, and that the positive action measure serves to correct this disadvantage.[116]

In the recent case law analysed in this chapter the Court combines two aspects of the Roma/Travellers groups, precisely as ethnic minority groups with a specific identity and culture, but also as 'underprivileged' social groups. Since the *D.H.* case, indeed, the Court has recognised protection for Roma and Travellers not merely as individuals, but as a *group*.[117] In this case, the

115 C.Wilkie and M. Zisman Gary, *supra*, 55.

116 U. Archibong, M. Bell, L. Waddington, et al., *supra*, at 26.

117 On a critical analysis of this point and on the issue of structural discrimination resulting in a particular group being systematically placed in a disadvantaged position in various areas of social life, see R. Medda-Windischer, 'Dismantling Segregating Education and the European Court of Human Rights. D.H. and Others vs. Czech Republic: Towards an Inclusive Education?', *supra*, at 39–42; J. Marko, *supra*, at 99–103.

Court clearly affirmed that because the applicants are members of the Roma community they 'necessarily suffered the same discriminatory treatment ... [and therefore the Court] ... does not need to examine their individual cases.'[118]

Clearly, an approach based on *difference* rather than *sameness* implies that applicants are required to find a group to which they could belong because of a personal characteristic that separates that group from other groups. And this, for some, is problematic because the specificity engendered by such an application of the comparator analysis 'precludes complexity, intersectionality or any analysis of layers of oppression.'[119]

From the analysis conducted in this chapter on the Strasbourg case law on Roma/Travellers and housing, the overall picture is quite puzzling: the glass can equally be seen as half empty and as half full. New applications lodged by Roma and Travellers will oblige the Strasbourg Court to further clarify the scope of the housing obligations on states towards Roma and Travellers as a specific underprivileged minority and there are signs that the Court is slowly going in this direction. The limitations placed on the use of state's margin of appreciation, even in the case of housing policies, and the reference to other international and European mechanisms requiring alternative accommodation in the event of forced eviction of Roma and Travellers, are important bricks in the construction of a solid set of case law favouring the most underprivileged minority group living in Europe.

118 ECtHR (Grand Chamber), D.H. and Others v. The Czech Republic, *supra*, para. 209.

119 C.Wilkie and M. Zisman Gary, *supra*, at 49.

THE RIGHT TO WORK OF PEOPLE WITH DISABILITIES

The Obligation to Accommodate as an Emanation of the Contemporary Approach to Disability

Sébastien VAN DAMME

'The problem is not how to wipe out all differences,
but how to unite with all differences intact.'
Rabindranath Tagore

Over the years, the position of people with disabilities in society has changed. Following the emergence of the social model of disability, people with disabilities have become full holders of human rights, including the right to work. Since the labour market is largely inaccessible to them, this right remains as yet rather a theoretical right. In order to remedy this situation, a number of legal instruments provide for a 'right to reasonable accommodation'. This right entitles an employee to demand a number of reasonable adjustments to his work environment. The duty to accommodate is the central theme of this chapter. Prior to discussing this matter, it is important to provide the reader with a good insight into the concept of disability.

1. INTRODUCTION

The right to work is incorporated in various European and international sources of law.[1] Article 23(1) of the Universal Declaration of Human Rights, for instance, stipulates that everyone has the right to work. The right to work can also be found in Article 1 of the Revised European Social Charter, Article 22 of the Covenant

[1] D. Ashiagbor, 'The Right to Work' in G. De Búrca and B. De Witte, *Social Rights in Europe*, (Oxford: Oxford University Press, 2005), 241.

on Civil and Political Rights and Articles 6–8 of the Covenant on Economic, Social and Cultural Rights. In Belgium, this right has even acquired the status of a constitutional right by its introduction in the Constitution in 1994 (Art. 23,1°).

The fact that the right to work is incorporated in many sources of law can be explained by the importance of work.[2] Irrespective of the fact that work is an essential factor in terms of being able to earn a living, it also has other important functions. Work is a fundamental activity that allows human beings to develop themselves.[3] In a way, people derive their identity from their work. Furthermore, it is the supreme means of participating fully in society.[4] Finally, the right to work is essential for realising other human rights and constitutes an inseparable and inherent part of human dignity.[5]

Due to the universal scope of the legal instruments mentioned above,[6] the right to work applies to every person. Nonetheless, several population groups are still excluded from exercising this right, in particular people of a different origin, women and people with disabilities.[7] This chapter deals with the latter group. In 2007, the International Labour Organization concluded that 52% of people with a disability in Europe do not have the opportunity to participate in the labour market.[8] In developing countries, this rises to 80%. Persons with disabilities are not only discriminated against on the labour market, but they also face discrimination in other sectors of society such as education.[9]

In reaction to this social discrimination, a new dynamic started to develop in the 1970s *vis-à-vis* people with a disability.[10] They were no longer considered

---

2 W. Myhill, 'Employment of People with Disabilities', (2010) *International Encyclopedia of Rehabilitation*, 1; K. Reyniers, *(Verboden) arbeid*, (Antwerp-Oxford: Intersentia, 2012), 90.

3 Concl. A-G M. Poiares Maduro, Case C-303/06, *Coleman v. Attridge Law*, EU: C: 2008, para 11.

4 Recital 9 Directive 2000/78/EC of 27 November 2000 establishing a general framework for equal treatment in employment and occupation, *Official Journal L 303*, 2 December 2000, *P. 016–022*; R. Malhotra, 'The Implications of the Social Model of Disablement for the Legal Regulation of the Modern Workplace in Canada and the United States', (2009) *Manitoba Law Journal*, 1.

5 A. McColgan, *Discrimination, Equality and the Law*, (Oxford: Hart Publishing, 2014), 23; Committee on Economic, Social and Cultural Rights, *The right to work*, General Comment No. 18, adopted 24 November 2005, para 3.

6 For example Article 6(1) of the Covenant on Economic, Social and Cultural Rights speaks of 'everyone' has the right to work; M.A. Stein, 'Disability Human Rights', (2007) *California Law Review* 2007, 79.

7 Title 42, chapter 126, sec. 12101, (a) findings, (3) Americans with Disabilities Act 1990, as amended.

8 International Labour Organization, *Disability Discrimination at Work – Fact Sheet*, December 2007, available at www. Ilo.org/publications.

9 European Commission, *Education and Disability/Special Needs. Policies and practices in education, training and employment for students with disabilities and special educational needs in the EU – An independent report prepared for the European Commission by the NESSE network of experts*, Brussels, 2012, available at www.nesse.fr/nesse/activities/reports/activities/reports/disability-special-needs-1.

10 C. Barnes and G. Mercer, 'Theorizing and Researching Disability from a Social Model Perspective' in C. Barnes and G. Mercer, *Implementing the Social Model of Disability: Theory*

'receivers of care' and 'subjects in need of help', but rather 'equal rights holders'.[11] This resulted in a number of specific legislative initiatives, such as the 2006 UN Convention on the Rights of Persons with Disabilities (hereafter 'Convention')[12] and, on the European Union level, Directive 2000/78/EC which establishes a general framework for equal treatment in employment and occupation (hereafter 'Directive').[13] Both texts address the right to work and transpose this right to the specific situation of person with disabilities. The Directive[14] and the Convention[15] acknowledge that the labour market is insufficiently adapted to the needs of these people and consequently provide for a 'right to reasonable accommodation'.[16] In order to avoid the fundamental social right to work remaining merely a theoretical right for people with a disability, it is of vital importance to offer these people the opportunity to work in an environment adapted to their needs.

The objective of this chapter is to elucidate this abstract right to reasonable accommodation in relation to the right to work. To this end, the contemporary approach to disability will be discussed first.

2. CONTEMPORARY APPROACH TO DISABILITY

2.1. MODERN DISCRIMINATION LAW

Modern discrimination law is based on the idea that all people have equal intrinsic value and that, on the basis of their 'human nature', all citizens should participate equally in society.[17] In accordance with this equality principle all people are born with equal value and equal rights. Human rights would be meaningless if they did not apply to all people equally.

---

and Research, (Leeds: Leeds: The Disability Press, 2004), 1–17; C. Barnes and G. Mercer, 'Understanding Impairment and Disability: towards an international perspective' in C. Barnes and G. Mercer (eds.), *The Social Model of Disability: Europe and the Majority World, (*Leeds: Leeds, The Disability Press, 2005), 1.

11 T. Degener and G. quinn, *A Survey of International, Comparative and Regional Disability Law Reform,* paper presented at the 'From principles to practice' symposium, Washington, 2000; G. Quinn, 'A short guide to the United Nations Convention on the Rights of Persons with Disabilities' in G. Quinn and L. Waddington (eds.), *European Yearbook of Disability Law. Volume 1,* (Antwerp: Intersentia, 2009), 90.

12 Convention on the Rights of Persons with Disabilities, G.A. Res. 61/106 (2007).

13 A. Kanter, *The Development of Disability Rights Under International Law* (Abingdon: Routledge, 2015), 7–8.

14 Art. 5 Directive.

15 Art. 2 Convention; Art. 27(I) Convention.

16 L. Waddington, 'Equal to the task? Re-Examining EU Equality Law in Light of the United Nations Convention on the Rights of Persons with Disabilities' in L. Waddington, G. Quinn and E. Flynn (eds.), *European Yearbook of Disability Law, vol. 4,* (Cambridge-Antwerp: Intersentia, 2013), 184.

17 T. Loenen, *Equality as a legal principle,* (The Hague: Boom Juridische Uitgevers, 2009) 11.

The fundamental equality of all human beings did not prevent people with disabilities remaining invisible in terms of the application of human rights.[18] They were either not considered to be holders of rights, or these rights were applied less strictly to them.[19] Research has shown that people with disabilities are disproportionately affected by violations of human rights.[20]

For a long time, discrimination law – whether on a national, European or international level – was conceived to be a total prohibition of discrimination, leaving no room to take into account protected characteristics like gender, race and disability.[21] Due to the emergence of fundamental social rights, this has gradually changed: discrimination law now includes various positive obligations, such as the obligation to provide for a right to reasonable accommodation and promote the employment of persons with disabilities through affirmative action programmes and incentives.[22] Moreover, the realisation of the right to work for vulnerable groups requires more than a prohibition on discrimination only.[23] This is reflected in Article 27 of the Convention, which transposes the universal right to work to the specific situation of persons with disabilities. Pursuant to this article, people with disabilities have the right to a safe and healthy work environment, the right to choose freely a profession, the right to equal pay for work of equal value, the right to get the same benefits of labour law, etc. By the same token, the Directive does not simply require that a person with a disability should be treated in exactly the same way as a non-disabled person.[24] Thus, the model of equality underlying the Convention and the Directive is not a strict formal equality model based on treating people with no relevant difference in the same way, but it reaches beyond this, towards some notion of substantive equality.[25] This model of equality requires that some attempts be made to remove

18 F. Megret, 'The Disabilities Convention: towards a holistic concept of rights, (2008) *International Journal of Human Rights* 6; G. de Búrca, 'The European Union in the negotiation of the UN Disability Convention', (2010) *E.L. Rev.*, 175.

19 H. Mannan, M. MacLachlan and J. McVeigh, 'Core concepts of human rights and inclusion of vulnerable groups in the United Nations Convention on the rights of persons with disabilities', (2012) *European Journal of Disability Research*, 161.

20 J. Clifford, 'The UN Convention and its Impact on European Equality Law', (2011) 6 *The Equal Rights Review,* 13.

21 L. Waddington, 'Equal to the task? Re-Examining EU Equality Law in Light of the United Nations Convention on the Rights of Persons with Disabilities' in L. Waddington, G. Quinn and E. Flynn (eds.), *European Yearbook of Disability Law, vol. 4*, (Cambridge-Antwerp: Intersentia, 2013), 184; L. Waddington, *From Rome to Nice in a Wheelchair. The Development of a European Disability Policy*, (Groningen: European Law Publishing, 2006), 27.

22 Art. 27 Convention.

23 R. Buitenweg, K. Buitenweg and J. Temperman, *Het Sociale Gezicht van Europa*, (The Hague: Boom Juridische uitgevers, 2013), 53.

24 A. Lawson, 'The EU rights based approach to disability: strategies for shaping an inclusive society', (2005) 6 *International Journal of Discrimination and the Law*, 274–275.

25 J.E. Lord and R. Brown, 'The Role of Reasonable Accommodation in Securing Substantive Equality for Persons with Disabilities: The UN Convention on the Rights of Persons with Disabilities', (2010) available at Social Science Research Network, 1–4; T. Loenen, *Equality*

the barriers that exclude persons with disabilities. Therefore, the underlying thought of the right to reasonable accommodation is that the strict application of the formal principle of equality will not lead to increased participation in the labour market. On the contrary, people with a disability require an environment that is adapted to their needs.[26]

2.2. CONCEPT OF DISABILITY

The change in the way in which disabilities are perceived, better known as the transition from a medical model to a social model of disability, had a major influence on the concept of disability.[27]

2.2.1. *From a Medical to a Social Model of Disability*

At the time the medical model held sway, disabilities were considered to be an individual problem, as an abnormality and a personal tragedy.[28] People were given the label 'disabled' on the basis of a clinical and medical diagnosis. Since the emphasis was on the person's 'disorder', legislation was predominantly oriented towards the recovery and healing of the disability.[29] If the disability was of such a nature that the person in question was not able to generate an income, he was entitled to disability benefits.[30] Following the emergence of fundamental social rights and the inclusion idea (not the 'us-them' model but an all-inclusive model), this medical model was gradually abandoned.

In the 1970s, a new approach to disability started to develop, mainly in the United States and Canada.[31] Disability scholars no longer considered a disability

as a legal principle, (The Hague: Boom Juridische Uitgevers, 2009) 13–14; A. McColgan, *Discrimination, Equality and the Law*, (Oxford: Hart Publishing, 2014), 20–23.

26 S. van Damme, 'Tewerkstelling van personen met een handicap: het recht op redelijke aanpassingen onder de loep genomen', (2014) 7 *Soc.Kron.*, 329; K. Henrard, 'De verhouding tussen de concepten redelijke aanpassing, indirecte discriminatie en proportionaliteit' in C. Bayart, S. Sottiaux and S. Van Droogenbroeck, *De nieuwe federale antidiscriminatiewetten*, (Bruges: die Keure, 2008), 267–277.

27 P. Barlett, 'The United Nations Conventions on the Rights of Persons with Disabilities and Mental Health Law', (2012) *Modern Law Review*, 758.

28 A. Sawadsri, '"Do I Look Like an Object?" A Quest of Exploring Person-Place Relationship of Disabling', (2012) 50 *Procedia – Social and Behavioral Sciences* 2012, afl. 50, 419–42; R.K. Scotch, 'Models of Disability and the Americans with Disabilities Act', (2014) *Berkeley J. Emp. & Lab. L.*, 214.

29 R. Kayess and P. French, 'Out of the darkness into light? Introducing the Convention on the Rights of Persons with Disabilities', (2008) *Human Rights Law Review*, 5.

30 S. van Damme, 'Klik maken voor de inclusie van personen met een handicap', (2015) 310 *Juristenkrant*, 10; A. Lawson, 'The EU rights based approach to disability: strategies for shaping an inclusive society', (2005) 6 *International Journal of Discrimination and the Law*, 272.

31 C. Barnes and G. Mercer, 'Theorizing and Researching Disability from a Social Model Perspective' in C. Barnes and G. Mercer, *Implementing the Social Model of Disability: Theory*

to be an individual problem, but rather contemplated the social and cultural aspects of disability.[32] They studied the extent to which environmental obstacles and social attitudes were responsible for the creation of a disability.[33] In this contemporary social model it is not the individual, but rather both the obstacles that are created by society and discrimination, prejudices and exclusion, that constitute the problem.[34] Adherents of the social model try to make the transition from exclusion and segregation to inclusion. This also has tangible consequences for the right to work. For instance, this right should preferably be exercised in an 'open' work environment (Art. 27(1) Convention). Nevertheless, in most – even European – countries persons with disabilities are employed in sheltered workshops.[35]

2.2.2. *To a Broad Definition of Disability*

The contemporary approach to disability has led to a new and broader definition of disability.[36] An example of such a wide notion can be found in Article 1 of the Convention: 'Persons with disabilities include those who have long-term physical, mental, intellectual or sensory impairments which in interaction with various barriers may hinder their full and effective participation in society on an equal basis with others'. The fact that the term disability should be interpreted broadly is also emphasised in the preamble (recital e), which states that: 'disability is an evolving concept and that disability results from the interaction between persons with impairments and attitudinal and environmental barriers that hinder their full and effective participation in society on an equal basis with others'. The European Directive does not include a definition of the term 'disability', but the Court of Justice of the European Union and the European Commission have already held that the European legal instruments have to be

---

and Research, (Leeds:Leeds: The Disability Press, 2004), 1–17; J.-S.Beaudry,'Beyond (Models of) Disability?', (2014) *McGill University*, Working paper series, 1; M.A. Stein, 'Disability Human Rights', (2007) *California Law Review*, 85.

32 D. Cuypers, S. Keunen and S. van Damme, 'Het Herziene Europees Sociaal Handvest en de verbetering van de mensenrechtenpositie van personen met een handicap' (2016) 1 *TSR*, 13–17; A. Wiesbrock,'Disability as a Form of Vulnerability under EU Law and CoE Law: Embracing the 'Social Model'?' in F. Ippolito and S.I. Sánchez, *Protection Vulnerable Groups. The European Human Rights Framework*, (Oxford: Hart Publishing, 2015), 72.

33 R. Lang, 'The United Nations Convention on the right and dignities of persons with disability: A panacea for ending disability discrimination?', (2009) 3 *European Journal of Disability*, 268.

34 R. Traustadóttir, 'Disability studies, the Social Model and Legal Developments' in O.M. Arnardóttir and G. Quinn (eds.), *The UN Convention on the Rights of Persons with Disabilities. European and Scandinavian Perspectives*, (Leiden-Boston: Martinus Nijhoff Publishers, 2009) 8.

35 On this point see: S. Ferraina, 'Analysis of the Legal Meaning of Article 27 of the UN CRPD: Key Challenges for Adapted Work Settings', (2012) available at http://digitalcommons.ilr.cornell.edu/cgi/viewcontent.cgi?article=1559&context=gladnetcollect, 35p.

36 R.K. Scotch, 'Models of Disability and the Americans with Disabilities Act', (2014) *Berkeley J. Emp. & Lab. L.*, 217.

read in the light of the Convention.[37] In 2010, the European Union even acceded to the Convention as an independent entity.[38] It is also worth mentioning that the European Court of Human Rights used the Convention in the past to clarify the meaning of the ECHR in relation to people with disabilities.[39]

It is apparent from the definition of disability that both the Convention and – following the Court of Justice's case law – the Directive opt for the social approach to disability.[40] Rather than stressing a person's limitations, emphasis is placed on their ability to participate on the understanding that accommodations are made to the environment. The right to reasonable accommodation should therefore be considered a manifestation of the social model of disability and the substantial model of equality.[41] Due to the obligation to accommodate, employers are forced to take the employee's individual characteristics into account.[42] Consequently, even though person A and B may be suffering from the same visual disorder, an application form printed in Braille may only constitute an appropriate adjustment for person B, who is able to read Braille. Under the medical model this differentiation was impossible. There was only one way of dealing with a certain type of disorder. It is precisely this differentiation that leads to effective equality.

This redefinition has practical implications, since people who used to be considered ill can now be regarded as disabled.[43] The difference between both concepts is of significant importance since people with an illness do not fall within the scope of disability protection. Consequently, those persons cannot invoke the right to reasonable accommodation. EU law does not provide for a

---

37 Case C-354/13, *Kaltoft v. Kommunernes Landsforening*, EU: 2014; Case C-356/12, *Wolfgang Glatzel v. Freistaat Bayern*, EU:2014; Case C-363/12, *Z v. A Government Department*, EU: 2014; European Commission, *Joint Report on the application of Council Directive 2000/43/EC and of Council Directive 2000/78/EC*, (Brussels: COM (2014) 2 final), 14.

38 G. de Búrca, 'The European Union in the negotiation of the UN Disability Convention', (2010) *E.L. Rev.*, 174–196.

39 For example: ECtHR, 17 July 2014, Valentin Câmpeanu v. Romania, no. 47848/08 and ECtHR, 29 January 2013, S.H.H. v. United Kingdom, no. 60367/10.

40 R. Lang, M. Kett, N. Groce and J.-F. Trani, 'Implementing the United Nations Convention on the rights of persons with disabilities: principles, implications, practice and limitations', (2011) 5 *European Journal of Disability Research*, 208; A. Kanter, *The Development of Disability Rights Under International Law* (Abingdon: Routledge, 2015), 7; L. Waddington, 'A New Era in Human Rights Protection in the European Community: the Implications the United Nations' Convention on the Rights of Persons with Disabilities for the European Community', *Maastricht Faculty of Law. Working Paper nr. 2007–4*, 17.

41 J.E. Lord and R. Brown, 'The Role of Reasonable Accommodation in Securing Substantive Equality for Persons with Disabilities: The UN Convention on the Rights of Persons with Disabilities', (2010) available at Social Science Research Network, 4; L. Waddington, *From Rome to Nice in a Wheelchair. The Development of a European Disability Policy*, (Groningen: European Law Publishing, 2006), 3 and 27.

42 S. van Damme, 'Tewerkstelling van personen met een handicap: het recht op redelijke aanpassingen onder de loep genomen', (2014) 7 *Soc.Kron.*, 329.

43 N. Betsch,'The Ring and Skouboe Werge: A Reluctant Acceptance of the Social Approach of Disability', (2013) *ELLJ*, 138.

prohibition on discrimination on the basis of disease as such.[44] In a number of judgments, the European Court of Justice has shed light on the unclear distinction between the concepts of disability and disease.[45] In the (quite old) *Chacòn Navas* case, the Court adhered to the medical modal of disability and established a strict separation between illness and disability.[46] In the joined cases *Ring* and *Skouboe Werge* the same Court held for the first time that the Directive should be read in combination with Article 1 of the Convention.[47] The dividing line between both concepts has become even more blurred since the Court of Justice's *Kaltoft* case, in which the Court found that serious forms of obesity can be considered a disability.[48] The Court held that it should be verified whether the disorder hinders the person's full and effective participation in professional life on an equal basis with other workers, and that this hindrance has to be a long-term one. It is not required that the inability to participate is absolute. For the applicability of the Directive and the Convention it is also not required that there is a connection between the specific work and the disability.

Following the broad definition, the following disorders may be categorised as disabilities within the meaning of the Convention and the Directive: auditory and visual impairments, autism,[49] depression, diabetes, obesity,[50] dyslexia, ADHD, serious forms of learning disabilities, etc.[51] Chronic illnesses, such as cardiovascular diseases, might also meet the two criteria mentioned above (long-term and hindering aspects of the disorder). According to the European Court of Human Rights, HIV-positive persons also fall within the scope of the protection.[52] Furthermore, several authors raise the question whether people with cancer should also be considered disabled.[53] In that case, there is a danger of the entire population being labelled disabled and of the protection being undermined. According to the Court of Justice, not being able to conceive naturally does not constitute a disability within the meaning of the Directive and the Convention.[54] Although this might be a source of great suffering, it does not prevent women

---

44 Case C-13/05, *Chacòn Navas v. Eurest Colectividades SA*, EU: 2006.

45 Case C-13/05, *Chacòn Navas v. Eurest Colectividades SA*, EU: 2006; Case C-335/11–337/11, *Ring and Skouboe Werge*, EU: 2014; Case 354/13, *Kaltoft v. Kommunernes Landsforening*, EU: 2014.

46 Case C-13/05, *Chacòn Navas v. Eurest Colectividades SA*, EU: 2006; L. Waddington and M.S. Gijzen, '(Her)definitie van het begrip 'handicap' in de EG en Nederlandse gelijkebehandelingswetgeving', *NTER* 2006, 272.

47 Case C-335/11–337/11, *Ring and Skouboe Werge*, EU: 2014.

48 Case C-354/13, *Kaltoft v. Kommunernes Landsforening*, EU: 2014.

49 European Committee on Social Rights, 11 September, European Action of the Disabled (AEH) v. France, no. 81/2012.

50 Case C-354/13, *Kaltoft v. Kommunernes Landsforening*, EU: 2014.

51 S. van Damme, 'Het (theoretisch) recht op inclusief onderwijs', (2013–2014) *TORB*, 418.

52 ECtHR, 10 March 2011, Kiyutin v. Russia, no. 2700/10.

53 D. Foster, 'Understanding Workplace Accommodations for Disabled Employees: The Law and Good Practice' in T. Wright and H. Conley (eds.), *Gower Handbook of Discrimination at Work*, (Burlington: Gower Publishing Limited, 2011, 174.

54 Case C-363/12, *Z v. A Government Department*, EU: 2014.

from carrying out a professional activity. It should be noted that under Canadian law, pregnant employees are entitled to request an accommodation to their work environment, because they fall within the scope of the disability protection.[55] Further, the Convention itself excludes *short-term disabilities* resulting from trauma or illness and *people with occasional disabilities*. The introduction of a comprehensive list of illnesses and disorders into the Convention and Directive could solve the question as to what constitutes a disability. However, this would detract from the merits of the social model of disability, namely from the idea that society is disabled rather than the individual.[56] Moreover, the question whether a disorder constitutes a disability depends on the nature of society, the context and of course also the nature of the work.[57] A visual impairment may be considered a disability in a society where it is not easy to obtain glasses because it hinders a person's participation in said society. Finally, such a list will not remain up-to-date very long, given the continuous progress of medical science.[58]

The division between short-term and long-term disabilities and the condition of the hindering aspect cannot be found in Canadian legislation.[59] In Canada, people with a fractured foot, people who suffer from stress and people with a fear of flying are entitled to reasonable accommodations too.[60] However, the Canadian system also has its limits. Employees who are, for instance, fatigued cannot enjoy disability protection, even when they have a medical certificate. It should also be noted that Canadian courts and human rights tribunals have held that even people who are addicted to nicotine, alcohol and drugs are entitled to demand accommodations to their work environment.[61] The United States also defines disability broadly to include people who are *regarded* as disabled,[62] as well as those with drug and/or alcohol addiction.[63]

According to the European Commission, the Directive also prohibits a situation where a person is directly discriminated against on the basis of wrong perception or assumption of protected characteristics, for example if

55 M. Lynck, *Disability and the Duty to accommodate in the Canadian Workplace*, 2001, available at http://ceiu.net/duty_to_accommodate.pdf, 24.

56 T. Shakespeare, and N. Watson, 'The social model of disability: an outdated ideology?', (Leeds: Disability Studies Leeds, 2002), 5, available at http://disability-studies.leeds.ac.uk/.

57 D. Cuypers and S. van Damme, 'Het VN-Verdrag inzake de Rechten van Personen met een Handicap. Bron van inspiratie voor het Unierecht en het Belgisch sociaal recht', (2014) 1 *TSR* 2014, afl. 1, 62.

58 J. Damamme, 'La socialisation de la notion de handicap en droit de la non-discrimination', (2013) 5 *Journal européen des droits de l'homme*, 842.

59 M. Lynck, *Disability and the Duty to accommodate in the Canadian Workplace*, 2001, available at http://ceiu.net/duty_to_accommodate.pdf, 6.

60 M. Lynck, *Disability and the Duty to accommodate in the Canadian Workplace*, 2001, 6.

61 M. Lynck, *Disability and the Duty to accommodate in the Canadian Workplace*, 2001, 7–8.

62 Title 42, subchapter I, sec. 12101, (3) Americans with Disabilities Act 1990, as amended. See also Art. 16 of the Flemish regulation of 10 July 2008 about a framework for an equal opportunities and equal treatment policy.

63 A. Kanter, *The Development of Disability Rights Under International Law* (Abingdon: Routledge, 2015), 37–38.

a candidate for a job is not selected because the employer wrongly believes he has a disability.[64] The Court of Justice did not (yet) dare to make this step in the *Kaltoft* judgment. Unfortunately, the Court did not touch on the issue of stereotype-based discrimination either, even though the Advocate-General had raised this issue in his opinion. The extension to people who are regarded as disabled might provide a good way to counter the discussion as to whether someone has a disability or not. Furthermore, the Court of Justice notes that it would be contrary to the purpose of the Directive to make its applicability dependent on the cause of a person's disability.[65] Indeed, the concept of disability does not depend on the question whether the person involved contributed to his disability. Belgian case law shares this view.[66] This does raise questions for alcohol, nicotine and drugs addiction.[67] Essentially, such addictions do meet the Convention's cumulative requirements (long-term and hindering aspect), but would it be fair to make an employer bear the consequences thereof?

Employers in Canada and the Netherlands can be released from their obligation to accommodate if they can prove that the employee in question does not want to work on his destructive behaviour (for instance, premature withdrawal from treatment).[68] It is also worth mentioning that Canada is one of the only countries that included the prohibition of discrimination on the grounds of disability in its Constitution.[69]

3. RIGHT TO REASONABLE ACCOMMODATION

Now that it is clear who can invoke the right to reasonable accommodation, the question arises as to what this right entails.

3.1. ORIGIN

The right to reasonable accommodation first emerged in US and Canadian discrimination law.[70] Originally, this right was not intended to improve the participation possibilities for people with disabilities, but to accommodate

64 European Commission, *Joint Report on the application of Council Directive 2000/43/EC and of Council Directive 2000/78/EC*, (Brussels: COM (2014) 2 final), 10.

65 Case C-335/11–337/11, *Ring and Skouboe Werge*, EU: 2014.

66 Arbh. Brussels 18 December 2012, no. 2001/AB/1089, available at www.Juridat.be.

67 R.K. Scotch, 'Models of Disability and the Americans with Disabilities Act', (2014) *Berkeley J. Emp. & Lab. L.*, 220.

68 M. Lynck, *Disability and the Duty to accommodate in the Canadian Workplace*, 2001, 29.

69 Section 15 of the Canadian Charter of Rights and Freedoms; M. Lynck, *Disability and the Duty to accommodate in the Canadian Workplace*, 2001, 6.

70 E. Bribosia and I. Rorive, 'Reasonable Accommodation beyond Disability in Europe?', (2013) *Office for Official Publications of the European Union*, 2013, 12–19; L. de Campos Velho

religious diversity.[71] Employers were obliged to make certain accommodations so that employees who adhere to a particular religion were able to practice. Such accommodations could consist of, for instance, providing a prayer room and coordinating the work schedule with religious obligations. In order to prevent an overload of unreasonable requests regarding accommodations to the work environment, a proportionality test was introduced. If the suggested adjustment led to a 'disproportionate burden', the employer could refuse.[72] Since the exception rule was broadly interpreted, accommodations became the exception rather than the rule.

At the international level the concept of reasonable accommodation first appeared in General Comment 5 of the Committee on Economic, Social and Cultural Rights.[73] Most European countries did not introduce the duty to accommodate until the 2000 Directive, which provides for a right to accommodation exclusively for people with a disability and only in relation to the right to work.[74] As from 2008, when the Convention came into force, the obligation to accommodate started to take root.[75] The Convention provides reasonable accommodations in all sectors of day-to-day life (e.g. education and recreation). Belgian discrimination law is broadly in line with the broad interpretation of the Convention's duty to accommodate.[76] The United States and Canada even recognise a right to reasonable accommodation beyond disability (religion, gender and race).[77, 78]

3.2. PRINCIPLES

We shall now examine the types of accommodations that fall under this right and the extent of the employer's obligation to accommodate.

Martel, ''Reasonable Accommodation: The New Concept from an Inclusive Constitutional Perspective', (2011) 8 *Sur International Journal on Human Rights*, 88–89.

71 G.L. Beaman, (ed.), *Reasonable accommodation. Managing Religious Diversity*, (Vancouver: UBC Press, 2012), 13–29.

72 R. Malhotra, 'The Legal Genealogy of the Duty to Accommodate American and Canadian Workers with Disabilities: A comparative study', (2007) 23 *Wash. U. J. L. & Pol'y* 2007, 24.

73 Office of the High Commissioner for Human Rights, *CESCR General Comment No. 5: Persons with Disabilities*, Geneva, United Nations, adopted on 9 December 1994.

74 L. Waddington, 'When is it reasonable for Europeans to be confused: understanding when a disability accommodation is 'reasonable' from a comparative perspective' in E.F. Emens and M.A. Stein (eds.), *Disability and Equality Law*, (Farnham: Ashgate, 2012), 294.

75 L. de Campos Velho Martel, ''Reasonable Accommodation: The New Concept from an Inclusive Constitutional Perspective', (2011) 8 *Sur International Journal on Human Rights*, 99.

76 Belgian law of 10 May 2007 combating certain forms of discrimination.

77 M. Lynck, *Disability and the Duty to accommodate in the Canadian Workplace*, 2001, available at http://ceiu.net/duty_to_accommodate.pdf, 1.

78 E. Bribosia and I. Rorive, 'Reasonable Accommodation beyond Disability in Europe?', (2013) *Office for Official Publications of the European Union*, 2013, 63.

3.2.1. *What is an Accommodation?*

Both the Convention and the Directive give a definition of the concept reasonable accommodation. Article 2 of the Convention stipulates that: 'Reasonable accommodation means necessary and appropriate modification and adjustments not imposing a disproportionate or undue burden, where needed in a particular case, to ensure to persons with disabilities the enjoyment or exercise on an equal basis with others of all human rights and fundamental freedoms'. The Directive provides a similar definition and adds that these accommodations have to ensure that persons with disabilities have access to work and are able to participate to work or training.[79]

Within the context of work, reasonable accommodations are therefore concrete and appropriate measures, granted by the employer, that allow an employee with a disability to participate on an equal basis with others to a work-related activity.[80] It is worth mentioning that the duty to accommodate is not limited to execution of the employment contract, but also applies to all social events at the workplace, such as teambuilding activities.[81] There are many possible accommodations and they can be both of a *material* nature (accommodations to the work station, such as a special desk, installing a stair lift, parking space near the entrance of the company, aids, etc.) and an *immaterial* nature (manner of service, assistance, adjustment of the work schedule, etc.).[82] Furthermore, employers are not only obliged to provide reasonable accommodations from the time of actual employment, but also during the selection procedure.[83] It is often much harder for people with disabilities to make it through selection tests successfully. Accommodations during the selection procedure may include: oral instead of written tests, allocating additional time to fill out a list of questions and adjusting the font size of those lists.[84] Although the term suggests otherwise, an adjustment can also mean forbearance. In that case, the employer will tolerate certain behaviour from the employee. Further, providing reasonable accommodation is not a one-off obligation. The obligation remains for the entire duration of the labour

---

79 Art. 5 Directive.

80 M.V. Liisberg, *Disability and employment. A contemporary disability human rights approach applied to Danish, Swedish and EU law and policy,* (Cambridge-Antwerp-Portland: Intersentia, 2011), 108.

81 G. de Beco, 'Het recht op arbeid voor personen met een handicap volgens artikel 27 van het VN-Verdrag inzake de rechten van personen met een handicap met een toepassing in Vlaanderen', (2013) 4 *BTSZ*, 574; K. Van Den Langenbergh, 'Discriminatie van gehandicapten bij aanwerving: een verkennende analyse' in D. Cuypers, *Gelijkheid in het arbeidsrecht: gelijkheid zonder grenzen?*, (Antwerp: Intersentia, 2003), 184.

82 A. D'Espallier, 'Tolkuren voor dove en slechthorende leerlingen', (2010) *NJW*, 608.

83 A. Rahmé (ed.), *Discriminatie op basis van handicap en gezondheidstoestand in de arbeidsverhouding,* (Antwerpen-Oxford: Intersentia, 2009), 97.

84 S. van Damme, 'Tewerkstelling van personen met een handicap: het recht op redelijke aanpassingen onder de loep genomen', (2014) 7, *Soc.Kron.*, 329.

relation.[85] Consequently, the employer has to evaluate the accommodations that have been provided on a regular basis and, if necessary, make additional accommodations for the employee.

Unlike the Convention and the Directive,[86] the Americans with Disabilities Act provides a list of accommodations.[87] This list includes part-time work, special training material and the presence of an interpreter.[88] These examples of accommodations are also mentioned by courts in various European countries. This is no surprise since the authors of the Convention and the Directive were inspired by the Americans with Disabilities Act.[89] It is both impossible and undesirable to formulate an exhaustive list of accommodations, just as it is impossible to draw up an exhaustive list of disorders.[90] When accommodations are provided for an employee, his specific needs should be taken into account and these needs are different for every person with a disability. As a result, case law – in particular the case law of the European Court of Justice – plays an important role in exploring this vague concept of accommodation.[91] Since the obligation to accommodate was picked up from common law legal systems, this judicial activism is no surprise.

Additionally, accommodations can be of an individual nature or a collective nature.[92] *Individual* accommodations are accommodations that are made exclusively for one employee. The adjustment should be geared towards the individual's abilities and limitations as far as possible. Individual accommodations can include an adapted telephone for someone with an auditory disability, a larger computer screen for someone with a visual disability and a flexible timetable with a sufficient number of breaks for someone who needs to take his medication. *Collective* accommodations, on the other hand, are

85 K. Van Den Langenbergh, 'Discriminatie van gehandicapten bij aanwerving: een verkennende analyse' in D. Cuypers, *Gelijkheid in het arbeidsrecht: gelijkheid zonder grenzen?*, (Antwerp: Intersentia, 2003), 184; A. Rahmé (ed.), *Discriminatie op basis van handicap en gezondheidstoestand in de arbeidsverhouding*, (Antwerpen-Oxford: Intersentia, 2009), 106.

86 Except for the non-binding recital 20.

87 L. Waddington, *From Rome to Nice in a Wheelchair. The Development of a European Disability Policy*, (Groningen: European Law Publishing, 2006), 29.

88 Title 42, Chapter 126, Subchapter I, Sec. 12111 Americans with Disabilities Act 1990, as amended.

89 M.A Stein and P.J.S Stein, 'Beyond Disability Civil Rights', (2007) 58 *Hastings Law Journal* 1203–1204; L. Waddington, 'When is it reasonable for Europeans to be confused: understanding when a disability accommodation is 'reasonable' from a comparative perspective' in E.F. Emens and M.A. Stein (eds.), *Disability and Equality Law*, (Farnham: Ashgate, 2012), 296.

90 L. Waddington and A. Lawson, *Disability and non-discrimination law in the European Union*, (Luxembourg: Publications Office of the European Union, 2009), 25.

91 L. de Campos Velho Martel, 'Reasonable Accommodation: The New Concept from an Inclusive Constitutional Perspective', (2011) 8 *Sur International Journal on Human Rights*, 88–89.

92 S. van Damme, 'Tewerkstelling van personen met een handicap: het recht op redelijke aanpassingen onder de loep genomen', (2014) 7, *Soc.Kron.*, 329.

not intended for a particular person but for a group of people.[93] A wide entrance door through which both mothers with prams and people with wheelchairs can enter is an example of a collective accommodation. Collective accommodations cannot be considered *sensu stricto* to be reasonable accommodations since they do not take the employee's individual situation into account. Therefore, these types of accommodations rather fit the principle of *universal design*, which aims at guaranteeing an accessible society.[94]

Finally, many EU Member States have introduced the Directive's terminology into their national legislation when transposing Article 5. In the United Kingdom, for example, legislation requires the making of reasonable 'accommodations'. However, in some legal systems the word 'accommodations' has been replaced with another term. Finnish law refers to 'steps' and the French Labour Code speaks of 'appropriate measures'. The use of these alternative words is not an issue as long as the right to reasonable accommodation is not undermined. Consequently, these countries do not need to adapt their national terminology in light of the ratification of the Convention.

3.2.2. *What is a 'Reasonable' Accommodation?*

The right to an adapted work environment is limited in two ways.[95] On the one hand, its non-absolute nature results from the fact that this right is an intrinsic part of, and not an exception to, the prohibition of discrimination.[96] Differences in treatment on the basis of protected characteristics may be permitted if they are justified by a legitimate objective, and if the means of achieving that objective are proportionate.[97] Within the context of work, the Directive stipulates that an employer can only give a different treatment on the basis of a protected characteristic (such as a disability) with regard to a particular job where such a characteristic constitutes a 'genuine and determining' occupational requirement.[98] A classic example of this is the person with a visual disability who wants to be a pilot or a cab driver.[99] The non-absolute nature of the right to

---

93 A. Rahmé (ed.), *Discriminatie op basis van handicap en gezondheidstoestand in de arbeidsverhouding*, (Antwerpen-Oxford: Intersentia, 2009), 98; S. van Damme, 'Tewerkstelling van personen met een handicap: het recht op redelijke aanpassingen onder de loep genomen', (2014) 7, *Soc.Kron.*, 329.

94 Art. 2 Convention.

95 S. van Damme, 'Recht op arbeid voor personen met een handicap', (2015) 333 *NJW*, 888–890.

96 K. Henrard, 'De verhouding tussen de concepten redelijke aanpassing, indirecte discriminatie en proportionaliteit' in C. Bayart, S. Sottiaux and S. Van Droogenbroeck, *De nieuwe federale antidiscriminatiewetten*, (Bruges: die Keure, 2008), 277–278.

97 C. Bayart, *Discriminatie tegenover differentiatie. Arbeidsverhoudingen na de Discriminatiewet. Arbeidsrecht na de Europese Ras-en Kaderrichtlijn*, (Brussels: Larcier, 2004), 58; Fra, *Handbook on European non-discrimination law*, (Luxembourg: Imprimerie Centrale, 2011), 44.

98 Art. 4 Directive.

99 J. Vrielinck, S. Sottiaux, and D. De Prins, 'De anti-discriminatiewet. Een artikelsgewijze analyse (Deel 1) ', (2003) *NJW*, 269.

reasonable accommodation is also apparent from the text of the Directive and the Convention. Both instruments relieve the employer of his obligation if the suggested adjustment would impose a 'disproportionate or undue burden'.[100] A proportionality test is also implied in the concept itself, which does not concern the right to accommodation, but the right to 'reasonable' accommodation. The Netherlands, among others, has attached even more importance to the proportionality test by referring to 'effective' rather than 'reasonable' accommodations in its legislation. Employers are thus urged to focus more on the efficacy of the accommodation and less on the cost.[101] The fact that various European countries do not mention 'effective' accommodation certainly does not mean that accommodations should not be effective. An ineffective adjustment is not an adjustment at all. The obligations laid down in the Convention and the Directive are not met until the adjustment is an *effective* one and leads to the *full and independent* participation of a person with a disability.[102] An adjustment is *effective* if it allows the person with a disability to perform his tasks better. If an adjustment leads to hardly any specific improvements, the employer can conclude that in that particular case the adjustment is not effective.[103] The criterion of *independence* means that the adjustment needs to enable the employee to participate within the company with as little help as possible from third parties (e.g. opening the door without help from a passer-by). Finally, the employee with a disability should be able to use the facilities and services within the company on an *equal basis* with others (e.g. being able to enter the building with a wheelchair through the main entrance, or eating with colleagues in the company canteen and not in a separate room).

The meaning of the term 'reasonable' is complex and unclear.[104] Neither the Convention nor the Directive (apart from the non-binding recital 21) contain a list of criteria to assess an accommodation's 'reasonableness'. In 2007, the United Nations produced a handbook for politicians on how to implement the Convention in domestic law.[105] This book listed a number of criteria for

---

100 Art. 2 Convention; Art. 5 Directive.

101 A. D'Espallier, 'Tolkuren voor dove en slechthorende leerlingen', (2010) *NJW*, 608.

102 A. Rahmé (ed.), *Discriminatie op basis van handicap en gezondheidstoestand in de arbeidsverhouding*, (Antwerpen-Oxford: Intersentia, 2009), 98–99.

103 N. Denies and V. Ghesquière, 'Les aménagements raisonnables en matière de handicap au sens de la loi du 10 mai 2007 tendant à lutter contre certaines formes de discrimination' in C. Bayart, S. Sottiaux and S. Van Drooghenbroeck, *Actuele topics discriminatierecht*,(Bruges: die Keure, 2010), 398.

104 L. Waddington and A. Lawson, *Disability and non-discrimination law in the European Union*, (Luxembourg: Publications Office of the European Union, 2009), 26.

105 Office of the High Commissioner for Human Rights, *From Exclusion to Equality Realizing the rights of persons with disabilities. Handbook for Parliamentarians on the Convention on the Rights of Persons with Disabilities and its Optional Protocol*, (Geneva: United Nations, 2007), 150p.

assessing whether a disproportionate burden is placed on the employer.[106] The first important factor is the *cost* of the suggested adjustment. When considering the financial impact of the adjustment, the employer's capacity (size, nature and resources of the company) should be taken into account. A small grocery is not subject to the same obligations as a multinational or a body governed by public law.[107] Installing an elevator in a corner shop probably goes beyond reasonableness. Moreover, the *organisational impact* of such accommodation should be considered, as well as its *influence on the environment and other users*. For instance, the fact that an elevator is also beneficial to other users, such as elderly people or people with prams, should be taken into consideration.[108] Suppliers would also benefit from an elevator, since heavy boxes would no longer have to be carried upstairs. Another important aspect that should be taken into account is the influence of the accommodation on *safety* and *health* in the workplace. People with a disability are often considered a safety hazard and an enterprise risk.[109] Therefore, including the safety aspect in the assessment is possibly risky, since there is a chance of employers trying to ignore the obligation to provide reasonable accommodation by arguing that the presence of a person with a disability increases the chances of industrial accidents.[110] It should be pointed out that it is not the objective of the right to reasonable accommodation to force an employer to hire or prevent him from dismissing an employee who does not meet the essential occupational requirements due to his disability or who cannot perform the required tasks even with the aid of reasonable accommodations.[111] This can also be found in the non-binding recital 17 of the Directive and in *Chacòn Navas* case.[112] Recital 21 further stipulates that the availability of government subsidies should also be taken into account. Indeed, if an employer is entitled to government subsidies, the adjustment is less likely to be qualified as unreasonable. In Belgium – more specifically in Flanders – the government subsidises accommodations in the work place.[113] Finally,

---

106 Office of the High Commissioner for Human Rights, *From Exclusion to Equality Realizing the Rights of Persons with Disabilities. Handbook for Parliamentarians on the Convention on the Rights of Persons with Disabilities and its Optional Protocol,* (Geneva: United Nations, 2007), 62–63.

107 S. van Damme, 'Tewerkstelling van personen met een handicap: het recht op redelijke aanpassingen onder de loep genomen', (2014) 7 *Soc.Kron.*, 330.

108 N. Denies and v. Ghesquière, 'Les aménagements raisonnables en matière de handicap au sens de la loi du 10 mai 2007 tendant à lutter contre certaines formes de discrimination' in C. Bayart, S. Sottiaux and S. Van Drooghenbroeck, *Actuele topics discriminatierecht,*(Bruges: die Keure, 2010), 402.

109 A. O'Reilly, *The Right to Decent Work of Persons With Disabilities*, (Geneva: International Labour Office), 2007, 66.

110 A. Hendriks, *Gelijke toegang tot arbeid voor gehandicapten, (*Deventer: Kluwer, 1999) 38–39.

111 C. Hiel and G. Boot, 'The application of the EU framework for disability discrimination in 18 European countries', (2013) 4 *ELLJ*, 127.

112 Case C-13/05, *Chacòn Navas v. Eurest Colectividades SA*, EU: 2006, para 49.

113 See on this point: S. van Damme, 'Tewerkstelling van personen met een handicap: het recht op redelijke aanpassingen onder de loep genomen', (2014) 7 *Soc.Kron.*, 330.

there is nothing that prevents the employer from opting for the least expensive solution if there are multiple and equivalent options available. The fact that a suggested adjustment can be qualified as unreasonable does not imply that the employer does not need to take any action at all.[114] In that case, an adjustment that helps to remove the barriers as efficiently as possible is required, without it being an excessive burden. It is worth mentioning that an American consulting bureau found that it is exceptional for the cost of a reasonable accommodation to exceed the sum of US $500.[115] Hence, the idea that the recruitment of a person with a disability always involves expensive accommodations is a general misconception.[116]

It is disputed whether the stigmatising effect of denial of an accommodation also has an influence on the proportionality test.[117] In Canada, the stigmatising element is clearly reported. It is justified to consider this element in the test, because the refusal of an accommodation often leads to the continued existence of certain prejudices.[118] Denial emphasises the non-ability once more. Other people – who at some point in their life might need accommodations in their work environment – can also benefit from the stigma ceasing to exist. However, it should also be noted that the right to reasonable accommodation is an individual right and its objective is to adjust the labour market that was created on the basis of dominant norms to the needs of a specific employee. The obligation to provide reasonable accommodation as such is a vague concept to begin with. It is a concept that proves to be difficult for employers to interpret in practice. Hence, it might be a bridge too far to expect them to also take immeasurable elements such as stigma into consideration.

There are also a number of other limitations to the proportionality test. It is, for instance, difficult to give an estimate of the costs of an immaterial adjustment, such as changes to the work schedule.[119] It is also possible that a

---

114 D'Espallier, A., 'Draagkracht is geen toverwoord. Duidelijkheid vanuit een juridisch oogpunt', (2011) 9 *Momenten*, 22.

115 JAN (Job Accommodation Network), *Workplace Accommodations: Low Cost, High Impact*, 2013, http://askjan.org/media/lowcosthighimpact.html. See also: C. Hiel and G. Boot, 'The application of the EU framework for disability discrimination in 18 European countries', (2013) 4 *ELLJ*, 128.

116 Office of the UN High Commissioner for Human Rights, *Thematic Study on the Work and Employment of Persons with Disabilities*,b17 December 2013, A/HRC/22/25, 10; www.ohchr.org/Documents/Issues/Disability/A-HRC-22-25_en.pdf.

117 S.R. Bagenstos, 'Subordination, stigma and 'disability'', (2000) 86 *Virginia Law Review*, 437; See also on this point: C.R. Sunstein, 'Cost-benefit analysis without analyzing costs or benefits: reasonable accommodation, balancing, and stigmatic harms', (2007) 74 *University of Chicago Law Review*, 1895–1909.

118 A. D'Espallier, 'Stigma in de weegschaal? Over het gewicht van het stigma in antidiscriminatierecht en in redelijke aanpassingen' in A. Alen and J. Theunis (eds.), *Leuvens Staatrechtelijke Standpunten*, (Bruges: die Keure, 2012), 210.

119 A. D'Espallier, 'Stigma in de weegschaal? Over het gewicht van het stigma in antidiscriminatierecht en in redelijke aanpassingen' in A. Alen and J. Theunis (eds.), *Leuvens Staatrechtelijke Standpunten*, (Bruges: die Keure, 2012), 209.

third party might be required to make an adjustment rather than the employer. This is the case, for example, if the employer does not own but rather rents the building in which the person with a disability would be employed.[120] In these circumstances, the owner of the building has to give permission to install an elevator. But should he also contribute towards the costs since the presence of an elevator is likely to raise the value of the property? What if the owner refuses to make an adjustment? All this shows that it is not easy to find a fair balance. Another interesting point concerns the question whether the proportionality test only applies to the accommodation as such or also to the procedure of granting accommodations.[121] Since the objective of an accommodation is to meet individual needs, all applications should be examined separately. For the suppliers of goods and services, who receive multiple applications requesting accommodations, this could involve a lot of work. Case law seems to have a rather negative response to this issue. In my opinion, this is the correct approach. Otherwise, the entire concept of reasonable accommodation would be undermined. Since this is not really an issue within the context of work, we will not discuss this further.

3.3. PROCEDURE FOR GRANTING ACCOMMODATIONS

Neither the Directive nor the Convention mention the procedure that should be followed in granting an accommodation. Nevertheless, this procedure should meet a number a requirements. These conditions are based on the nature of the duty to accommodate.

First, the procedure should focus on a particular and individual case.[122] As mentioned several times above, the objective of the obligation to provide reasonable accommodation is to list and remove the specific barriers for a certain employee. Hence, the needs of a specific person are the basis of the obligation. There is no universal adjustment that is suitable for all people with a disability. The same disability can even require different treatment and accommodations depending on the individual involved.[123] This approach fits in with the transition

---

120 K. Van Den Langenbergh, 'Discriminatie van gehandicapten bij aanwerving: een verkennende analyse' in D. Cuypers, *Gelijkheid in het arbeidsrecht: gelijkheid zonder grenzen?*, (Antwerp: Intersentia, 2003), 186.

121 A. D'Espallier, 'Directe of indirecte discriminatie, overeenstemming van de regelgeving met het discriminatieverbod en redelijke aanpassingen', (2012) 96 *DCCR*, 123.

122 J. Vrielinck, S. Sottiaux and D. De Prins, 'De anti-discriminatiewet. Een artikelsgewijze analyse (Deel 1) ', (2003) *NJW* 2003, 268.

123 A. D'Espallier, 'Stigma in de weegschaal? Over het gewicht van het stigma in antidiscriminatierecht en in redelijke aanpassingen' in A. Alen and J. Theunis (eds.), *Leuvens Staatrechtelijke Standpunten*, (Bruges: die Keure, 2012), 210.

from the medical to the social model of disability. The obligation to provide reasonable accommodation is obviously a result of this new model.[124]

Next, the accommodations should be granted by mutual agreement.[125] The employer and the employee should engage in a dialogue.[126] This dialogue has to be transparent and public. The employer knows best what his company can do and the person with a disability knows best what will be most beneficial to him. Therefore, where an employee suffers from a disability that is not obvious at first sight, he will have to divulge the condition in question. This proves to be problematic in a number of cases, since this can immediately expose the employee to discrimination.[127] It is, however, not feasible to take a different approach to the matter. Employers cannot be expected to grant accommodations without being informed of the employee's disability and his specific needs. According to Belgian case law a disabled employee has a twofold obligation to inform: he has to prove that he has informed his employer about his disability and he must explicitly request accommodations.[128] In my opinion, this view is correct.[129] During the conversation between an employer and his employee, the tricky matter of the proportionality test will arise. If the parties do not come to an agreement, it is up to the judge to find a balance between the employee's needs and the employer's costs. However, it can be problematic if a judge needs to decide which accommodations need to be made, especially if the employer in question is the government. This could raise questions as to the principle of the separation of powers.[130]

3.4. SANCTION FOR NOT GRANTING ACCOMMODATIONS

Now that it is clear which persons are entitled to invoke the right to reasonable accommodation and what this right implies with regard to the right to work, there is only one more issue that needs to be addressed: what if the employer

124 M.A. Stein, 'Disability Human Rights', (2007) *California Law Review*, 91.

125 A. D'Espallier, 'Tolkuren voor dove en slechthorende leerlingen', (2010) *NJW*, 608.

126 L. de Campos Velho Martel, ''Reasonable Accommodation: The New Concept from an Inclusive Constitutional Perspective', (2011) 8 *Sur International Journal on Human Rights*, 106; M.V. Liisberg, *Disability and employment. A contemporary disability human rights approach applied to Danish, Swedish and EU law and policy*, (Cambridge-Antwerp-Portland: Intersentia, 2011), 109; S. Karlan and G. Rutherglen, 'Disabilities, Discrimination, and reasonable accommodation', (1996) 46 *Duke Law Journal*, 33.

127 K. Van Den Langenbergh, 'Discriminatie van gehandicapten bij aanwerving: een verkennende analyse' in D. Cuypers, *Gelijkheid in het arbeidsrecht: gelijkheid zonder grenzen?*, (Antwerp: Intersentia, 2003), 185–186.

128 Arbrb. Antwerp 8 May 2014, nr. 13/469/A; Arbrb. Bergen 9 March 2015, nr. 14/436/A; Arbh. Liege 13 November 2014, 2013/AL/573. These decisions are available at the website of the Belgian Centre for Equal Opportunities: www.diversitybelgium.be/.

129 For a contrary view: L. Vermeulen, *Discriminatie in arbeidsrelaties*, (Ghent: Cahiers Antwerp-Brussels-Ghent, Larcier, 2015), 72–73.

130 A. D'Espallier, 'Tolkuren voor dove en slechthorende leerlingen', (2010) *NJW*, 609.

fails to perform an accurate proportionality test and incorrectly qualifies the accommodation as unreasonable?

The Convention puts an unjustified denial on a par with an act of discrimination.[131] This alignment is logical given the nature of the right to reasonable accommodation. After all, this right is an intrinsic part of the prohibition of discrimination. The EU turned out to be a strong advocate of this equalisation during the negotiation of the Convention.[132] This is quite surprising, since the EU's Directive does not include such equalisation. The EU's change of course could imply that non-discrimination towards people with a disability has been given a more prominent place on the agenda. The proposal of Directive 2008 on equal treatment between persons irrespective of disability or other grounds of discrimination also considers the unjustified denial of accommodation as an act of discrimination.[133] This directive complements Directive 2000/78 which only applies to work.[134] Negotiations on the new directive, however, have reached total deadlock.[135] A majority vote has reportedly been reached, however, on disability as a ground of protection.[136] It is likely that, through the Convention, the EU wanted to incorporate equalisation into Union law. Such a development can only improve the position of people with a disability.

The Convention does not provide a specific sanction for violating the prohibition of discrimination. It is up to the parties to the Convention to take all legislative and administrative measures to implement its provisions.[137] Consequently, it is the national legislator that determines the applicable sanctions. This is in accordance with Article 17 of the Directive.[138] Nevertheless, all sanctions should be effective, proportionate and dissuasive, and not merely symbolic. In the *Accept* case, the European Court of Justice held that Directive 2000/43 precludes national law under which sanctions are purely symbolic and, under certain circumstances, law by virtue of which it is only possible to give a warning in a case of discrimination.[139] Belgian discrimination law predominantly provides civil

131 Art. 2 Convention.

132 G. de Búrca, 'The European Union in the negotiation of the UN Disability Convention', (2010) *E.L. Rev.*, 191–192.

133 Art. 2 proposal for a Council Directive on implementing the principle of equal treatment between persons irrespective of religion or belief, disability, age or sexual orientation, COM (2008) 426.

134 Art. 1 proposal for a Council Directive on implementing the principle of equal treatment.

135 D. Cuypers and S. van Damme, 'Het VN-Verdrag inzake de Rechten van Personen met een Handicap. Bron van inspiratie voor het Unierecht en het Belgisch sociaal recht', (2014) 1 *TSR*, 68.

136 L. Waddington, 'Future prospects for EU Equality Law: Lessons to be Learnt from the Proposal Equal Treatment Directive', (2011) 36 *E.L.Rev.*, 170.

137 Art. 4(a) Convention.

138 European Commission, *Joint Report on the application of Council Directive 2000/43/EC and of Council Directive 2000/78/EC*, (Brussels: COM (2014) 2 final), 7.

139 Case C-81/12, *Asociaţia ACCEPT v. Consiliul Naţional pentru Combaterea Discriminări*, EU:2013.

sanctions for refusing reasonable accommodation, damages being one of them. In the event of a wrongful refusal of accommodation, an employer risks being ordered to pay six months' remuneration to his employee.[140] The denial of accommodations becomes more and more an issue before the Belgian labour courts.[141] Therefore, we can conclude that the right to reasonable accommodation has the power to change the precarious labour situation of persons with disabilities.

4. CONCLUSION

This chapter has focused on the right to work for people with a disability and more particularly on the important role of the right to reasonable accommodation. If the fundamental social right to work is to be more than just a theoretical right, it is essential for people with a disability to be able to request adjustments to their work environment.

Before we discussed the duty to accommodate, we highlighted the concept of disability. We explained that the term disability should be interpreted broadly today. Due to this extensive interpretation, classic illnesses are increasingly categorised as disabilities. This growing protection fits in with the transition from a medical to a social model of disability. According to this new model, this group of people who are traditionally discriminated against has to be able to enjoy the fundamental rights on an equal basis with others. This idea is also explicitly recorded in the UN Convention on the Rights of Persons with Disabilities. Contrary to Directive 2000/78, the right to reasonable accommodation – as laid down in the Convention – concerns all domains of social life.

The concept of reasonable accommodation is problematic in practice, mainly because of its vagueness. Interpretation is largely up to the judges. Case law shows that the obligation to accommodate is increasingly taking hold. However, employers are still not always sure how to deal with a request for accommodation. The reasonability test in particular has proven to be a problem. We have tried to clarify this proportionality test, but it will always remain a complex balance. After all, various factors, such as cost, have to be taken into consideration. Moreover, the range of possible accommodations is huge given the fact that every person with a disability has different needs. There is no such thing as a universal accommodation.

Finally, the duty to accommodate is an important part of the social model of disability. People with a disability are no longer forced to watch from the side-lines but can rather fully participate in society now. Society should include them and remedy its own inaccessibility by granting accommodations. It is

140 Art. 18(2)(2) Belgian law of 10 May 2007 combating certain forms of discrimination.

141 These decisions are available on the website of the Belgian Centre for Equal Opportunities: www.diversitybelgium.be/.

not the person who is disabled, but society, through its lack of adjustment. The increasing protection of persons with disabilities can only be welcomed.

INDIRECT DISCRIMINATION, REASONABLE ACCOMMODATION AND RELIGION*

Erica HOWARD

1. INTRODUCTION

In this chapter, it is argued that there is no reason why the duty to make reasonable accommodation for people with disabilities, which exists in European Union (EU) law,[1] could not be extended to include religious people and people with other characteristics which attract protection under anti-discrimination law. However, even if this duty is not extended, it is suggested that something which comes close to such a duty is part of the provision of indirect discrimination. This chapter specifically focuses on the accommodation of religious manifestations and practices, but the duty could be expanded to include all grounds of discrimination covered by EU law (sex, race, religion or belief, age and sexual orientation). It can be said that EU law itself makes certain accommodations in relation to sex, for example, in the regulations protecting pregnant and breast-feeding women, and in relation to age, where it protects younger workers.

2. EXISTING DUTIES OF REASONABLE ACCOMMODATION

In EU law, a duty of reasonable accommodation in relation to disabled people is laid down in Article 5 of Directive 2000/78/EC. Employers must 'take appropriate measures, where needed in a particular case, to enable a person with a disability to have access to, participate in, or advance in employment,

* This chapter is a shortened and updated version of an article published in 2013 the European Law Review. See: E. Howard 'Reasonable Accommodation of Religion and other Discrimination Grounds in EU Law' (2013) 38, 3, *European Law Review*, 360–375.

1 See Article 5 of Directive 2000/78/EC of 27 November 2000, Establishing a General Framework for Equal Treatment in Employment and Occupation [2000] OJ L 303/16.

or to undergo training, unless such measures would impose a disproportionate burden on the employer'. The first sentence of Article 5 provides that reasonable accommodation must be made 'in order to guarantee compliance with the principle of equal treatment', so this duty is clearly placed within a discrimination context and a failure to provide accommodation can thus be seen as a form of discrimination. However, this duty applies only in relation to disability and does not extend to any of the other grounds covered by Directive 2000/78/EC (religion or belief, age and sexual orientation), nor does it extend beyond the employment field.

In contrast, in the USA, a duty of reasonable accommodation short of 'undue hardship' was first laid down in law for cases of discrimination on the ground of religion and then later extended to cases of disability discrimination.[2] The duty made its way over from the USA to Canada, and, in *Simpson-Sears*, the Canadian Supreme Court accepted a duty of reasonable accommodation in relation to religion short of undue hardship, explaining the latter as meaning 'without undue interference in the operation of the employer's business and without undue expense to the employer'.[3] In 1998, the duty of reasonable accommodation was laid down in Section 15(2) of the Canadian Human Rights Act 1985. This duty is not restricted to cases of discrimination based on religion or creed but is applicable to all the grounds of discrimination prohibited in the Human Rights Act.[4] In both the USA and in Canada, the duty is thus linked to a finding of discrimination.

It has been suggested that EU law and national law in European countries should contain a duty of reasonable accommodation for all the grounds covered by anti-discrimination law. This duty would be subject to the proviso that this should not impose a disproportionate burden on employers or service providers.[5] There does not appear any reason why the provisions for reasonable accommodation in relation to disability in EU anti-discrimination legislation could not be extended to include religion or belief or any of the other grounds covered by this legislation. But does it need to be extended?

---

2 Section 701j, Title VII, Civil Rights Act 1964.

3 *Ontario Commission of Human Rights and Theresa O'Malley (Vincent) v Simpson-Sears Ltd* [1985] 2 S.C.R. 536, para 23.

4 Race, national or ethnic origin, colour, religion, age, sex (including pregnancy and childbirth), sexual orientation, marital status, family status, disability and conviction for an offence for which a pardon has been granted or in respect of which a record suspension has been ordered (S 3).

5 See, for example, Council of Europe, Opinion of the Commissioner for Human Rights on National Structures for Promoting Equality, CommDH(2011)2, under 6.1, point 2, https://wcd.coe.int/ViewDoc.jsp?id=1761031#P66_5638; and, Equinet (2008) *Beyond the Labour Market New Initiatives to Prevent and Combat Discrimination*, Equinet, Brussels, at 8, www.equineteurope.org/IMG/pdf/EN_-_Beyond_the_Labour_Market_-_Opinion_2008.pdf (both last visited 22 May 2015).

3. EXISTING DUTIES OF ACCOMMODATION REQUIRE A BALANCING OF INTERESTS

As Waddington writes, most EU Member States provide for a duty of reasonable accommodation in relation to disabled people only and thus do not go beyond the minimum requirement of Directive 2000/78/EC.[6] But Bulgaria, Poland and Spain have recognised a (limited) right to accommodation in the employment context for people who wish to practice their religion, while the Decree for the Flemish Community in Belgium of 8 May 2002 contains a general right to claim reasonable adjustments in employment which is not confined to people with disabilities.[7] The fact that some EU Member States have included a duty of reasonable accommodation in relation to religion or belief or other grounds suggests that there is no reason why this could not also be done in the legal provisions at EU level or at national level in the other EU Member States, as has been done in Canada and the USA.

In 1976, long before the duty to accommodate the needs of disabled people was introduced by Directive 2000/78/EC, the Court of Justice of the European Union (CJEU) had held that the EU administration, when setting dates for competitive examinations for jobs, should inform itself in a general way of dates which might be unsuitable for religious reasons and should seek to avoid fixing such dates for these exams.[8] This might be seen as a duty on EU institutions to reasonably accommodate religious practices. However, Directive 2000/78/EC only contained a duty in relation to disability.

In *Ring and Werge*, the CJEU held that a reduction in working hours could be a reasonable accommodation but that it was up to the national court to decide on the facts of the case whether this imposed a disproportionate burden on the employer.[9] So the CJEU did not indicate when a burden would be disproportionate. It did, however, state that the concept of 'reasonable accommodation' must be interpreted broadly, in accordance with Article 2(2) of the UN Convention on the Rights of Persons with Disabilities, which determines that '"reasonable accommodation" means necessary and appropriate modification and adjustments not imposing a disproportionate or undue burden, where needed in a particular case, to ensure to persons with disabilities the enjoyment or exercise on an equal basis with others of all human rights

6 L. Waddington, 'Reasonable Accommodation', in D. Schiek, L. Waddington and M. Bell (eds.), *Cases, Materials and Text on National, Supernational and International Non-Discrimination Law* (Oxford, Hart Publishing, 2007), at 629 and 755.

7 Ibid., Bulgaria, Poland and Spain: at 697–699; Belgium: at 667 and 701.

8 Case C-130/75, *Vivien Prais v Council of the European Communities*, EU:C:1976:142, para 18.

9 Cases C-335/11 and C-337/11, *HK Danmark, acting on behalf of Jette Ring v Dansk Almennyttigt Boligselskab* and *HK Danmark, acting on behalf of Lone Skouboe Werge v Dansk Arbejdsgiverforening, acting on behalf of Pro Display A/S, in Liquidation*, EU:C:2013:222, para 64.

and fundamental freedoms'.[10] Article 2 of the Convention also makes clear that discrimination on the basis of disability includes the denial of reasonable accommodation.

Recital 20 of the Preamble to Directive 2000/78/EC gives as examples of accommodations: effective and practical measures to adapt the workplace to the disability, for example adapting premises and equipment, patterns of working time, the distribution of tasks or the provision of training or integration resources. Recital 21 then states that 'to determine whether the measures in question give rise to a disproportionate burden, account should be taken in particular of the financial and other costs entailed, the scale and financial resources of the organisation or undertaking and the possibility of obtaining public funding or any other assistance'. Advocate General Jääskinen opined that 'it is worth recalling that Article 5 of Directive 2000/78 merely requires employers to provide 'reasonable accommodation' to persons with disabilities'.[11] All the above and the terms used in Article 5 of Directive 2000/78/EC itself – *reasonable* accommodation, *appropriate* measures and *disproportionate* burden – strongly suggest that a balancing of the interests of both parties is required and the benefit for the employee must be weighed against the burden for the employer and his organisation. If the latter is disproportionate, no accommodation has to be made. The test can thus be seen as a proportionality test: the burden on the employer must be proportionate to the benefits to be achieved for the employee.

This is the same for the duties in US law and Canadian law. These also require a balancing of the interests of both parties to establish whether there is 'undue hardship'. Thus, the rights of the employee or service user must be weighed against those of the employer or service provider and the efficient management of their organisation. The Canadian Supreme Court indicated in *Simpson-Sears* that there is also a duty on the employee to take 'some accommodating steps on his own part'.[12] This, again, points to a proportionality test but it also suggests that there is an onus on both parties to compromise and to make concessions and this could be at some cost to both parties. As Vickers points out, the non-discrimination principle does not require that 'religious adherence be cost-free for the employee'.[13] So the duty is clearly a mutual duty and requires a proportionality test or balancing exercise to be carried out.

---

10 Ibid. para 53.

11 Opinion Advocate General Jääskinen, Case C-354/13, *Fag og Arbejde acting on behalf of Karsten Kaltoft v Kommunernes Landsforening, acting on behalf of the Municipality of Billund*, EU:C:2014:2106, para 49.

12 *Simpson-Sears Ltd*, above note 3, para 23.

13 L. Vickers, *Religious Freedom, Religious Discrimination and the Workplace* (Oxford, Hart Publishing, 2008), at 199.

Chakrabarti gives a good example which can be used to illustrate the above.[14] This is:

> the case of the Christian bus driver who refused to drive buses carrying the slogan "There's probably no god." His employer recognized that this might be upsetting for him and agreed to try to put him on other routes, as long as this did not inconvenience other drivers. The driver accepted this and agreed that if it became impracticable to accommodate him, he would have to find another job.

So, here an accommodation is made, taking into account its impact on other drivers. The religious employee accepted that there were limits to the accommodation and that he might, if accommodation is no longer possible, have to change jobs.[15]

All the above suggests that there is no reason why a duty of reasonable accommodation in law could not cover grounds of discrimination other than disability. But is there a need to extend the duty in EU anti-discrimination law in such a way? Or, could a consideration whether a religious (or other) practice or manifestation can be accommodated be seen as part of the justification test for indirect discrimination?

4. INDIRECT DISCRIMINATION IN EU LAW

EU anti-discrimination law makes a distinction between direct and indirect discrimination. Article 2(2)(a) of Directive 2000/78/EC determines that direct discrimination shall be taken to occur where one person is treated less favourably than another is, has been or would be treated in a comparable situation, on one of the grounds covered by the Directive (religion or belief, disability, age or sexual orientation). According to Article 2(2)(b), indirect discrimination, for example on the ground of religion or belief, shall be taken to occur where an apparently neutral provision, criterion or practice would put persons having a particular religion or belief at a particular disadvantage compared with other persons unless that provision, criterion or practice is objectively justified by a legitimate aim and the means of achieving that aim are appropriate and necessary. So, in EU law, indirect discrimination can be objectively justified and the test for this is given in Article 2(2)(b). It will be clear that this justification test also contains a proportionality test. But can this justification test be interpreted as including an implicit duty to make reasonable accommodation?

---

14 S. Chakrabarti, 'Faith in the Public Sphere', (2014) 22, 2 *Journal of Law and Policy*, 483, at 501.

15 See on this case also: *Man Refuses to Drive "No God" Bus*, BBC NEWS (Jan. 16, 2009): http://news.bbc.co.uk/1/hi/england/hampshire/7832647.stm (last visited 22 May 2015).

There appears to be a clear link between the concepts of indirect discrimination and reasonable accommodation. As Jackson-Preece points out, reasonable accommodation entered the USA jurisprudence via the indirect discrimination provisions.[16] And from the *Simpson-Sears* case[17] it is clear that this was the same in Canada. Other authors have mentioned this link as well For example, Vickers writes that 'it is arguable that the Directive [2000/78/EC] creates an indirect duty to make reasonable accommodation',[18] as 'a failure to accommodate a request for different treatment by religious employees may amount to indirect discrimination, unless the refusal to accommodate is justified'.[19] And, Waddington writes that 'the obligation not to discriminate indirectly against a worker or other individual can, on occasions, result in positive duties to accommodate difference'.[20] This already suggests that a duty of reasonable accommodation could be part of the test whether indirect discrimination is justified.

Bribosia and Rorive express this even more clearly where they point out that reasonable accommodation has resurfaced in the EU as an issue in certain cases involving indirect religious discrimination. They continue that:

> in order to assess the justification of indirect discrimination, judges are sometimes called on, when applying the proportionality test, to examine whether the legitimate objective underlying the difference in treatment can be achieved by measures that are less detrimental to the principle of equality or religious freedom.[21]

Elsewhere, Rorive writes 'the question is nowadays whether an indirect discrimination could be justified where reasonable accommodation is conceivable'[22] and argues that EU anti-discrimination law has developed with 'the emergence of the concept of reasonable accommodation to test whether an indirect discrimination is objectively and reasonably justified'.[23] All this

---

16 J. Jackson-Preece 'Emerging Standards of Reasonable Accommodation towards Minorities in Europe?' in Council of Europe, *Trends in Social Cohesion, No 21, Institutional Accommodation and the Citizen: Legal and Political Interaction in a Pluralist Society* (Strasbourg, Council of Europe Publishing, 2009), at 123.

17 *Simpson-Sears Ltd*, above note 3.

18 L. Vickers, *Religion and Belief Discrimination in Employment – EU Law* (Luxembourg, Office for Official Publications of the European Communities, 2006), at 22.

19 Ibid. at 21.

20 L. Waddington, above note 6, at 754.

21 E. Bribosia and I. Rorive, *In search of a Balance between the Right to Equality and Other Fundamental Rights*, EU DG Employment, Social Affairs and Equal Opportunities (Luxembourg, Publications Office of the European Union, 2010), at 9. See also E. Bribosia, J. Ringelheim and I. Rorive, 'Reasonable Accommodation for Religious Minorities: a Promising Concept for European Antidiscrimination Law?', (2010) 17, 2 *Maastricht Journal of European and Comparative Law*, 137at 156–158.

22 I. Rorive, 'Religious Symbols in the Public Space: in Search of an European Answer' (2009) 30 *Cardozo Law Review*, 2669, at 2693.

23 Ibid. at 2695.

suggests that an implicit duty of reasonable accommodation can be read in the EU provisions against indirect discrimination.

5. CASE LAW

In *Bilka Kaufhaus*[24] which concerned indirect sex discrimination, the CJEU explained that there are three parts to the objective justification test for indirect sex discrimination: first of all, the means chosen must correspond to a real need; secondly, these means must be appropriate with a view to achieving the objective pursued; and, thirdly, they must be necessary to that end. Schiek writes that 'from this, one can conclude that where there is a less discriminatory alternative, the measure is not objectively justified'.[25] So, if the legitimate aim can be achieved in an alternative, less discriminatory way, the provision is not necessary and thus not justified. The objective justification test for indirect sex discrimination is worded in the same way as the tests for indirect discrimination on the other grounds protected by EU law and thus there appears to be no reason why this should not also apply to indirect discrimination on those other grounds.[26] It is argued here that considering whether there is a less discriminatory alternative is very similar to considering whether the religious (or other) practice which does not conform to the measure taken, can be accommodated.

Some support for the above can be found in case law from EU Member States. For example, in cases concerning indirect discrimination, national courts sometimes suggest that alternative ways should have been explored, or, in other words, that possible accommodation should have been examined. The following case from the Swedish Equality Ombudsman can be given to illustrate this. In this case, a female student was not allowed to take part in an educational training programme for pre-school teachers because she wanted to wear a *niqab* (a face covering veil) in class for religious reasons. The school claimed that the *niqab* made it harder to teach since the teacher could not read the student's face. The Equality Ombudsman decided that a prohibition of *niqabs* could amount to indirect discrimination unless it was objectively justified, for example, for safety reasons. It was held that a general ban was not acceptable and that the education

24 Case C-170/84, *Bilka Kaufhaus GMBH v Karin Weber von Hartz*, EU:C:1986:204, para 36.

25 D. Schiek, 'Indirect Discrimination', in D. Schiek, L. Waddington and M. Bell (2007), above note 6, at 357.

26 Compare Articles 2(1)(b) Council Directive 2006/54/EC on the Implementation of the Principle of Equal Opportunities and Equal Treatment of Men and Women in Matters of Employment and Occupation (Recast) [2006] OJ L 204/23, and 2(b) Council Directive 2004/113/EC implementing the Principle of Equal Treatment between Men and Women in the Access to and Supply of Goods and Services [2004] OJ L 373/37 with Articles 2(2)(b) of both Council Directives 2000/78/EC and 2000/43/EC of 29 June 2000 implementing the Principle of Equal Treatment between Persons irrespective of Racial or Ethnic Origin [2000] OJ L 180/22.

provider must try to solve any pedagogical problems by measures less obtrusive for the student if possible. In other words, the provider must consider whether the wearing of the *niqab* by students could be accommodated. In this case, the student and the education provider agreed on a practical solution: the student sat at the front and could remove her *niqab*. The teacher could see her face, but male students were seated behind her so that they could not see her face.[27]

Another case to illustrate this is the British case of *Fugler v MacMillan-London Hair Studios Ltd.*[28] Here, a hair salon introduced a rule that no leave could be taken on Saturdays, as this was the busiest day of the week. Mr Fugler, who was Jewish, requested to have a Saturday off to celebrate *Yom Kippur* but this was refused. The Employment Tribunal (ET) held that the rule indirectly discriminated against Jewish people and that the refusal was not justified because the employer had failed to consider whether the staffing needs on this particular occasion could have been met in some other way.

In some other cases, courts or adjudicating bodies have gone further: not only did they hold that indirect discrimination was not objectively justified because there were alternative and less restrictive ways to achieve the aim of the measure but they also made suggestions as to alternative ways. So the court or body makes it clear that the practice can be accommodated or can be dealt with in a less discriminatory way. A good example of this is a case of the Dutch Equal Treatment Commission, where a local council swimming pool refused access to someone who was wearing a *burkini*[29] because the pool dress rules prohibited body covering clothing during public swimming times. The aim of the dress rule was to maintain a good atmosphere – differences in cover could create uneasiness amongst swimmers – and to maintain security in the swimming pool, by making the person in charge stand out through being dressed fully, which would be undermined by swimmers wearing *burkinis*. The Commission held that the rule was indirectly discriminatory and was not objectively justified because there were other ways of maintaining the atmosphere and the security. The person in charge could stand out, for example, by wearing clothes with a distinctive colour, text or logo.[30] This would achieve the same objective without the need for a ban on the wearing of *burkinis* and, as the Commission stated, would also be more in keeping with the inclusive policies of the pool as a municipal swimming pool. So, here the Equal Treatment Commission suggested

27 Equality Ombudsman, Case 2009/103, 30 November 2010.

28 *Fugler v MacMillan-London Hair Studios Ltd*, Employment Tribunal, Case Number: 2205090/2004. For another example see the article referred to in footnote 1 above.

29 A *burkini* is a swimsuit which covers the body up to the wrists and ankles and with a hood to cover the hair.

30 *Commissie Gelijke Behandeling*, Judgment 2009-15. Since 2 October 2012 the Equal Treatment Commission has become part of the *College voor de Rechten van de Mens* (Netherlands Institute for Human Rights). All judgments of the Commission are available (in Dutch) from the Institute's website: mensenrechten.nl. For more examples see the article referred to in footnote 1 above.

a way of accommodating the wish to wear a *burkini* without endangering the achievement of the legitimate aim of the pool dress policy.

So, in these cases, a duty to consider accommodation can be said to be implicitly accepted in the analysis of whether the indirectly discriminatory measure is justified. The British *Azmi* case[31] is an example where a measure was considered justified because alternative means to achieve the legitimate aim had been considered. Ms Azmi was a teaching assistant, employed by a school as a bilingual language support worker, who wanted to wear a *niqab* while teaching when male teachers were present. The school did not immediately prohibit her from wearing the *niqab*, but only did so after two classroom observations during which it was found that the children were seeking visual clues from Ms Azmi and that her diction was not as clear as it would have been without the face veil. The school also only banned her from wearing the *niqab* when she was working with children and she was allowed to wear it at all other times. So the Employment Tribunal held that the ban on the wearing of the *niqab*, although indirectly discriminatory, was justified taking into account the fact that the school had considered alternatives and had made great efforts to accommodate Ms Azmi's wishes. On appeal, the Employment Appeal Tribunal agreed.

Based on the above, it can be argued that the objective justification and proportionality test for indirect discrimination is not only similar to the test used for reasonable accommodation in EU, US and Canadian law, but also that this test includes a consideration of the attempts made to accommodate the religious practices or manifestation of an employee or service user. Whether the employer or service provider has considered ways of accommodating a religious practice would thus be one of the issues to be taken into account to establish whether the means used to achieve a legitimate aim are appropriate and necessary and thus whether the indirect discrimination is objectively justified. If this is the case, then there would be no need for a separate provision for reasonable accommodation in relation to religion and belief, and, by analogy, in relation to the other grounds of discrimination covered by EU anti-discrimination law. But are there any arguments against this?

6. GROUP DISADVANTAGE

It has been argued that indirect discrimination is defined by and requires evidence of group disadvantage. Vickers, for example, points out that there might be a problem with using the concept of indirect discrimination to create a duty to accommodate a religious individual because 'indirect discrimination is defined in terms of group disadvantage. Thus the claimant must show that a requirement would put *persons* [emphasis in original] of a particular religion

31 *Azmi v Kirklees Metropolitan Borough Council* [2007] IRLR 484 (EAT).

or belief at a particular disadvantage compared with others'.[32] In contrast, reasonable accommodation as described in Directive 200/78/EC is made for an individual disabled person. However, the latter does not have to be the case: many countries also impose anticipatory duties of reasonable accommodation, for example for service providers, who are required to take proactive steps to make their services accessible for disabled people. A good example would be libraries installing access ramps or allowing access for guide dogs. Therefore, the concept of reasonable accommodation is not necessarily linked to an individual person.

But does the fact that indirect discrimination is defined by group disadvantage mean that we cannot use the concept of indirect discrimination to create a duty to accommodate a religious individual? First of all, in most cases, an individual requesting reasonable accommodation of their religious manifestation will do so because they believe that this is required by their religion and they generally share this belief with at least some other people of the same religion or belief. As mentioned, indirect discrimination, for example on the ground of religion or belief, shall, according to Article 2(2)(b)of Directive 2000/78/EC, be taken to occur where an apparently neutral provision, criterion or practice would put persons having a particular religion or belief at a particular disadvantage compared with other persons unless that provision, criterion or practice is objectively justified by a legitimate aim and the means of achieving that aim are appropriate and necessary. This article mentions 'persons' but does not give any indication of how many 'persons' should be put at a disadvantage. Neither does it prescribe that the whole of a religious group should be affected, so it could presumably be a very small sub-group. But could it even refer to an individual?

The requirement of group disadvantage for a successful claim of indirect (religious) discrimination was discussed in the British case of *Eweida v British Airways Plc*.[33] Ms Eweida worked for British Airways as check-in staff. She was a devout Christian and wanted to wear a small silver cross with her uniform in a visible manner, but this was against the uniform policy prohibiting visible religious symbols unless their wearing was required by the particular religion involved and could not be concealed under the uniform. Both the Employment Tribunal and the Employment Appeal Tribunal rejected the claim of indirect discrimination because Eweida had not shown that the uniform requirement put persons of the same religion at a disadvantage.[34] So, as there was no evidence

32 L. Vickers, above note 18, at 21, footnote 59. See also: L. Waddington, above note 6, at 742.

33 *Eweida v British Airways Plc* [2009] IRLR 78 (EAT); [2010] IRLR 322 (CA).

34 The Employment Equality (Religion and Belief) Regulations 2003 were applicable at the time. Reg. 3(1)(b) on indirect discrimination determined that a provision, criterion or practice which 'puts or would put persons of B's [the person suffering the discrimination] religion or belief at a particular disadvantage compared with others' could be indirectly discriminatory

of group discrimination, there was no indirect discrimination.[35] The Court of Appeal rejected Eweida's appeal and held that the term 'persons', both in the British Regulations and in Directive 2000/78/EC, could not be read as including a single person.[36] The detriment in this case was suffered by Eweida alone: neither evidentially nor inferentially was anyone else similarly disadvantaged.[37]

Although, in *Eweida,* the absence of group disadvantage led to the conclusion that there was no indirect discrimination and thus there was no need to examine any justification, the Employment Tribunal did consider justification. It held that, although the uniform policy had a legitimate aim, the means used to achieve this aim were not proportionate. The Tribunal considered that, in this context, it was 'important to assess whether the respondent has demonstrated that any discriminatory impact has been assessed and reduced to the barest minimum'.[38] It continued that it did not consider that 'the blanket ban on everything classified as "jewellery" struck the correct balance between corporate consistency, individual need and *accommodation of diversity*[39] [emphasis added]'. So here, again, it is suggested that alternative, less discriminatory means must be considered and that the accommodation of diversity is seen as part of the justification test for indirect discrimination.

Recently, the British Court of Appeal, in *Home Office v Essop*, confirmed that, under the British Equality Act 2010, group disadvantage is required and that it is 'necessary in indirect discrimination claims for the claimant to show *why* the PCP [provision, criterion or practice] has disadvantaged the group [emphasis in original]' and that 'group disadvantage cannot be proved in the abstract'.[40]

So, is group disadvantage required for a finding of indirect discrimination? It is submitted that the wording of Directive 2000/78/EC differs from the wording in the British Employment Equality (Religion and Belief) Regulations 2003 and the Equality Act 2010. The latter two instruments use the words 'puts or would put persons ... at a particular disadvantage...', while the Directive only states: 'would put persons...'. This could suggest, as Bamforth et al. argue,[41] that:

> the new UK definition is more restrictive by appearing to require evidence that there is a *group* defined by a particular characteristic which is disadvantaged, while under the wording of the Directives, indirect discrimination could potentially occur when only *one person* defined by the particular characteristic was put at a disadvantage.

---

unless the provision, criterion or practice was objectively justified. The same formulation can now be found in S 19(2) of the Equality Act 2010.

35 *Eweida* (EAT), above note 33, paras 61–64.

36 *Eweida* (CA), above note 33, para 15.

37 Ibid. para.28.

38 *Eweida* (EAT), above note 33, para 18.

39 Ibid. para 19.

40 *Home Office (UK Border Agency) v Essop and Ohters* [2015] EWCA Civ 609, paras 57 and 59.

41 N. Bamforth, M. Malik and C. O'Cinneide, *Discrimination Law: Theory and Context Text and Materials* (London, Sweet and Maxwell, 2008), at 307–308.

The British Equality and Human Rights Commission also contends that the definition of indirect discrimination in Directive 2000/78/EC 'does not require a person to show that others who share the religion are actually put at a disadvantage by the employer's actions'.[42] Therefore, it appears that group disadvantage is not a requirement for indirect discrimination under EU law.[43]

Vickers points to a possible problem with the approach to indirect religious discrimination of allowing a claim in situations where there is only one person who has been put at a disadvantage: there could be a 'danger that a wide range of behaviours linked to individual beliefs could generate claims of discrimination'. However, she continues that 'employers need not anticipate and meet every wish of employees with any belief, as indirect discrimination can always be justified where proportionate'.[44] In other words, this problem is solved by the fact that indirect discrimination can be justified by a legitimate aim and the use of proportionate means to achieve this aim. And, as Vickers writes, 'it is arguable that the number of individuals affected by any requirement can be taken into account in assessing proportionality'.[45]

The requirement of group disadvantage, therefore, does not seem to be part of the EU definition of indirect discrimination and there is thus no reason why the objective justification test for indirect discrimination in EU law should not be seen as including a duty of reasonable accommodation. Can support for inclusion possibly be found in the European Convention for the Protection of Human Rights and Fundamental Freedoms (ECHR) and its interpretation by the European Court of Human Rights (ECtHR)?

7. EUROPEAN COURT OF HUMAN RIGHTS

The ECHR contains a number of guarantees of fundamental rights as well as a prohibition of discrimination on a large number of grounds in the enjoyment of these rights (Article 14). Article 14 itself does not contain any reference to

---

42 Submission of the Equality and Human Rights Commission in the European Court of Human Rights Eweida and Chaplin v the United Kingdom, App. Nos 48420/10 and 59842/10, (2012), para 28.

43 This author has argued elsewhere that the Court of Appeal in *Eweida v British Airways*, above note 33, should have referred the question whether group disadvantage is required for indirect discrimination under Directive 2000/78/EC, to the CJEU, see: E. Howard, 'Protecting Freedom to Manifest One's Religion or Belief: Strasbourg or Luxembourg?', (2014) 32, 2, *Netherlands Quarterly of Human Rights*, 159 at 161–163.

44 L. Vickers 'Religious Discrimination in the Workplace: an Emerging Hierarchy?', (2010) 12, 3, *Ecclesiastical Law Journal*, at 289; see also: M. Rubenstein 'Banning Cross not Directly Discriminatory', (2010) 199, *Equal Opportunities Review*, 199, at 25–26.

45 L. Vickers, ibid. at 289. This appears to have been confirmed for the British Equality Act 2010 in *Mba v London Borough of Merton* [2013] EWCA Civ 1562, paras 31 and 33 (Lord Justice Elias).

justification. The ECtHR has held that the principle of equality of treatment is violated if the distinction has no objective and reasonable justification. And, to be objectively justified, a difference in treatment must not only pursue a legitimate aim, there must also be a reasonable relationship of proportionality between the means employed and the aim sought to be realised.[46] Bosset and Foblets write about the ECtHR that

> there is every reason to believe that the Court's requirement for proportionality between the means applied and the purpose sought when supervising the application of the Convention plays a role similar to that of reasonable accommodation.[47]

This suggests that something similar to the (American and Canadian) reasonable accommodation duty might implicitly be present in the justification and proportionality test under Article 14 ECHR.

It has been argued that the ECtHR came close to accepting a concept of reasonable accommodation of religious practices in *Thlimmenos v Greece*.[48] Thlimmenos, who, as a Jehovah's Witness, conscientiously objected to military service, was convicted for his failure to wear military uniform. Six years later, after passing the exams necessary to become a chartered accountant, he was refused entry into the profession because of this criminal conviction. The ECtHR stated that the right under Article 14 not to be discriminated against was not only violated 'when States treat differently persons in analogous situations without providing an objective and reasonable justification' but also 'when States without an objective and reasonable justification fail to treat differently persons whose

---

46 ECtHR, 23 July 1968, *Case Relating to Certain Aspects of the Laws on the Use of Languages in Education in Belgium v Belgium*, nos 1474/62; 1677/62; 1691/62; 1769/63; 1994/63; 2126/64, under THE LAW, B, para 10.

47 P. Bossett and M-C. Foblets, 'Accommodating Diversity in Quebec and Europe: Different Legal Concepts, Similar Results?' in Council of Europe (2009), above note 16, at 61.

48 ECtHR, 6 April 2000, *Thlimmenos v Greece*, no. 34369/97. See: O. De Schutter, *The Prohibition of Discrimination under European Human Rights Law Relevance for EU Racial and Employment Equality Directives*, EU Directorate General, Employment, Social Affairs and Equal Opportunities, (Luxembourg, Office for Official Publications of the European Communities, 2005), at 16–17; L. Vickers, above note 18, at 21; L. Vickers, above note 13, at 221; M. Bossett and M.-C. Foblets, above note 47, at 59; F. Ast, 'European Legal Frameworks Responding to Diversity and the Need for Institutional Change. Indirect Discrimination as a Means of Protecting Pluralism: Challenges and Limits', in Council of Europe (2009), above note 16, at 97; E. Ruiz Vieytez, 'Reasonable Accommodation: Going Beyond the European Convention on Human Rights to Reflect the Plurality in National Institutional Settings', in Council of Europe (2009), above note 16, at 133; J. Wright, 'European Legal Frameworks that Respond to Diversity and the Need for Institutional Change: To what Extent are the Canadian Concept of "Reasonable Accommodation" and the European Approach to "Mutual Accommodation" Reflected in those Frameworks? Which Conceptual Approach Provides the Better Way Forward in the European Context?', in Council of Europe (2009), above note 16, at 150–151; E. Bribosia, J. Ringelheim and I. Rorive, above note 21, at 160; and, Bribosia and Rorive, above note 21, at 64.

situations are significantly different'.[49] This recognises that Article 14 covers not only direct but also indirect discrimination. The ECtHR then considered that:

> it was the State having enacted the relevant legislation which violated the applicant's right not to be discriminated against in the enjoyment of his right under Article 9 of the Convention. That State did so *by failing to introduce appropriate exceptions to the rule* barring persons convicted of a serious crime from the profession of chartered accountants [emphasis added].[50]

Greece's failure to treat Mr Thlimmenos differently, its failure to accommodate difference therefore amounts to unequal treatment, because it amounts to a refusal to treat different people differently'.[51]

This may thus be seen as approaching a duty to accommodate religious practices as part of the justification test under Article 14 ECHR: if no attempt is made to accommodate a religious manifestation, the means used to achieve a legitimate aim cannot be considered appropriate. The ECtHR also appears to have accepted that a duty of reasonable accommodation exists in relation to disability discrimination.[52]

Jakobski v Poland[53] seems to suggest that the ECtHR is moving towards a duty of reasonable accommodation as part of the justification test under Article 9(2) ECHR. This article allows for restrictions on the right to freely manifest one's religion if the restriction is prescribed by law and is necessary in a democratic society in the interests of public safety, for the protection of public order, health or morals or for the protection of the rights of others. The expression 'necessary in a democratic society' has been interpreted to mean that the interference complained of must correspond to a pressing social need; be proportionate to the legitimate aim pursued and be justified by relevant and sufficient reasons.[54] So, here again, there is a justification test which includes whether the means used are proportionate to the legitimate aim pursued. This test is thus similar to the objective justification test under Article 14 ECHR and for indirect discrimination in EU law.

In *Jakobski*, a Buddhist prisoner requested to be served meat-free meals in order to follow his religious dietary requirements. When this request was refused, he claimed that this was a violation of his right to manifest his religion under

---

49 *Thlimmenos v Greece*, above note 48, para 44.

50 Ibid., para 48.

51 L. Vickers, above note 18, at 21.

52 ECtHR 30 April 2009, *Glor v Switzerland*, no. 13444/04, paras 96–97. See also on this case: F. Ast, above note 48, at 98.

53 ECtHR, 7 December 2010, *Jakobski v Poland*, no. 18429/06.

54 ECtHR, 7 December 1976, *Handyside v. the United Kingdom*, no.5493/72, paras 48–50. This case concerned a claim under Article 10(2) ECHR (freedom of expression), but the test has been held to be applicable to Article 9(2) as well. See, for example, ECtHR, 15 February 2001, *Dahlab v. Switzerland*, no. 42393/98, at 12.

Article 9 ECHR. The ECtHR considered that, whether the case was analysed in terms of a positive duty on the state to take reasonable and appropriate measures to secure the rights guaranteed under Article 9(1) or in terms of an interference justified under Article 9(2):

> *the applicable principles are broadly similar.* In both contexts regard must be had to the fair balance that has to be struck between the competing interests of the individual and of the community as a whole [emphasis added].[55]

Therefore, the ECtHR saw the analysis of the duty to take reasonable and appropriate measures and the justification test under Article 9 ECHR as broadly similar.

The Polish Government in *Jacobski* argued that the preparation of meat-free meals for one person would have been too expensive (because of extra costs and hygiene requirements) and would have placed an excessive burden on the prison's kitchen staff, but the ECtHR was not 'persuaded that the provision of a vegetarian diet to the applicant would have entailed any disruption to the management of the prison or to any decline in the standards of meals served to other prisoners'.[56] The ECtHR concluded that no fair balance had been struck between the interests of the prison authorities and those of the applicant and thus that the interference was not justified and was a breach of Article 9.[57] These considerations are very similar to the considerations which must be made to establish 'undue hardship' or a 'disproportionate burden' in relation to a duty of reasonable accommodation. Much of what was said in *Jakobski* was repeated in *Gatis Kovalkovs*.[58] Therefore, the ECtHR appears to have gone some way towards accepting that a duty of reasonable accommodation is part of the justification test under Article 9(2) and under Article 14 ECHR.

However, not all ECtHR judges followed this line. In *Francesco Sessa v Italy*,[59] a Jewish lawyer was not able to represent his client at a domestic hearing because the two dates offered by the Court were both Jewish religious festivals. The majority of the ECtHR's judges (4 out of 7 judges) held that Sessa's right to manifest his religion had not been infringed and, even if it had, this would have been justified for the protection of the rights and freedoms of others, in particular the public's right to a proper administration of justice and the principle that cases be heard within a reasonable time. However, the three dissenting judges

---

55 *Jakobski v Poland*, above note 53, para 47.

56 Ibid. para 52.

57 Ibid. paras 54 and 55.

58 ECtHR, 31 January 2012, *Gatis Kovalkovs v Latvia*, no. 35021/05, para 64. This case also concerned the exercise of religious practices in prison, this time loud chanting and reading of prayers and burning of incense sticks in a prison cell shared with other prisoners, but the outcome of the balancing exercise was different and no violation of Article 9 ECHR was found.

59 ECtHR, 3 April 2012, *Francesco Sessa v Italy*, no. 28790/08.

stated that proportionality requires that, where there are several alternative means to achieve the pursued legitimate aim, the authorities should choose the one that is least restrictive to the rights and liberties protected. The search for reasonable accommodation could lead to a less restrictive means to achieve the aim sought, and, in this case, such a reasonable accommodation could have been made quite easily and this would have avoided an interference with the freedom of religion of the applicant, according to the dissenting judges.[60]

In *Eweida and Others v. the United Kingdom*,[61] the ECtHR referred to the duty of reasonable accommodation as it exists in US and Canadian law[62] and mentioned that a number of interveners had argued that a proportionality analysis by the ECtHR should take account of the possibility of an accommodation of an individual's beliefs and practices.[63] However, the ECtHR did not mention this again when it assessed the individual cases, nor did it indicate whether such a duty was part of the justification tests under Articles 9 and 14 ECHR. The ECtHR has been criticised for not clarifying this issue in this case,[64] although it could very tentatively be argued that the ECtHR appeared to suggest that British Airways could and should have accommodated Ms Eweida's wish to wear a small cross where it considered that:

> Ms Eweida's cross was discreet and cannot have detracted from her professional appearance. There was no evidence that the wearing of other, previously authorised, items of religious clothing, such as turbans and hijabs, by other employees, had any negative impact on British Airways' brand or image. Moreover, the fact that the company was able to amend its uniform code to allow for the visible wearing of religious symbolic jewellery demonstrates that the earlier prohibition was not of crucial importance.[65]

The ECtHR came to the conclusion that, in relation to Ms Eweida, a fair balance had not been struck between her right to freely manifest her religion and British Airways's wish to protect its corporate image and that the domestic courts had given too much weight to the latter.[66]

---

60 Ibid. dissenting opinion, paras 9 and 10. A request for deferral to the Grand Chamber in this case was rejected so the judgment is final.

61 ECtHR, 15 January 2013, *Eweida, Chaplin, Ladele and McFarlane v. the United Kingdom*, nos 48420/10, 59842/10, 51671/10 and 36516/10.

62 Ibid. paras 48–49.

63 Ibid. para 78.

64 See, for example: D. McIlroy, 'A Marginal Victory for Freedom of Religion, Case Comments' (2013) 2,1, *Oxford Journal of Law and Religion*, at 213; S. Smet, '*Eweida, Part II: The Margin of Appreciation Defeats and Silences All*', Blog Strasbourg Observers, 23 January 2013; and, R. Wintemute, 'Accommodating Religious Beliefs: Harm, Clothing or Symbols, and Refusal to Serve Others', (2014) 77, 2, *Modern Law Review*, at 243.

65 *Eweida and Others v UK*, above note 61, para 94.

66 Ibid.

As mentioned, the ECtHR has been criticised for not clarifying this issue in this case. For example, Smet criticises the ECtHR for not settling this argument as the case 'was the perfect case to both firmly ground reasonable accommodation of religion in the Convention *and* at the same time explain its limitations'.[67] McIlroy finds that the lack of discussion of reasonable accommodation is 'the most unsatisfactory part of the decision',[68] while Wintemute writes that the ECtHR 'chose an ambiguous, potentially neutral position: accommodation is not required but might be permitted'.[69]

On the other hand, *Eweida v the United Kingdom* appears to have been read and explained by both the British Supreme Court and by the British Equality and Human Rights Commission as meaning that something close to a duty of reasonable accommodation can be part of the proportionality test which has to be performed to establish whether an interference with the Article 9 ECHR right is justified. In the Supreme Court case of *Bull and Another v. Hall and Another*,[70] Lady Hale stated:

> I am more than ready to accept that *the scope for reasonable accommodation is part of the proportionality assessment*, at least in some cases. This is reinforced by the decision in Eweida v United Kingdom (2013) 57 EHRR 8, where the Strasbourg court abandoned its previous stance that there was no interference with an employee's right to manifest her religion if it could be avoided by changing jobs. Rather, that possibility was to be taken into account in the overall proportionality assessment, *which must therefore consider the extent to which it is reasonable to expect the employer to accommodate the employee's right* [my italics].[71]

The British Equality and Human Rights Commission issued guidance to employers after the *Eweida* judgment.[72] In this guidance it is stated that employers are not required to comply with religious requests on all occasions, but that they need to consider such requests seriously.[73] Employers are 'encouraged to take as their starting point consideration as to how to accommodate the request, unless there are cogent and compelling reasons not to do so … '.[74] The factors that should be taken into account are the impact of accommodation on other employees, on customers and on service users and on the operation of the business, including costs, disruption and health and safety issues. The employer

67 S. Smet, above note 64.
68 D. McIlroy, above note 64, at 213.
69 R. Wintemute, above note 64, at 243.
70 *Bull and Another v. Hall and Another* [2013] UKSC 73.
71 Ibid, para 47.
72 Equality and Human Rights Commission, Religion and Belief in the Workplace: A Guide for Employers Following Recent European Court of Human Rights Judgments, equalityhumanrights.com.
73 Ibid, at 5.
74 Ibid.

should also consider whether work policies and practices to ensure uniformity and consistency are justifiable.[75]

So, *Eweida v the United Kingdom* appears to be open to interpretation on the question whether something close to a duty of reasonable accommodation can be part of the proportionality test which has to be performed to establish whether an interference with the Article 9 ECHR right is justified. But, this case and some of the other cases could suggest that the ECtHR is slowly moving towards the view that a duty of reasonable accommodation is part of the proportionality test under both Articles 9 and 14 ECHR, although the Court itself has not expressed itself very clearly on this. But this development could also support the argument that it is part of the objective justification test for indirect discrimination in EU law.

8. CONCLUSION

In this chapter, the question whether the duty of reasonable accommodation, as found in EU anti-discrimination law for disability, should be expanded to include religious manifestations and practices has been analysed The duties as these exist in EU, US and Canadian law have been used to illustrate how such a duty can be laid down in law. All three duties are linked to a finding of discrimination and all three require a balancing of all different interests involved. The duty in the US and Canada is seen as a mutual duty which requires some accommodation on the side of the religious employee or service user as well, and accommodation does not have to be made if the hardship for the employer or service provider is undue. In EU law, accommodation does not have to be made if the burden on the employer is disproportionate. The CRPD also mentions 'disproportionate or undue burden'. So the balancing test required in all these instruments can be seen as a proportionality test; the burden on the employer or service provider must be proportionate to the benefits to be achieved for the employee or service user.

The analysis of existing duties suggested that there is no reason why the duty should only exist in relation to disability and why it should not be extended to religion or belief and other grounds of discrimination. However, it was argued that such an extension might not be necessary as an implicit duty to make reasonable accommodation could be seen as part of the justification test for indirect discrimination under EU law. Under EU law a measure is not indirectly discriminatory if it is objectively justified by a legitimate aim and the means of achieving that aim are appropriate and necessary. So, here too, a proportionality test is applied. In *Bilka Kaufhaus*,[76] the CJEU has held that the justification test

75 Ibid, 5–6.

76 *Bilka Kaufhaus*, above note 24, para 36.

for indirect discrimination includes examining whether less discriminatory alternatives are available and this, it was concluded, is very similar to considering whether a practice which does not conform to the measure taken, can be accommodated. This is supported by the fact that very similar tests need to be performed to establish whether the burden of accommodation is disproportionate or whether indirect discrimination is justified: both require proportionality tests and a balancing of all interests involved. Further support for the proposition that an implicit duty of reasonable accommodation is part of the justification and proportionality test for indirect discrimination can be found, albeit tentatively, in the case law of the ECtHR.

It is thus submitted that the objective justification test for indirect discrimination includes a consideration of the attempts made to accommodate the religious or other practices of an employee or service user and, if no attempts to accommodate are made, the discrimination should not be held to be justified. Extending the duty of reasonable accommodation beyond disability to other grounds of discrimination explicitly in law is thus not necessary as such a duty is already part of the justification test for indirect discrimination. On the other hand, there does not seem to be any objection to extending the law. An anti-discrimination law which would clearly state that the duty of reasonable accommodation applies to all grounds of discrimination covered by that law, would make it absolutely clear that accommodation should be attempted and that reasonable requests from employees or service users should be considered. But, based on the above, the author would argue that reasonable accommodation needs to be considered, even if the anti-discrimination law does not state this.

RECONSIDERING CIVIC INTEGRATION POLICIES FOR MIGRANTS THROUGH THE LENS OF SOCIO-ECONOMIC STATUS

Examples of Belgian and Dutch Legal Orders

Sarah GANTY*

For about the past 15 years, civic integration policies have been implemented in some European countries[1] as an alternative or a new strategy to improve integration. The logic of civic integration is to 'treat migrants as individuals who are depicted as responsible for their own integration'.[2] It refers 'to the legal framework applying in a country aimed at the participation of immigrants in the society by proficiency of the language and general knowledge of the host

* The present paper was written in the framework of the interdisciplinary Project 'action de recherche concertée': 'Sous le signe du mérite et de la conformité culturelle, les nouvelles politiques d'intégration des immigrés en Europe' (Université Libre de Bruxelles). I would like to thank Jogchum Vrielink, David Barrett, Prof. Kees Groenendijk as well as the two peer-reviewers for their valuable and helpful comments and suggestions on an earlier version of this paper. I am also grateful to Marie-Caroline Mendez for her support with the wording of this paper. I take full and sole responsibility for what is written here. The present article was written in December 2014, presented at the *Equal is not Enough* conference in February 2015 and submitted for peer review in May 2015. It has been updated and modified in order to include two important rulings handed down by the Court of Justice of the European Union in June and July 2015.

1 Notably in Germany, France, Denmark, the United Kingdom, Belgium, the Netherlands and Austria.

2 C. Joppke, 'Transformation of Immigrant Integration: Civic Integration and Antidiscrimination in the Netherlands, France, and Germany' (2007) *World Politics* Vol 59:2, 247–248.

country, including its cultural values'.[3] Those policies are linked to the concept of participation in society[4] and more generally to the concept of 'citizenship'.[5]

In many EU countries, the integration requirements held to be compulsory are imposed as a prerequisite for receiving a residence permit, citizenship and other social rights.[6] Those civic integration policies are thus, most of the time, part of other policies such as immigration, social welfare and citizenship policies.

The integration requirements described as 'civic requirements'[7] generally imply a minimum level of knowledge of the national language and knowledge of the host country and its values. Those requirements are usually evaluated through integration tests. In some cases, migrants have to attend integration courses and do not have to pass a test at the end of the integration process. As the case may be, requirements and the way they are drawn and issued (strictly or leniently) differ depending on the country and the right or status at stake. In most cases, if an applicant does not respect those integration requirements, she is penalised and sees her rights or status refused. In some countries, migrants can instead be fined or have their social benefits reduced.[8]

It has already been underlined in the literature that those policies result in direct and indirect differences in treatment, favouring certain migrants while hindering others. Scholars and NGOs have in particular addressed the differences in treatment on grounds of nationality and ethnic origin under discrimination law.[9] Among others, they have denounced the exemption of

---

3 G. Vonk & S. Van Walsum, 'Access denied, towards a new approach to social protection for formally excluded migrants' in G. Vonk (ed.), *Cross-Border Welfare State. Immigration, Social Security and Integration* (Cambridge/Antwerp/Portland, Intersentia, 2012), 8.

4 K. Groenendijk, 'Legal Concepts of Integration in EU Migration Law' (2004) *European Journal of Migration and Law* Vol 6, 114.

5 S. Carrera, *A typology of different integration programmes in the EU, Briefing paper (*European Parliament, 2006); K. De Vries, *Integration at the Border, The Dutch Act on Integration Abroad and International Immigration Law* (Oxford, Hart Publishing, 2013), 2 and 72 & seq.

6 E. Guild, K. Groenendijk, S. Carrera, 'Understanding the Contest of Community : Illiberal Practices in the EU?' in E. Guild, K. Groenendijk, S. Carrera (eds.), *Illiberal Liberal States: Immigration, Citizenship, and Integration in the EU* (England, Ashgate Publishing, 2009); R. Van Oers, E. Ersbøll, D. Kostakopoulou (eds.), *A redefinition of Belonging?* Language and integration tests in Europe (Leiden/Boston, Martinus Nijhoff, 2010).

7 S.W. Goodman, 'Integration Requirements for Integration's Sake? Identifying, Categorising and Comparing Civic Integration Policies' (2010) *Journal of Ethnic and Migration Studies* 36:5, 753–772.

8 Notably in Belgium.

9 E. Bribosia, 'Les politiques d'intégration à l'épreuve du principe de non-discrimination' in T. Strik, Y. Pascouau (eds.) *Which Integration Policies for Migrants? Interaction between the EU and its Member States* (The Netherlands/Nijmegen, Wolf Legal Publishers, 2012); K. De Vries, 'The Dutch Act on Integration Abroad: a case of racial or ethnic discrimination?' in S. Morano-Foadi and M. Malena (eds), *Integration for third-country nationals in the European Union, the Equality Challenge* (Edward Elgar Publishing, 2012); K. Groenendijk, 'Are third-country nationals protected by the Union law prohibition of discrimination on grounds of nationality?' in K. Barwig & R. Dobbelstein (eds.), *Den Fremden akzeptieren.*

OECD nationals from passing integration tests to get a Dutch family reunion visa. But it is striking that, most of the time, little attention is paid to the social and economic situation of migrants even though this is a determining factor in civic integration policies.

In the first section, I address civic integration policies by focusing on the differences in treatment between migrants, especially regarding their socio-economic situation. I base my analysis on examples of some Belgian and Dutch civic integration policies (section 1). In the second section, I discuss the importance of addressing those differences in treatment under European and international discrimination law and particularly the status ground of 'social condition' (section 2).

1. SOCIO-ECONOMIC STATUS AND CIVIC INTEGRATION POLICIES: DUTCH AND BELGIAN LEGAL ORDERS

The Netherlands has adopted civic integration policies at different levels, including at immigration policy level. It has notably made integration a condition for the acquisition or the extension of a non-permanent residence permit (section 1.1). In contrast, Belgium, including the Flemish Community, does not directly link integration and immigration policies (section 1.2). Therefore, both countries address the issue of civic integration in their own way. Yet the two countries seem to treat migrants differently depending on their socio-economic situation (section 1.3).

1.1. DUTCH PRE-ENTRY AND INLAND TESTS AS A CONDITION FOR THE ACQUISITION OF A NON-PERMANENT RESIDENCE PERMIT

At immigration level, Dutch civic integration policies require migrants to pass pre-entry and inland tests as a prerequisite for getting or extending a non-permanent residence permit.[10]

Firstly, applicants, especially those seeking family reunification or formation with a Dutch citizen or with a third-country national (TCN), are required to

Festschrift für Gisbert Brinkmann (Schriften zum Migrationsrecht, 6) (Baden-Baden/ Nomos, 2012), 131–142; Human Rights Watch, *The Netherlands: Discrimination in the Name of Integration Migrants' Rights under the Integration Abroad Act* (Human Rights Watch, 2008).

10 In the following part, I only discuss the integration conditions required to obtain a non-permanent residence permit.

take and pass a pre-departure civic integration test to prove they possess a basic knowledge of the Dutch language and of Dutch society.[11] The level required for the language test is A1 of the Common European Framework of Reference (CEFR). If applicants do not fulfil these conditions, the permit will be refused and they will not be admitted to Dutch territory.[12]

Moreover, Dutch law also requires that family members of Dutch citizens or of TCNs pass a civic integration test within three years of their arrival – called the 'inland test'.[13] This examination tests their knowledge of the national language and of Dutch society. The level required is higher than the pre-entry test: A2 of the CEFR. Migrants who fail to comply can be fined.[14] The fine imposed depends on the municipality where the migrants live and can cost up € 1,250.[15] As an example, in Amsterdam in 2014, the fine could reach € 200 and could be imposed several times if the migrants did not comply with their integration obligations.[16] Before January 2013, the municipalities could also sanction migrants by reducing their social benefits instead of asking them to pay a fine.[17]

Since January 2013,[18] the sanction has gone even further. In the event of failing the test, the residence permit of family members who do not meet the requirements within three years of their arrival can be withdrawn or not extended.[19] As a result, the migrant will most probably be left with no legal status and may have to leave the country. However, we will have to wait until 2016 to see how this new rule will be applied since the first migrants who are subject to this rule will have completed their three-year stay in 2016. However, it is worth highlighting that the Dutch Council of State considered in its advice on the draft project that such a sanction is unlawful and notably breaches the right to family life.[20]

It is striking that migrant workers and their family members, as well as Western migrants, do not have to comply with pre-entry and inland tests, in

11 The *Wet inburgering buitenland* (Dutch Act integration abroad, WIB) entered into force on 15 March 2006. This Act constitutes an amendment to the *Vreemdelingenwet 2000* (Dutch Aliens Act). See Art 16(1)(h) Dutch Aliens Act; Wet *inburgering* (Integration Act) adopted on 1 January 2007. See Art 3(1)(a) Integration Act; *Vreemdelingenbesluit 2000* (Aliens Decree); *Vreemdelingencirculaire 2000* (Aliens Circular).

12 Article 3.98a (3) Aliens Decree.

13 Article 7 Integration Act.

14 Article 31 Integration Act.

15 Article 34 Integration Act.

16 E. Besselsen & B. De Hart, *Verblijfsrechtelijke consequenties van de Wet inburgering. Een onderzoek naar de ervaringen van migranten in Amsterdam* (Wolf Legal Publishers, 2014), 19–20.

17 Former Article 44 Integration Act.

18 E. Besselsen & B. De Hart, above note 16, at 24. Amending Act of 13 September 2012, *Staatblad*, 29 September 2012, 430.

19 Article 31 Integration Act and Articles 18 and 19 Aliens Act.

20 Advies van de Raad van State, *Kamerstukken* II 2011–2012, 33086, n°4, 9. E. Besselsen & B. De Hart, above note 16, at 24.

whole or in part (section 1.1.1). As a consequence, Dutch civic integration policies mainly target family members of Dutch citizens and TCNs – non migrant workers – and may constitute an important burden for them (section 1.1.2).[21]

1.1.1. OECD Nationals, TCN Migrant Workers and their Family Members

TCN migrant workers other than religious leaders, whether they are (non-) skilled[22], 'knowledge'[23] or highly skilled workers[24], as well as their family members, do not have to pass the pre-entry test to be admitted to Dutch territory.[25] They do not have to pass the inland test after three years of residence either. The Netherlands only imposes language requirements when these categories of migrants want to obtain a permanent residence permit after a five-year stay on Dutch territory,[26] or if they want Dutch citizenship.[27]

This exemption is explained by the fact that these workers and their families are in the Netherlands for temporary purposes, in contrast to the family members of Dutch citizens or TCNs.[28] It is true that the nature of labour migration has changed significantly in the Netherlands since the 60s and 70s: most migrant workers are Western 'knowledge' workers and they usually do not stay on Dutch territory permanently.[29] However, the concept of 'temporary purposes' is a very relative one. Indeed, according to statistics from the Dutch central Bureau of Statistics, a quarter of the TCN workers who arrived in 2000–2002 were still in the Netherlands in 2007.[30] Moreover, migrant workers and their families – except seasonal ones – are eligible to be granted a permanent residence permit after five years of residence on Dutch territory. In this context, why is it that TCN workers and their family members who are staying for several years do not have to integrate with Dutch society within the three years of their arrival – i.e. to comply with integration tests – while the other categories of TCNs do?

---

21 I do not speak about EU citizens, asylum seekers and the family members of both of those groups as specific rules apply to them under European Union law and international treaties.

22 By reference to Articles 1–10 *Wet arbeid vreemdelingen* (Aliens Employment Act).

23 By reference to the Dutch *kennismigrantenregeling* (Knowledge Migrant Programme).

24 By reference to the Blue Card Directive.

25 Article 16(1)(h), 17 Aliens Act; Article 3.5(2) Aliens Decree; Article 3(1)(a) Integration Act 2007.

26 Article 45b (2) Aliens Act; Article 13 Integration Act 2007.

27 Article 8 (1) (d) *Rijkswet op het Nederlanderschap* (Citizenship Act) and Decree of 15 April 2002 on Besluit naturalisatietoets (Citizenship test Decree). See also T. Strik, A. Böcker, M. Luiten & R. Van Oers, *Integration and Naturalisation tests: the new way to European Citizenship, Country report: The Netherlands* (INTEC Project, 2010 (b)), 12 and16.

28 For the list of temporary purposes under the Integration Act, see Art 2.1(1) *Besluit inburgering* (*Inburgering* Decree) and Annex 1 to *Regeling inburgering* (Integration Regulations).

29 S. Verschuren, R. Van Gaalen & H. Nicolaas, *Arbeidsmigratie, volgmigratie en* retour migratie *in de periode 2000–2006* (Bevolkingstrends, 2e kwartaal 2011, Centraal Bureau voor de Statistiek, 2011), 74.

30 *Ibid.*, 72.

As the Council Directive 2009/50/EC of 25 May 2009 (the so-called 'Blue Card Directive')[31] stipulates the measures aiming to attract and retain qualified highly skilled TCN workers as part of an approach based on the needs of Member States to achieve the 'objective of becoming the most competitive and dynamic knowledge-based economy in the world'.[32] While to some extent the exceptions made for highly skilled workers and their families not having to pass civic integration tests became necessary through the transposition of the Blue Card Directive, they are also clearly a response to the country's national interests and current labour market needs.[33] Indeed, as an example, when it comes to families of highly skilled workers, the Blue Card Directive only forbids 'pre-entry' civic integration conditions but does not forbid inland integration measures;[34] however, they are exempted from both tests in the Netherlands. They have to pass integration tests only if they want to apply for a permanent residence permit or naturalisation.

As mentioned above, this exception not only applies to highly skilled workers and their family members. The 'Dutch Knowledge Migrant Programme', which is not a transposition of any EU law, also exempts knowledge migrants and their families from integration requirements. This programme even outstrips in application volume that of the European Blue Card in the Netherlands.[35] It is worth noting that in the Netherlands in 2010 one out of seven migrant workers was a highly skilled/knowledge worker while the proportion was only one out of 11 in 2005.[36]

In addition, TCN workers who are not 'highly skilled' or 'knowledge' workers can also be given work and residence permits on several conditions. The administration has a wide margin of appreciation in that field and takes into account the areas of shortages in the labour market[37] and thus the added value the applicant might bring. Yet those workers and their families do not have the advantages of the fast-track procedure that knowledge/highly skilled migrants benefit from, but they are exempted from the integration requirements on entry and after three years of residence.

---

31 Council Directive 2009/50/EC of 25 May 2009 on the conditions of entry and residence of third-country nationals for the purposes of highly qualified employment, OJ L 155/17, 18 June 2009. The transposition can be found in Article 3.30b Aliens Act.

32 Recital 6 of the Blue Card Directive.

33 R, Schweitzer, *A Stratified Right to Family Life? Patterns and Rationales behind Differential Access to Family Reunification for Third-Country Nationals Living within the EU* (University of Sussex, 2014), 14.

34 Article 15 (3) of the Blue Card Directive.

35 M. Reurs, 'EBC or HSMP? The Netherlands' transposition of Directive 2009/50' in T. Strik, & C. Grütters, *The Blue Card Directive: Central Themes, Problem Issues, and Implementation in Selected Member States* (The Netherlands, Wolf legal Publishers, 2012), 86.

36 Europese migratienetwerk, *De organisatie van het asiel-en migratiebleid in Nederland* (Rijswijk/Indiac, NL EMN NCP/2012), 27. See also: www.cbs.nl (last visit on 3 December 2014).

37 See notably Articles 8 and 9 Aliens Employment Act.

Besides that, TCNs who are exempted from visa requirements, namely those who come from so-called 'Western countries' (OECD citizens) do not need to take the pre-entry test.[38] This distinction is directly based on the ground of nationality. But it is also indirectly based on the grounds of race and ethnic origin since some ethnic minorities, such as Moroccans, are mainly those for whom integration measures are applicable.[39] It also indirectly differentiates between migrants based on their socio-economic status, since migrants who come from OECD countries are more likely to be in a better socio-economic situation than those who come from less developed countries. The government explains the exemptions for OECD nationals by the fact that they come from cultural, economic and social situations from which it can be expected that they would have a good understanding of Dutch social relations, norms and values.[40]

As a consequence, the above-mentioned exemptions seem to show that the economic 'added value' of migrants for the Netherlands is at the forefront of Dutch civic integration policies. Indeed, migrant workers and their family members, as well as OECD nationals, who are seen as an economic 'added value' for the country or in 'similar' social, economic and cultural situations are much better treated than other categories of migrants. This difference in treatment is questionable when considering integration purposes which are supposed to involve the society as a whole.

1.1.2. Burden of the Dutch Integration Tests

Both pre-entry and inland tests are costly for the target groups that are obliged to take them. Language courses and lessons on Dutch society are not offered by the State. At pre-entry test level, applicants attend courses in their own countries where teaching quality and rates vary significantly. According to different studies, participation in a course costs € 800 on average.[41] Moreover, the cost of the exam is € 350.[42] If the applicant fails the test, she will not be granted admission to Dutch territory. Moreover, the costs of the pre-entry test involve not only the test itself and the course but also travelling to the embassy, often more

38 Articles 16(1)(h) and 17(1)(a) Aliens Act. See also, K. De Vries, above note 5, at 53.

39 K. De Vries, above note 5, at 53.

40 *Ibid.*, 53 and 309; H. Entzinger, C. Ivanescu, P. Scholten & S. Suvarierol, *The Impacts of Restrictions and Entitlements on the Integration of Family Migrants (IMPACIM), National report, The Netherlands* (Rotterdam, Erasmus University, 2013); K. De Vries, above note 9, at 326. See also *Parliamentary Papers II* 2004– 2005, 29 700, N° 6, 31–32 and *Parliamentary Papers II* 2003–2004, 29700, N°3, 19.

41 P.W.A. Scholten et al, *Integration from abroad? Perception and impacts of pre-entry tests for third country nationals. Final report of PROSINT Workpackage 4* (PROSINT, 2012), 66; T. Strik & al., *Integration and Naturalisation tests: the new way to European Citizenship, Country report: The Netherlands* (INTEC Project, 2010 (b)), 12 and 109; K. De Vries, above note 5, at 62. See also Annex to *Parliamentary Papers II* 2008–2009, 32 005, N°1, 8.

42 Article 3.98 b (2) Aliens Decree.

than once, and travelling and staying for weeks or months in a large city to take a course.[43] At the inland test level, it is even more expensive. Courses can cost up to € 5,000. Migrants have to cover the cost of the tuition and fees. If migrants do not have enough money to pay to prepare for their test, they can obtain a 'social loan' from the government.[44] Since January 2013, the *inburgering* (civic integration) budget has been reduced drastically.[45] Only asylum seekers who pass the inland test within three years – or five years for illiterate/analphabetic asylum seekers – do not have to repay the loan.

Furthermore, both of the tests include a reading test without any exemption or assistance for illiterate/analphabetic individuals.[46] For the inland test, the three-year term can be extended by two years if migrants are illiterate.[47] Some people can also face the difficulty of the digital divide since all the tests have to be taken on a computer. Finally, Work Instruction no. 2013/9[48] relating to the hardship clause – enshrined in the Aliens Decree[49] – also specifies that the clause cannot be successfully invoked when the applicant is unable to pass the test because she does not have sufficient financial or technical means.

As a consequence, the pre-entry and inland integration tests are likely to hinder under-educated and low-earning TCNs, since they are costly and difficult particularly when considering the required reading skills and associated costs.[50]

It is worth highlighting that the rules relating to the financial and practical burden of the pre-entry test might change in the future following the judgment of the Court of Justice of the European Union (CJEU) handed down in July 2015, where the Court ruled that Dutch legislation related to the pre-entry test is not compatible with EU law and especially Family Reunification Directive 2003/86 (see hereafter).[51]

---

43 T. Strik & al., *Integration and Naturalisation Tests: The New Way to European Citizenship, Synthesis Report* (INTEC Project, 2010), 95.

44 Articles 16 and 17 Integration Act 2007.

45 R. Van Oers, *Deserving citizenship, citizenship Tests in Germany, the Netherlands and the United Kingdom* (Wolf legal Publishers, 2013). *Parliamentary Papers II* 2013– 2014, 32824, N°62. See also E. Besselsen & B. De Hart, above note 16, at 23.

46 Article 3.98 a (3) Aliens Decree; IND-werkinstructie Wet inburgering in het buitenland nr. 2013/9 (AUA), 1st June 2013, para. 2.3, 7–9 (Work instruction); K. De Vries, above note 5, at 55 and 61.

47 Article 7 (3) (b) Integration Act 2007.

48 IND-werkinstructie Wet inburgering in het buitenland nr. 2013/9 (AUA), 1st June 2013, para. 2.3, 7–9 (Work instruction).

49 Article 3.71 a, d), Aliens Decree.

50 T. Strik et al., *Integration and Naturalisation Tests: The New Way to European Citizenship, Synthesis Report* (INTEC Project, 2010), 95 and 100; T. Strik & al., *Integration and Naturalisation tests: the new way to European Citizenship, Country report: The Netherlands* (INTEC Project, 2010), 71. K. De Vries, above note 5, at 66 & seq; Human Rights Watch, above note 9.

51 CJEU, Judgment in P&S, C-579/13, EU:C:2015:369; CJEU, Judgment in K&A, C-153/14, EU:C:2015:453.

1.2. FLEMISH INBURGERING

In Belgium, because of the federal structure, the competence of integration of migrants is divided between the following federated entities: the Flemish Community (in the Flemish Region and the Region of Brussels-Capital), the French Community Commission (in the Region of Brussels-Capital), the Walloon Region, and the German Community. There is no civic pre-entry test necessary to access Belgian territory or any civic test to obtain or extend a temporary or permanent residence permit to stay in Belgium. In contrast to many European countries, immigration and integration policies are not (yet) directly linked to each other.

Between 2012 and 2014, each of the above-mentioned Belgian entities[52] adopted new rules relating to the integration of migrants. However, I only focus on the Flemish civic integration policies in the present contribution, as it has some unique features since Flemish authorities have been implementing mandatory integration courses for more than 10 years. This policy is officially called *inburgering.*[53] The Flemish Decree of 28 February 2003[54] (2003 *Inburgering* Decree) establishes the policy of 'civic integration' (*inburgering*) in the Flemish part of Belgium.

The 2003 *Inburgering* Decree provides that the civic integration process is composed of one primary programme and a secondary one.[55] More specifically, the first one[56] is compulsory for some groups of migrants – unlike the second one, which is not compulsory – and includes societal,[57] vocational[58] and language[59] courses.[60] A New Decree was adopted on 7 June 2013[61] but the main provisions have not yet entered into force. It does not make any major amendments to the substance of the *inburgering* programme or to the target groups.

52 Except for the German Community.

53 On the contrary, the integration policies of the other federated entities are not (yet) mandatory, except for some new small exceptions for the Walloon Region.

54 Flemish Decree of 28 February 2003 concerning the Flemish policy of civic integration (2003 *Inburgering* Decree).

55 Article 4, §2 of the 2003 *Inburgering* Decree.

56 Article 10 and 5, §1 of the 2003 *Inburgering* Decree.

57 Article 13, §1er, para. 2 of the 2003 *Inburgering* Decree.

58 *Ibid.*, para. 4.

59 *Ibid.*, para. 3.

60 Z. Yanasmayan & M.-C., Foblets, *Integration and Naturalisation tests: the new way to European Citizenship. Country Report Belgium*, (INTEC Project, 2011) 4; See also Article 13, §1, para. 1 of the 2003 *Inburgering* Decree.

61 (Recast) Flemish Decree of 7 June 2013 concerning the Flemish integration and civic integration policies. It merges the Flemish integration policy that is ruled by the Decree of 1998 and the Flemish civic integration one that is ruled by the 2003 *Inburgering* Decree and cancels, at the same time, the two mentioned Decrees. This new law is called 'Decree concerning the Flemish integration and civic integration policies'. The Decree is expected to entry into force in its entirety in 2016.

As in the Netherlands, the Flemish *inburgering* policy makes a distinction between workers and their families and other migrants (1.2.1). For the latter, the burden of integration requirements varies and is a lot less heavy and hard to deal with than it is in the Netherlands (1.2.2).

1.2.1. TCN Migrant Workers and their Families

Migrants who are obliged to attend such an *inburgering* process are TCN 'newcomers'[62] and newcomers who are 'Belgian nationals of immigrant origin'.[63] If this obligation to attend courses is not respected, people can be fined.[64] The fine may vary between € 100 and € 150 and can reach up to € 5,000 in the event of repeated infringement.[65] Moreover, newcomers who receive social benefits and who do not fulfil their obligations are not likely to be fined but can lose their benefits in whole or in part, on the basis of other legal provisions.[66] Migrants can also be sanctioned regarding their social housing.[67]

Similarly to the Netherlands, the Flemish Government discharges TCN workers who can get a 'permanent and definitive job' and their family members from the obligation to attend the *inburgering* process.[68] The Flemish Government justifies this exemption by the 'temporary character of the stay'. Nevertheless, the Government adds in the Decree 'that the stay can become permanent though'.[69] Therefore, there is a direct difference in the treatment of newcomer TCN workers who can get a 'permanent and definitive job' and their family members and other categories of migrants. Although the temporary character of the stay justifies

---

62 Migrants registered in the national registry for the first time and who are long-term residents (not in the sense of the Council Directive 2003/109/EC of 25 November 2003). Article 5, §1, 1° of the 2003 *Inburgering* Decree.

63 Adult Belgian individuals who were born outside of Belgium with at least one parent not born in Belgium who are registered in the national registry for the first time in less than 12 months. Article 5, §1, 1°, 2°, 3° of the 2003 *Inburgering* Decree.

64 E. Somers, 'Le parcours d'intégration civique en Flandre : les personnes visées et leurs obligations' in J. Ringelheim (ed.) *Le droit et la diversité culturelle* (Bruxelles, Bruylant, 2011), 302; Article 25, §2 of the 2003 *Inburgering* Decree and Article 10 of the Flemish Government Decree of 12 September 2008 concerning administrative fines imposed on persons integrating who are among the prioritised group and the mandatory group (Flemish Government Decree of 12 September 2008).

65 Article 10 of the Flemish Government Decree of 12 September 2008.

66 E. Somers, above note 64, at 302; Article 25 of the 2003 *Inburgering* Decree and Article 1, §2 of the Flemish Government Decree of 12 September 2008.

67 Article 92, para. 2, 8° of the Flemish Housing Code.

68 See Vlaams Minderheden Centrum, Brochure Doelgroep inburgering 18+ in Vlaanderen en Brussel vanaf 2/3/2008 Juridische afbakening, 2008, www.vvsg.be/sociaal_beleid_en_werk/Etnisch-culturele_diversiteit/inburgering/Documents/doelgroep%20inburgering/VMCbrochure%20doelgroep%20inburgering_.pdf.

69 Except religious ministers. See Article 5, §1 of the Flemish Government Decree of 15 December 2006 concerning the implementation of the Flemish civic integration policy and Article 9 of the Royal Decree of 9 June 1999.

this exception, like the Dutch policies, it is worth highlighting a contradiction: TCN workers and their family members are seen to stay temporarily and thus they do not have to comply with integration requirements, but ultimately they can stay permanently if they want to. In that case, they do not have to take part in any *inburgering* process even if they apply for a permanent stay later. Again, as in the Netherlands, it seems that the 'added value' of the TCN workers plays an important role in the choice of whether or not to target certain groups with civic integration policies.

1.2.2. Burden of the Inburgering Process

In contrast to the Netherlands, in the Flemish Region of Belgium, TCNs and Belgian nationals of immigrant origin[70] who are obliged to attend the *inburgering* process are not asked to pay for it. So far what is required from migrants is a duty of best efforts and not a duty to achieve a specific result. But this might change with the entry into force of the New Decree of 7 June 2013.

Thus the *inburgering* process may appear accessible to socio-economically underprivileged TCNs not only as regards the costs but also as regards the difficulty of the process. This makes a huge and important difference in comparison with the Dutch policies.

Two nuances should be pointed out. First, the number of hours TCNs are likely to have to attend can reach up to 600 hours for illiterate/analphabetic people,[71] which is a lot when looking at the private and family life of TCNs. In addition, fines and some sanctions relating to social benefits and social housing are likely to affect the most vulnerable.[72] Therefore, in Belgium, under-educated and low-earning TCNs are also likely to be hindered by Flemish civic integration policies: while integration requirements are not linked to the acquisition of a residence permit, the costs of the courses are covered by the administration and no duty to achieve a specific result is required, the policies can be demanding in terms of time and sanctions.

There is therefore a tension between, on the one hand, the obligation to attend an *inburgering* process which might constitute a burden for some migrants – in terms of time, energy and possible sanctions – and, on the other hand, an opportunity to attend free language, vocational and societal courses that are likely to support migrants in their integration and their understanding of the society.

70 Cf. footnote 63.
71 Http://inburgering.be/inburgeringstraject (last visit on 3 December 2014).
72 Article 25 of the 2003 *Inburgering* Decree; Article 1, §2 of the Flemish Government Decree of 12 September 2008; Act of 26 May 2002 concerning the right of social benefit; Article 92, para. 2, 8° of the Flemish Housing Code.

1.3. THE IMPACT OF THE SOCIO-ECONOMIC SITUATION OF MIGRANTS WITHIN CIVIC INTEGRATION POLICIES

Dutch and Flemish civic integration policies seem to mirror new transnational 'classes'[73] of migrants by treating them (both directly and indirectly) differently depending on their socio-economic situation.

Firstly, migrant workers and their families are not targeted by Dutch and Flemish civic integration policies and are therefore advantaged in comparison to the target groups. In this context, I have seen that the argument of the 'temporary stay' of migrant workers is not very consistent in the instance of migrant workers who stay for several years or even permanently. Even though some will argue that workers do not need an integration process since working is the way to integrate *par excellence*, this assertion would not, however, be true for their family members. In my view, the differences in the treatment of family members of TCN migrant workers and the family members of Dutch/Belgian citizens or TCNs – non-migrant workers – are particularly worth questioning. Moreover, when looking at EU and national policies, the process of integration does not seem to be reduced to 'work' – even though work is an essential part of it. Indeed, civic integration policies are also presented in terms of the goals of promoting 'social' and 'cultural' integration – and not only economic participation. Yet, by exempting migrant workers and their family members from integration requirements, politicians seem to consider that there is no need for civic integration when migrants present an 'economic added value' for the State. This logic could be questioned regarding the aim of an 'integrated society'.

Finally, Dutch civic integration policies seem to particularly hinder socio-economically underprivileged migrants through the integration requirements and their costs. This situation seems to disadvantage a category of migrants that is already vulnerable. The legality of this is questionable under European and international human rights law, discrimination law and EU law. This assertion is more debatable for the Belgian *inburgering* process, which is practically and economically accessible to the target groups and is not a prerequisite for a residence permit, in contrast to the Dutch integration policies.

[73] A. Weiss, 'The Transnationalization of Social Inequality: Conceptualizing Social Positions on a World Scale' *Current Sociology* Vol 53 2005, 707 and seq.

2. SOCIO-ECONOMIC STATUS AND CIVIC INTEGRATION POLICIES: WHAT PROTECTION FOR MIGRANTS?

At the international, European and EU levels, few tools exist to expressly address and protect migrants when they are treated differently because of their socio-economic situation. In the following section, I discuss the question whether the tools of EU migration law and discrimination law are suitable to protect those migrants within civic integration policies (section 2.1). In the second section, I argue that although it is not widespread in practice, the prohibition of discrimination on grounds of social condition has some potential to protect migrants when they are disadvantaged because of their socio-economic position as regards civic integration policies (section 2.2).

2.1. EU MIGRATION LAW AND DISCRIMINATION LAW

Firstly, I examine the question whether EU migration law offers sufficient protection to migrants who are disadvantaged by civic integration policies because of their socio-economic status. I discuss this question in the light of two recent rulings of the CJEU (section 2.1.1). On this basis, I explain that international and European discrimination law might be an interesting additional protection tool (section 2.1.2).

2.1.1. EU Migration Law: a Sufficient Protection?

Very recently, the CJEU handed down two important rulings about Dutch integration tests. The difficulty of passing the integration tests because of the applicants' level of education or lack of financial means was central in the two cases.

The *P&S* case[74] concerns the integration test – the equivalent of the above-mentioned Dutch inland test – that long-term residents have to pass, failing which they can been fined. The preliminary ruling raised the question whether such a test was compatible with the long-term residence Directive 2003/109.[75] In its consideration, the Court does not discuss in depth the difficulty and the high cost of such a test taking into account the situation of socio-economically underprivileged migrants. It rules that the Directive does not preclude such an integration examination.[76] However, the means of implementing that obligation

74 CJEU, Judgment in P&S, C-579/13, EU:C:2015:369.

75 Council Directive 2003/109/EC of 25 November 2003 concerning the status of third-country nationals who are long-term residents, OJ L 16/44, 23 January 2004 (Long-term Residence Directive).

76 Para. 56.

cannot jeopardise the achievement of the objectives pursued by that Directive, taking into consideration many elements including the socio-economic status of migrants.[77] Furthermore, the payment of a fine, which can reach up € 1,000 in addition to the fees, is liable to jeopardise such objectives. Yet, according to the Court, it is for the referring court to verify it.[78]

In the *K&A* case[79], the Court goes far further in its scrutiny of the protection of migrants who are disadvantaged by integration policies because of their socio-economic position. The case is about the compatibility of the above-explained Dutch pre-entry tests with the Family Reunification Directive.[80] The Court holds that the pre-entry tests preclude the objectives of the Directive. It first recalls the general principle of proportionality.[81] The Court insists on the importance of taking into account specific individual circumstances – including the socio-economic situation of migrants[82] – and recalls the substance of Article 17 of the Directive, which requires that applications for family reunification be examined on a case-by-case basis.[83] However, the Dutch hardship clause is not capable of doing so.[84] Moreover, in contrast to the *P&S* case, the Court itself verifies whether the various costs and the fees relating to such an examination are compatible with the Directive. It judges that they are too high.[85]

As a consequence, in the two judgments, the Court addresses, more or less extensively, the situation of migrants likely to be disadvantaged by integration tests because of their socio-economic status. It does it indirectly – through the Long-term Residence and Family Reunification Directives, the objectives of which cannot be jeopardised. This is undoubtedly a first step in the protection of socio-economically underprivileged migrants. The two rulings also show that the CJEU is receptive, in some extent, to arguments raised by applicants about their socio-economic difficulties.

However, the protection afforded by EU migration law to people who are disadvantaged because of their socio-economic situation seems limited. In the *P&S* case, the CJEU limits the scope of the protection to a minimum. Indeed, it does not itself verify whether the fees and the amount of the fine are compatible with the Long-term Residence Directive. In addition, in the two cases, the scope of the protection afforded is limited to the two above-mentioned Directives. Indeed, the Court does not mention the EU Charter of Fundamental Rights

77 Paras. 49 and 56.

78 Para. 54.

79 CJEU, Judgment in K&A, C-153/14, EU:C:2015:453.

80 Council Directive 2003/86/EC of 22 September 2003 on the right to family reunification, OJ L 251/12, 3 October 2003 (Family Reunification Directive).

81 Paras. 51 and 56.

82 Para. 58.

83 Para. 60.

84 Para. 63.

85 Paras. 64–71.

and human rights more generally, which are part of the EU general principles.[86] Therefore, the protection can hardly be extended to similar cases involving other provisions. More generally, the above-mentioned direct and indirect differences in treatment within Dutch and Belgian civic integration policies appear as difficult to tackle under the Long-term Residence and Family Reunification Directives. Furthermore, many integration policies are developed by Member States outside the scope of these instruments or EU migration law in general. This is notably the case for integration conditions required of migrants who apply for social benefits or citizenship. Finally, given the opt-outs in EU law, the two-above mentioned Directives do not apply to some EU Member States, especially to the UK where such integration requirements also exist (see hereafter).

As a consequence, given the limited scope of protection from EU law, it seems important to examine some other tools likely to protect socio-economically underprivileged migrants, in order to ensure efficient protection and to avoid them falling through the cracks. In this context, discrimination law seems to be a suitable complementary protection tool.

2.1.2. Discrimination Law: as a Complementary Protection Tool?

International and European discrimination law appears to be a legal tool that is likely to safeguard the rights of disadvantaged migrants regarding civic integration policies. 'European and international discrimination law' refers in the present contribution to the anti-discrimination clauses that are enshrined in the following European and international human rights instruments and the case law related to it: the European Convention on Human Rights,[87] the Charter of Fundamental Rights of the European Union,[88] the two United-Nation Covenants,[89] and the European Social Charter.[90] Even though their scope and interpretation may vary, they bring a good overview of the existing tools that can be mobilised to protect socio-economically underprivileged people under discrimination law. In that sense, this approach follows the integrated method

86 See. not. CJEU, Judgment in Dülger, C-451/11, EU:C:2012:504, para. 53; CJEU, Judgment in Chakrou, C-578/08, EU:C:2010:117, para. 44; CJEU, Judgment in O&S, C-356/11 and C-357/1, EU:C:2012:776, paras. 75 and seq.; Judgment in Parliament v. Council, C-540/03, EU:C:2006:429, para. 35.; CJEU, Judgment in Kamberaj, C-571/10, EU:C:2012:233, paras. 79 and 80.

87 Article 14 of the European Convention on Human Rights and Fundamental Freedoms (ECHR). See also article 1 of Protocol n°12 to the ECHR.

88 Article 21 of the Charter of Fundamental Rights of the European Union (CFREU).

89 Article 26 and 2(1) of the Covenant on Civil and Political Rights (ICCPR); Article 2(2) of the Covenant of Economic, Social and Cultural Rights (ICESCR).

90 Article E of the European Social Charter (ESC).

that has been developed by some scholars such as Eva Brems, in the field of human rights law.[91]

The anti-discrimination clauses of the above-mentioned instruments are particularly relevant from a vertical perspective that concerns the discriminatory character of public policies, such as integration policies. Indeed, sometimes a disputed policy does not appear to be in itself unlawful or in violation of a Directive or freestanding human rights, but the differences in treatment resulting from that policy could be seen as being unlawful and thus discriminatory. It is especially true in immigration and integration law where States usually have a wide margin of appreciation: immigration and integration measures, which may be found to be compatible with EU directives and freestanding human rights may amount to unjustified discrimination. In other words, not only does the measure at stake have to be lawful, but the difference in treatment between one group and another also has to be justified. For instance, the civic integration requirement of attending integration courses in the Flemish part of Belgium could be considered as being lawful in itself but, simultaneously, the lawfulness of the differences in treatment as a result of this – for instance between family members of TCN migrant workers and family members of TCNs who are not migrant workers – could be questioned. Furthermore, the approach in discrimination law has the advantage that the courts do not have to examine the substance of domestic law to verify whether human rights law has been violated. As soon as there is a difference in treatment between two categories in comparable situations which cannot be objectively and reasonably justified, the domestic measure is supposed to be unlawful.[92]

Moreover, Member States and the EU have repeatedly highlighted that not discriminating against migrants – at vertical and horizontal levels – is one of the key points of their integration process.[93] As a matter of fact, when adopting integration policies, the Member States should be particularly careful not to discriminate, since discriminating against migrants could directly hinder the aim of integration itself. In addition, the targeted ethnic and socio-economic groups within civic integration policies are, for most of these groups, people who

---

91 E. Brems, 'Should Pluriform Human Rights Become One? Exploring the Benefits of Human Rights Integration', (2014) *J.E.D.H.* Vol 4, 447–470. For an example of the integrated approach of discrimination law, see E. Bribosia & I. Rorive, 'Chronique en droit de l'égalité et de la non-discrimination', (2014) *J.E.D.H.* Vol 2, 223–243.

92 N. Bernard, 'Les ressources – préjudicielles notamment – qu'offre l'article 34, paragraphe 3, de la Charte des droits fondamentaux de l'Union européenne (droit à une aide au logement)' (2014) *Rev. trim. dr. h.* Vol 97, 84.

93 See notably Commission communication to the European Parliament and the Council, 4th Annual Report on Immigration and Asylum (2012), COM (2013)422 final, 17 June 2013, para. III. 4, 8; Commission communication to the Council, the European Parliament, the European Economic and Social Committee and the Committee of the Regions Communication, An open and secure Europe: making it happen, COM(2014) 154 final, 3 March 2014, 4.

are facing discrimination in their daily lives in Belgium and the Netherlands. Therefore, they are likely to be even more excluded, stigmatised and stereotyped by compulsory integration policies.[94] As a consequence, integration policies appear to be the first policies where Member States should particularly pay attention to not discriminating.

A question that has already received some attention is the issue of discrimination by Dutch integration measures on the grounds of nationality and racial and ethnic origin.[95] Yet the grounds of ethnic origin and nationality are not sufficient in themselves to protect socio-economically disadvantaged migrants from discriminatory policies. For several years, scholars and NGOs have stated that disadvantaged people, mainly poor people, are increasingly discriminated against and excluded from access to many goods and services.[96] They have argued for the protection of the rights of those underprivileged people through discrimination law. The prohibition of discrimination on grounds of social condition seems, in this context, particularly relevant.

2.2. ADDRESSING THE USEFULNESS OF THE GROUND OF SOCIAL CONDITION TO QUESTION CIVIC INTEGRATION POLICIES

Social condition – and the other related characteristics – is one of the grounds least invoked by applicants and least scrutinised by supranational human rights bodies when dealing with alleged discrimination.[97] Authors specialising in discrimination law also seem to pay very little attention to this ground (section 2.2.1).[98] What about the application of this ground to civic integration policies? The

---

94 Human Rights Watch, above note 9.

95 K. De Vries, above note 9, at 327–328; See also Human Rights Watch, above note 9; Committee on the Elimination of Racial Discrimination, Consideration of reports submitted by states parties under article 9 of the Convention, Concluding observations of the Committee on the Elimination of Racial Discrimination, Netherlands, 16 March 2010, CERD/C/NLD/CO/, 17–18.

96 See notably W. MacKay & N. Kim, *Adding Social Condition to the Canadian Human Rights Act, Canadian human rights conditions*, (Canadian Human Rights Commission, 2009); D, Roman, 'Introduction – La justiciabilité des droits sociaux ou les enjeux de l'édification d'un État de droit social' (2011) *Lettre "Actualités Droits-Libertés" du CREDOF*; D, Roman, 'La discrimination fondée sur la précarité sociale, un nouvel outil en faveur de l'effectivité des droits?' (2013) *Lettre "Actualités Droits-Libertés" du CREDOF*; Commission nationale consultative des droits de l'homme, *Avis sur les discriminations fondées sur la précarité sociale, Assemblée plénière du 26 septembre 2013* (Commission nationale consultative des droits de l'homme, 2013).

97 S. Fredman, 'The potential and limits of an equal rights paradigm in addressing poverty' (2011(a)) *Stellenbosch L. Rev.* Vol 22, 566–590, 581 & seq; M. Cousins, 'The European Convention on Human Rights, Non-Discrimination and Social Security: Great Scope, Little Depth?' (2009) *Journal of Social Security Law* Vol 16/3, 120–138.

98 N. Bamforth, M. Malik & C. O'Cinneide, *Discrimination Law: Theory and Context* (London, Sweet & Maxwell, 2008); M. Bell, *Anti-Discrimination Law and the European Union* (Oxford,

British case *Chapti, Ali & Bibi* relating to integration tests is a good example where such discrimination could have been raised (section 2.2.2). Moreover, the ground of social condition is often part of multiple discrimination and plays an important role in this framework (section 2.2.3). On this basis, this ground could be useful in the context of civic integration policies to protect people who are disadvantaged because of their socio-economically underprivileged position (section 2.2.4).

2.2.1. Social Origin, Social Condition and Related Grounds

'Social origin' is usually quoted as a status ground in anti-discrimination clauses of the above-mentioned international and European instruments.[99] Yet the explanatory works of those legal instruments provide only a little clarification on what 'social origin' means.

Only General Comment No. 20 ('Non-discrimination in economic, social and cultural rights') of the UN Committee on Economic, Social and Cultural Rights provides an explanation.[100] According to the Committee, 'social origin' refers to a person's inherited social status, which is linked to the status of 'property', descent-based discrimination under 'birth' and 'economic and social status'.[101]

Thus, the ground of 'social origin' is likely to be applied to people in a socio-economically disadvantaged situation to a narrow extent since this situation should be 'inherited'. As MacKay and Kim specify on the basis of Canadian case law, social origin has 'a fairly common sense meaning, encompassing heritage/ancestry, "beginning or derived from a source", and having a geographical component'.[102] In this context, the authors consider that 'social origin' 'is a

Oxford University Press, 2002); Interight, *Non- Discrimination in International Law, A Handbook for Practitioners, Interights* (Interight, 2011); D. Schiek, L. Waddington, M. Bell, *Cases, Materials and Text on National, Supranational and International Non-Discrimination Law* (Oxford, Hart Publishing, 2007).

99 As an example, Articles 26 and 2(1) of the ICCPR expressly protect people against any discrimination on the grounds of 'social origin (…) or other status'. Article 2(2) of the ICESCR provides a similar protection as that of article 2(1) of the ICCPR.

100 At EU level, the explanatory report of the CFREU does not give a definition of this ground (Note from the Praesidium, Text of the explanations relating to the complete text of the Charter as set out in Charte 4487/00 Convent 50, Charte 4473/00 Convent 49, Brussels, 11 October 2000, www.europarl.europa.eu/charter/pdf/04473_en.pdf (last visit on 26 August 2014). Concerning the UN law, neither the Guide to the 'Travaux préparatoires' of the ICCPR (M.J. Bossuyt, *Guide to the 'travaux préparatoires' on the International Convenant on Civil and Political Rights* (Dordrecht, Martinus Nijhoff Publishers, 1987), 49–56 and 479–492. See also Craven, MCR, *The international Covenant on Economic, Social and Cultural Rights, a perspective on its Development* (Oxford, Clarendon Press, 1995), 153–193) nor the CCPR General Comment No. 18 'Non-discrimination' of the Human Rights Committee (HRC) give any detailing on the ground of social origin (H.R.C., CCPR General Comment No. 18.).

101 C.E.S.C.R., General Comment N°20 – Non-discrimination in economic, social and cultural rights, 2 July 2009, E/C.12/GC/20, §24.

102 W. MacKay & N. Kim, above note 96, at 37.

far narrower ground than social condition'.[103] Indeed, many people who are in such underprivileged situations which are not 'inherited' will not have the opportunity to invoke discrimination on the ground of social origin.

'Social condition' is a broader and more dynamic term. It 'refers to a present situation rather than one's background or history'.[104] It can be defined as the condition of inclusion of the individual, in a socially identifiable group that suffers from social or economic disadvantage resulting from poverty, low income, illiteracy, occupation, level of education or any other similar circumstance.[105]

Social condition is not quoted as a prohibited ground as such by the international and European instruments mentioned above. Therefore, could an applicant invoke discrimination on grounds of social condition? The answer seems to be 'yes' under the international and European instruments mentioned above. Indeed, their anti-discrimination clauses are open-ended[106] meaning that discrimination can be challenged on other grounds than those explicitly quoted in the texts. In other words, the grounds in those texts are meant to be illustrative rather than exhaustive by the inclusion of 'other status'.[107]

However, the 'open-ended character' of the anti-discrimination clauses enshrined in European and international human rights instruments is not that easily interpreted. In particular, regarding the case law of the European Court of Human Rights (ECtHR) on the non-exhaustive clause of Article 14 ECHR, Janneke Gerards explains that it is not consistent and coherent and is very confusing.[108] Nonetheless, it seems unlikely that the Court would refuse to consider a claim for discrimination based on the applicant's social condition such as low level of education, employment or wealth. Indeed, the Court has already acknowledged the grounds of employment[109] and wealth[110] as being personal characteristics in the sense of Article 14. As a result, 'social condition' – and all the related characteristics – is likely be considered as 'another status' within the meaning of Article 14 of the ECHR.

Finally, regarding EU law, despite Article 21(1) of the Charter of Fundamental Rights seeming to be an open-ended clause, a recent case of the CJEU involving

---

103 *Ibid.*

104 *Ibid.*, 17.

105 *Ibid.*, 127.

106 *Ibid.*, 86; R. Uitz, 'The old wine and the new cask: The implications of the Charter of Fundamental Rights for European non- discrimination law' (2013) *European anti-discrimination law review* Vol 16, 26; N. Bamforth, M. Malik & C. O'Cinneide, above note 98; J. Gerards, 'Chapter on discrimination Ground' in D. Schiek & L. Waddington and M. Bell (eds.) *Cases, Materials and Text on National, Supranational and International Non-Discrimination Law* (Oxford and Portland (Oregon), Hart Publishing, 2007.

107 W. MacKay & N. Kim, above note 96, at 127.

108 J. Gerards, 'The Discrimination Grounds of Article 14 of the European Convention on Human Rights' (2013) *Human Rights Law Review*, 6 and seq.

109 ECtHR, *B.S. v Spain*, 24 July 2012.

110 ECtHR, *Chabauty v. France*, 4 Octobre 2012; ECtHR, *Chassagnou and others v. France*, 29 April 1999.

discrimination on grounds of obesity casts a general doubt on it.[111] Moreover the application of Article 21 is limited by the constraint of Article 51(1) relating to the scope of the Charter. In addition, Article 19 of the Treaty on the Functioning of the European Union and the anti-discrimination directives[112] do not enshrine the criterion of social condition/origin or any related grounds and are exhaustive. The tools in EU law to protect people from discrimination on grounds of socio-economic position are thus very limited in contrast to the clauses enshrined in the other European and international human rights instruments.

In this respect, the general principle of equality and non-discrimination could be seen as an alternative. In the *Commission v. the Netherlands* case before the CJEU, which concerned the fees for getting long-term residence status (Directive 2003/109), the Advocate General indicated that 'the principle of non-discrimination seems to me to preclude the establishment of charges the amounts of which have a deterrent effect on third-country nationals who do not have sufficient financial resources'.[113] Unfortunately the Court did not examine the question under that principle in its ruling.[114] Nonetheless, the statement of the advocate general gives a first hint at the usefulness of the right of not being discriminated against because of one's socio-economic background according to the general principle of equality and non-discrimination.

2.2.2. Chapti, Ali & Bibi *case*

In the *Chapti, Ali & Bibi* case before the High Court of Justice of Birmingham, the claimants – Indian, Pakistanis and Yemeni – failed the language test required by the British Government to get a family reunification visa to join their respective partners on the British territory. They failed the test because of their illiteracy, because they had no computer skills (and the test was supposed to be taken on a computer) and because taking lessons was too burdensome in term of costs, distance and time. In that case, the High Court of Justice had to address the discriminatory aspect of the British pre-entry tests under Article 14 of the ECHR. *In casu*, the claimants and interveners submitted that the pre-entry language requirement was – directly and indirectly – unjustifiably discriminatory on

111 See notably CJEU, Judgment in Kaltoft, C-354/13, ECLI:EU:C:2014:2463.

112 Council directive 2000/78/EC of 27 November 2000 establishing a general framework for equal treatment in employment and occupation, OJ *L 303*, 2 December 2000; Directive 2006/54/EC of the European Parliament and of the Council of 5 July 2006 on the implementation of the principle of equal opportunities and equal treatment of men and women in matters of employment and occupation (recast), *OJ* L 204 26 July 2006; Council directive 2000/43/EC of 29 June 2000 implementing the principle of equal treatment between persons irrespective of racial or ethnic origin, *OJ* L 180/22, 19 July 2000.

113 Opinion of the Advocate General delivered on 19 January 2012, C-508/10, EU:C:2012:25, para. 69.

114 CJEU, Judgment in Commission v. the Netherlands, C-508/10, EU:C:2012:243.

grounds of nationality, ethnic origins, sex and gender. However, they did not invoke discrimination on the ground of their socio-economic status.[115]

In its judgment, the High Court, for procedural reasons, did not examine the grounds of gender and sex.[116] It dismissed the application by judging that pre-entry tests do not indirectly discriminate against people on the basis of ethnic origin and nationality. However, although the High Court did not conclude that the pre-entry tests had discriminatory effect *in casu*, it adopted an interesting point of view concerning under-educated migrants and migrants in precarious situations. Indeed, it stressed that: 'In relation to the other categories [nationality and ethnic origin], I have concluded that, while the rule has a disparate impact on some, that disparate impact arises from personal circumstances such as financial means, education or knowledge of English, and does not amount to discrimination contrary to Article 14.'[117]

So, without referring to discrimination on grounds of the social condition/origin of the applicants – since it was not raised in this case – the British judge appeared to acknowledge that the disparate effects are based on the social and economic situations of the migrants. It is worth mentioning that, in its ruling, the Court tackled the difficulties faced by the applicants, because of the difficulty and the cost of the test, indirectly and in a limited way, under the proportionality test of Article 8 ECHR. Mentioning the application of the 'exceptional compassionate circumstances exception', the Court ruled that if the British administration was not flexible enough with the applicant, the individual decision could be incompatible with Article 8 of the ECHR but 'this is not a ground for impugning the rule itself'.[118] Would the reasoning of the Court and the outcome of the decision have been similar if the applicants had invoked discrimination based on their socio-economic situation? At least, invoking discrimination on grounds of social condition would have obliged the Court to directly address the issue of applicants being disadvantaged by the tests because of their socio-economic position. The England and Wales Court of Appeal dismissed the appeal in its ruling of 12 April 2013.[119] The applicant appealed the decision before the UK Supreme Court, and that application is still pending.[120]

---

115 High Court of Justice (Administrative Court of Birmingham), *Chapti, Ali & Bibi v. Secretary of State for the Home Department*, 16 December 2011, [2011] EWHC 3370 (Admin), para. 117, see also paras. 122 and 125.

116 *Ibid.*, paras. 139 and 140.

117 *Ibid.*

118 Paras. 109–111.

119 Court of Appeal (Civil Division), Bibi & Ali v. Secretary of State for the Home Department, 12 April 2013, [2013] EWCA Civ 322, paras. 32 and 43–44.

120 Supreme Court of the United Kingdom, R (on the application of Ali) (AP) (Appellant) *v.* Secretary of State for the Home Department (Respondent) UKSC 2013/0266; R (on the application of Bibi and Another) (FC) (Appellants) *v.* The Secretary of State for the Home Department (Respondent) UKSC 2013/0270. On appeal from the Court of Appeal (Civil Division) (England and Wales). The Hearing was held on 5–26 February 2015.

2.2.3. *The Status Ground of Social Condition as Part of Multiple Discrimination*

As Sandra Fredman asserts 'Groups which suffer from discrimination on status grounds [gender, race, etc.] are disproportionately represented among people living in poverty'.[121] Moreover, as we have seen, poverty or more generally socio-economic situation might also be the cause of discrimination. In this context, the ground of social condition often adds to another protected ground such as disability, age, ethnic origin, nationality, residence status, etc. It rarely seems to be the only ground of discrimination at issue. In other words, the ground of social condition often seems to be part of 'additive' or intersectional discrimination.[122]

As MacKay and Kim underline, 'the "fit" of social condition with other prohibited grounds is not only appropriate, but also vital in recognizing and achieving the ameliorative purposes of human rights'.[123] Thus, failing to make an intersectional analysis could result in disadvantaged individuals falling through the cracks of human rights protection. In this context, the prohibited ground of social condition in discrimination law 'provides the potential of better reflecting the realities of discrimination in that it, in many ways, offers a means for recognizing the way social and economic disadvantage intersects with other grounds of discrimination'.[124]

That is particularly relevant in the case of civic integration policies. The impact of the socio-economic status of migrants overlaps with other grounds such as nationality and ethnic origin or even residence status. For example, Human Rights Watch provided statistical evidence in its 2008 report on the Dutch pre-entry tests, that 30% of Moroccan people living in the Netherlands live below the poverty line, in comparison with 8% of native Dutch citizens.[125] As a consequence, and as underlined by Human Rights Watch and de Vries,[126] people of Moroccan origin are especially affected by the integration tests because of their situation of poverty since it is harder for them to deal with the cost of the tests. They are therefore particularly affected by the integration tests because of their nationality, ethnic origin and socio-economic situation, which intersect with one another.

Consequently, the intersectional approach, though not widespread in Europe,[127] appears essential to take into account the whole situation of people

121 S. Fredman, above note 97, at 567.

122 S. Hannett, 'Equality at the intersections: the legislative and judicial failure to tackle multiple discrimination' (2003) *Oxford Journal of Legal Studies* Vol 23: 1, 68.

123 W. MacKay & N. Kim, above note 96, at 81.

124 *Ibid.*

125 Human Rights Watch, above note 9, at 30.

126 K. De Vries, above note 9, at 333.

127 The approach of Human Rights discrimination in a holistic and intersectional way has been promoted in many academic circles in Canada and the USA (N. Iyer, 'Categorical Denials: Equality Rights and Shaping of Social Identity', (1994) *Queen's L. J.* Vol 194:19; K.

hindered by civic integration policies. In this context, the role of the socio-economic situation of migrants seems a determining element.

2.2.4. *Social Condition: a Useful Tool to Tackle Civic Integration Policies*

The socio-economic situation of individuals plays a direct or indirect predominant role in the choices and differences in treatment made by policy makers, notably within Belgian and Dutch civic integration policies. These differences of treatment can directly or indirectly affect people because of their socio-economic situations and, to some extent, become discriminatory under international and European human rights law. The prohibited grounds traditionally invoked in discrimination law, such as race or gender, do not always appear suitable or, at least, adequate to fully protect individuals in socio-economic disadvantaged situations. The above-mentioned case *Chapti, Ali & Bibi* is illustrative in that regard.

This does not mean that courts completely ignore the difficulties migrants face in complying with civic integration requirements because of their socio-economic position. Depending on the rules involved, the courts, including the CJEU, sometimes seem to take this situation into account indirectly under EU directives or freestanding human rights. This is an important step. Yet the protection afforded is limited.

In this context, the prohibition of discrimination on grounds of social condition should be seen as a complementary protective tool to challenge policies, including civic integration policies, where people are disadvantaged because of their socio-economic position. It often plays a decisive role in cases of multiple or intersectional discrimination and helps to better reflect realities. Sometimes, it even stands alone without being combined with other grounds. It also protects migrants against stereotypes and stigma. In addition, it focuses on differences in treatment and not on the substance of the rule. Thus, it gives the applicants the opportunity to challenge a policy directly in order to impugn the rule itself because they are directly or indirectly disadvantaged on the basis of their socio-economic status in comparison with other categories. As an example, neither EU migration law nor Article 8 of ECHR seem to be suitable tools to challenge the differences in treatment between TCN migrant workers and their families and the other categories of migrants within Dutch and Belgian civic integration policies. The argument of direct discrimination on grounds of social condition appears to be particularly pertinent to raise in this case.

Crenshaw, 'Demarginalising the Intersection of Race and Sex' (1989) *University of Chicago Legal Forum* Vol 139) and more recently in Europe. However, intersectionality and multiple discrimination do not seem to have become widespread within European and National jurisdictions as such (S. Hannett, above note 122; S. Fredman, *Discrimination Law*, (Clarendon Series/ 2011), 139–143).

As a consequence, the status ground of social condition as legal tool deserves to be examined further by scholars, judges and lawyers, especially in the context of civic integration policies. Its justiciability will depend on creativity and new practices in this field.

3. CONCLUSION

Welfare, poverty and immigration have always been very sensitive and complicated subjects to deal with in international, European and domestic policies, especially in times of economic crisis when migrants and poor people are seen as the 'black sheep' of society. When it comes to socio-economically disadvantaged migrants who bring together both characteristics, this makes for even more complicated issues. The fact that no convention exists for the protection of poor people's rights and the protection of migrants' rights in general,[128] or more precisely a convention for the protection of migrants' rights ratified by the EU Member States,[129] is symptomatic of this phenomenon. The risk is that socio-economically underprivileged migrants might fall through the cracks without being able to claim protection of their rights and make their situation 'justiciable'.

Dutch civic integration policies, and to a lesser extent Flemish ones, are a good example of this phenomenon. Migrants appear to be particularly disadvantaged because of their socio-economic situation either because they are not workers or family members of a migrant worker and/or because they are socio-economically underprivileged. Traditional legal instruments invoked before courts do not always seem sufficient to denounce such differences of treatment and afford complete protection for those migrants.

In this context, even though it is not (yet) widely developed in practice, the discrimination ground of social condition may appear to be a suitable instrument to address and tackle, at international and European level, the potential direct and indirect discrimination that migrants are likely to suffer because of their socio-economic situation. This deserves to be developed by lawyers and practitioners along with multiple discrimination, since it could be an efficient way to ensure the protection of the rights of the most vulnerable migrants.

---

128 Except refugees and EU citizens with enough resources to ensure their livelihood, who both are 'privileged' migrants'.

129 International Convention on the Protection of the Rights of All Migrant Workers and Members of their Families, New York, 18 December 1990. No EU State has yet signed and ratified this Convention.

DOES EQUALITY LAW MAKE A DIFFERENCE?

Social Science Research on the Effect of Discrimination Law on (Potential) Victims

Jogchum VRIELINK*

Due to their nature and focus, legal scholarship and legal practice often neglect the actual societal effects of legislation. Research from within social sciences can, in this regard, provide a 'reality check', by revealing the 'complex nuances, challenges, and contradictions of the law and its implementation'.[1]

Social scientific research tends to complicate our understanding of important social facts and institutions, such as law, and its basic concepts, such as discrimination. In doing so, it calls into question explicit or implicit assumptions by lawyers and legislators about how humans and human interaction work. Law rarely (if ever) does exactly what it is envisioned to do. Discrimination law is no exception in this regard. Research shows that, at best, discrimination law provides partial protection and beneficial effects in some situations, while, at worst, having counterproductive effects or even inflicting its own harms on those it is supposed to protect.

This chapter focuses on some recent findings from within social sciences regarding discrimination law, and the way it impacts (potential) victims in particular.[2] It will firstly address research concerning the way in which (potential) victims make use of the legislation (or fail to do so), i.e. their claiming and litigation behaviour (section 1). Afterwards, a number of intended and

---

* This chapter is based, to a significant extent, on a prior publication in French: J. Vrielink, 'Le droit de l'égalité fait-il la différence? Les effets du droit antidiscriminatoire à la lumière des recherches en sciences sociales', in J. Ringelheim & G. Herman (eds.), *Politiques antidiscriminatoires*, Brussels: éditions De Boeck, 2015, 51–66. Research for this chapter was funded by the Flemish Ministry within the framework of the third Policy Research Centre Program (2012–2015).

1 E. Berrey, 'Sociology finds discrimination in the law', *Contexts* 2009, (1), 28.

2 Although this chapter does not focus on any particular country, much of the research that is discussed has been performed (only) in the US. The extent to which this impacts the validity of the research results for countries/systems outside the US is an open question, requiring replication of the research described.

unintended effects that empirical research suggests discrimination legislation may have on plaintiffs and potential victims are discussed (section 2).

1. GRIEVANCES, CLAIMING AND LITIGATING IN DISCRIMINATION LAW

What do social sciences tell us about the claiming and litigation behaviour of victims in situations of discrimination?

In a classic article Miller and Sarat[3] develop the concept of the 'dispute pyramid' to illustrate the way in which perceived injuries and grievances may or may not result in formal claiming behaviour and legal proceedings. The pyramid serves to demonstrate filtering effects due to a variety of influences and effects. Its bottom layer consists of *perceived injurious experiences*; these being the broad mass of personal injuries that people recognise. Only a small number of these perceived injurious experiences become *grievances*. Grievances are those injurious experiences of which the injured individual knows or believes that they involve an infringement of rights or entitlements. The next, and again more limited, level of the pyramid consists of *claims*: when an individual contacts and confronts the party responsible for the grievance in one way or the other, in order to seek redress. A certain segment of claims proceed to become *disputes*, i.e. when the party that is faced with a claim based on a grievance rejects it either in whole or in part. If subsequently a formal complaint is made, a dispute becomes a *filing*; and finally the smallest number of cases make it to the top of the pyramid as *trials*: cases that are in fact adjudicated by courts.

In their original article, Miller and Sarat made several observations concerning discrimination grievances in particular. More recently, Nielsen and Nelson[4] analysed the functioning of US discrimination law in greater depth, employing Miller and Sarat's model. In the following, their analysis is taken as a point of departure, and additional research is discussed where and when it seems useful.

1.1. PERCEIVED INJURIOUS EXPERIENCES

Researching perceived injurious experiences is often considered one of the most difficult aspects of the pyramid to analyse for any given issue. That being said, two main – and seemingly opposing – perspectives are present in the literature.

---

3 R.E. Miller & A. Sarat, 'Grievances, claims and disputes: assessing the adversary culture', *Law and Society Review* 1981, *15*, 525–566.

4 L.B. Nielsen & R.L. Nelson, 'Scaling the pyramid: a sociolegal model of employment discrimination litigation', in L.B. Nielsen & R.L. Nelson (eds.), *Handbook of employment discrimination research: rights and realities*, Dordrecht: Springer, 2005, 3–34.

The first perspective suggests that chronic or potential targets of prejudice tend to *minimise* or *underestimate* the extent to which they are personally victimised by discrimination. The second perspective suggests instead that chronic targets of prejudice are especially *vigilant* for, and sometimes *oversensitive* to, signs that they are being personally victimised by discrimination.

1.1.1. Underestimation

The most prevalent view in social science research finds that members of disadvantaged groups 'typically miss, underestimate, or deny the extent to which they are personally targets of prejudice'.[5] Major and Kaiser list a host of research findings that support this view. For instance, members of disadvantaged groups often have difficulty recalling times when they were targets of prejudice; they also tend to report that they *personally* experience less prejudice and discrimination than they perceive other members of their group to experience, and they often avoid labelling negative treatment that they have received as discrimination even when the treatment objectively qualifies as such.

Several factors are identified in research that may serve to explain this underestimation. These are both of a cognitive and of a more social or motivational nature.

1.1.1.1. Cognitive Factors

Several cognitive factors, partially specific to discrimination cases, contribute to people not recognising when they are victims of discrimination or underestimating the extent to which this is the case.

This may be due, firstly, to the fact that individuals are unaware of what qualifies as discrimination.[6] Harassment, disparate impact discrimination or indirect discrimination, and many other concepts employed in discrimination law, tend to be unfamiliar to many people in society. This so-called 'lack of rights awareness' is traditionally identified as one of the main factors for under-reporting: if you do not know what counts as discrimination, you are unlikely to be aware when you are being discriminated against.

This is further compounded by the fact that situations of (potential) discrimination tend to be highly ambiguous, when considered from an individual perspective. Overt expressions of prejudice and discrimination have become rare in most (Western) countries, since the initial introduction of

5 B. Major & C.R. Kaiser, 'Perceiving and claiming discrimination', in L.B. Nielsen & R.L. Nelson (eds.), *Handbook of employment discrimination research,* Dordrecht: Springer, 2005, 286.

6 A.-M. Marshall, 'Injustice frames, legality, and the everyday construction of sexual harassment', *Law and social inquiry* 2003, *28,* (3), 659–690.

discrimination legislation. Hence discrimination tends, these days, to be masked or disguised (cf. *infra* section 2.2.1). This leads to a situation, as Major and Kaiser describe, that 'whenever two individuals differ on multiple attributes that are relevant to outcome, such as seniority, performance, etc. there may be several possible explanations for their differential outcomes'.[7] Considered in isolation, actions that may be discriminatory (even *if* one is aware of the legal definitions) can usually have a number of possible causes. This almost inherent 'attributional ambiguity' makes it difficult to detect discrimination on a case-by-case basis.

Although a particular disadvantage or exclusion *may* be due to discrimination, a number of other explanations are usually possible as well. As such, targets of discrimination often do not know or are uncertain about whether they have been discriminated against: judgements of personal discrimination are subjective, susceptible to human error, and prone to dispute.

Finally, so-called 'social comparison biases' are also seen to cognitively work against the detection of discrimination. Identifying discrimination requires, both legally and contextually, that you compare your situation with that of others. This may also serve to mask discrimination, since people tend to compare their situation with people like themselves, who are statistically likely to be other in-group members, and who may be similarly treated unfairly.[8]

1.1.1.2. Social and Motivational Factors

Given the cognitive uncertainty that is almost inherent in individual cases of discrimination, several social and motivational factors that are identified in research can lead people to underestimate the extent to which and the frequency with which they are discriminated against.

Firstly, people tend to be motivated to believe that outcomes are under their personal control, and have difficulty acknowledging that they have limited control over events ('belief in personal control').[9] Secondly, people are usually motivated to perceive the world as a just place in which people get what they deserve ('just world belief').[10] Acknowledging that one has been a victim of discrimination requires acceptance that outcomes are controlled by capricious or even bigoted others, which threatens this need to regard the world as just. As a result, even when situations *may* be interpreted as discrimination, people

7 B. Major & C.R. Kaiser, 'Perceiving and claiming discrimination', in L.B. Nielsen & R.L. Nelson (eds.), *Handbook of employment discrimination research,* Dordrecht: Springer, 2005, 287.

8 *Ibid.*, p. 286–298.

9 E. Langer, 'The illusion of control', *Journal of personality and social psychology* 1975, *32*, 311–328; S.E. Taylor & J.D. Brown, 'Illusion and well-being: a social psychological perspective on mental health', *Psychological bulletin* 1988, *103*, (2), 193–210.

10 M.J. Lerner & D.T. Miller, 'Just world research and the attribution process', *Psychological Bulletin* 1978, *85*, (5), 1030–1051; M.J. Lerner, *The belief in a just world: a fundamental delusion,* New York: Plenum Press, 1980.

can nonetheless be motivated to neglect or ignore this, instead perceiving the situation as fair, or at least as due to causes other than discrimination.[11]

Finally, making a mistake in claiming discrimination bears the risk of being costly: seeing discrimination that does not exist can cause hostility and retaliation (*infra* section 1.2). This may not only lead people not to file a complaint, but it may also, unconsciously, lead them to be inclined not to *perceive* discrimination to begin with.[12]

1.1.2. Vigilance and Overestimation

A second view that can be found in the literature, although less commonly, is that the ambiguity that is inherent in many cases of discrimination not only results in under-reporting, but in *over*-reporting as well. This research indicates that potential victims become increasingly vigilant to cues in their environment indicating that they may be targets of prejudice and discrimination, and that they start seeing discrimination where it does not 'objectively', or at least legally, exist. Such findings may serve to explain why a relatively large number of discrimination complaints in most countries, both at the level of equality bodies and at the courts, are unfounded or inadmissible, as they bear insufficient relation to discrimination in the legal sense.

Major and Kaiser cite several studies that substantiate this idea. For instance, members of minority groups have been found to become 'on guard' to signs of prejudice in others, and to develop a 'hypersensitivity' to the smallest of prejudicial cues.[13] Other studies have demonstrated that people who realise that they may be discriminated against in a particular setting tend to become vigilant to a wide range of cues in that setting that might indicate the presence of prejudice and negative stereotypes.[14] Similarly, it has been suggested that previous experiences with discrimination can lead to members of stigmatised groups employing a so-called 'zero miss' strategy, in which even subtle cues of potential injustice trigger vigilance for discrimination, while also leading to increased perceptions of discrimination.[15]

---

11 B. Major, 'From social inequality to personal entitlement', in M. Zanna (eds.), *Advances in experimental social psychology,* San Diego: Academic Press, 1994, 293–355; J. Sidanius & F. Pratto, *Social dominance: an intergroup theory of social hierarchy and oppression,* New York: Cambridge University Press, 1999.

12 B. Major & C.R. Kaiser, 'Perceiving and claiming discrimination', in L.B. Nielsen & R.L. Nelson (eds.), *Handbook of employment discrimination research,* Dordrecht: Springer, 2005, 286–298.

13 G. Allport, *The nature of prejudice,* New York: Anchor Doubleday, 1954/1979.

14 C.M. Steele, S. Spencer & J. Aronson, 'Contending with group image: the psychology of stereotype and social identity threat', in M. Zanna (eds.), *Advances in experimental social psychology,* San Diego: Academic Press, 2002, 380–440.

15 L. Feldman-Barrett & J.K. Swim, 'Appraisals of prejudice and discrimination', in J.K. Swim & C. Stangor (eds.), *Prejudice: the target's perspective,* San Diego: Academic Press, 1998, 11–36.

Several factors are seen to contribute to this increased vigilance among potential targets of prejudice. Cognitively, some of the same issues regarding the uncertainty and lack of clarity surrounding potential cases of discrimination (cf. *supra*) are relevant here as well. However, depending on different motivational factors being triggered, this may lead to opposing outcomes.[16]

These motivational factors include the following: firstly, research suggests that when social environments are hostile, the costs of missing cues or indications of prejudice and discrimination are considered greater than the cost of a 'false alarm', leading to a high degree of vigilance. Secondly, a host of 'self-serving biases' also underlie vigilance to prejudice and to perceiving discrimination when this may not be 'legally warranted'. The self-serving bias, in general, entails individuals being motivated to protect self-esteem from threats. In the context of perceived discrimination, people have been shown to engage in a variety of strategies to protect and enhance their personal (individual) and social (collective) self-esteem. Relatedly, external attribution – that is, blaming negative outcomes on external causes – has been shown to be relevant as well: blaming the prejudice of others in ambiguous cases, rather than internal causes, such as one's own lack of ability, helps to protect self-esteem.[17]

Finally, for individuals from groups that have previously or historically been the object of discrimination, prejudice and discrimination are 'likely to be repeatedly primed and highly accessible cognitive constructs', which can be 'easily activated in ambiguous circumstances'.[18]

1.2. CLAIMING, DISPUTES, FILING AND TRIALS

Research indicates that even people who believe they have been targets of discrimination often fail to undertake further action. The fact that potential plaintiffs are reluctant to complain is a finding of virtually all studies performed in this field. Individuals who believe they have been victims of discrimination very rarely try to remedy this situation by directly confronting the perpetrator (claiming). This has shown to be the case even in situations in which the discrimination was blatant. Taking it a stage further, such

---

16 B. Major & C.R. Kaiser, 'Perceiving and claiming discrimination', in L.B. Nielsen & R.L. Nelson (eds.), *Handbook of employment discrimination research*, Dordrecht: Springer, 2005, 286–298.

17 B. Major, C.R. Kaiser & S.K. McCoy, 'It's not my fault: when and why attributions to prejudice protect self-esteem', *Personality and social psychology bulletin* 2003, *29*, (6), 772–781.

18 B. Major & C.R. Kaiser, 'Perceiving and claiming discrimination', in L.B. Nielsen & R.L. Nelson (eds.), *Handbook of employment discrimination research*, Dordrecht: Springer, 2005, 289.

as reporting discrimination to authorities, is rarer still. The (empirically corroborated) reasons for this are plentiful.

To begin with, there are the obvious factors of the high costs – both financially and time-wise – that tend to be associated with claiming, and litigating in particular. This is the case with litigation in general, but costs tend to be particularly high in discrimination cases, in which the plaintiff and the defendant – due to the moral and social stakes involved – tend to invest a lot of time, energy and resources.[19]

Furthermore, research has often revealed people to have a sense of shame regarding their victimhood, leading them to reject it,[20] and 'lump it', in the terminology of Miller and Sarat. This is compounded by the fact that friends, family and co-workers often also discourage potential claimants from thinking they were victims of discrimination; people often cannot count on support for their claim, but rather endure resistance and opposition when they try to even discuss the issue of discrimination. Connected to this is a frequent fear of not being believed.[21]

The reluctance to claim and litigate also has to do with the (feared) negative social and interpersonal impact that can be associated with making discrimination claims. Moreover, research demonstrates those fears to be justified. Individuals who claim they are victims of discrimination are viewed negatively by others, *even* when the claim is justified.[22] More generally, fears of retaliation by the perpetrator are often considered to constitute a greater risk than ignoring the problem.[23]

Another commonly identified issue in research is for potential victims of discrimination to display resistance to state institutions (such as courts and equality bodies) on personal or ideological grounds, which leads them to avoid claiming and litigating.[24]

---

19 J. Fink, 'Unintended consequences: how antidiscrimination litigation increases group bias in employer-defendants', *New Mexico Law Review* 2008, *38*, 333–372.

20 L. Bobo & S.A. Suh, 'Surveying racial discrimination', in M.L. Oliver et al. (eds.), *Prismatic metropolis,* New York: Russell Sage, 2000, 523–560; S.A. Suh, 'Women's perceptions of workplace discrimination: impacts of racial group, gender, and class', in M.L. Oliver et al. (eds.), *Prismatic metropolis. Inequality in Los Angeles,* New York: Russell Sage Foundation, 2000, 561–596.

21 L.F. Fitzgerald et al., 'Why didn't she just report him? The psychological and legal implications of women's responses to sexual harassment', *Journal of Social Issues* 1995, *51*, 117–138.

22 B. Major & C.R. Kaiser, 'Perceiving and claiming discrimination', in L.B. Nielsen & R.L. Nelson (eds.), *Handbook of employment discrimination research,* Dordrecht: Springer, 2005, 286–289.

23 J.K. Swim & L.L. Hyers, 'Excuse me – what did you say?! Women's public and private responses to sexist remarks', *Journal of experimental social psychology* 1999, *35*, (1), 68–88.

24 L.B. Nielsen, 'Situating legal consciousness: experiences and attitudes of ordinary citizens about law and street harassment', *Law & Society Review* 2000, *32*, (4), 1055–1090; L.B. Nielsen, *License to harass,* Princeton & Oxford: Princeton University Press, 2004. Conversely, individuals are more inclined and willing to report their experiences to in-group

Several additional considerations, especially those concerning the segment of claims that do make it to litigation and trial stages, will be discussed in the following section.

2. EFFECTS AND IMPACT

Legal scholarship often holds a formalistic conception of law,[25] in which the implicit assumption tends to be that discrimination law is 'effective', in the (instrumental) sense that it does what the legislator intended, and that it does *only* that. Scholarship from within social sciences tends to take a different perspective concerning the effects and effectiveness of legislation, looking instead at what legislation does in practice, thereby sometimes pointing out positive and even intended consequences (section 2.1), but paying attention to unintended consequences as well (section 2.2).

2.1. POSITIVE AND INTENDED EFFECTS

The 'net' positive effect of discrimination law is hard or even impossible to measure. This is due, in part, to the fact that social science research does not offer an unequivocal answer as to the exact impact that discrimination has on societal inequities to begin with.[26] Current research does not allow for generalised

members or close others (friends, family). Major and Kaiser point out that this suggests 'that contextual cues and settings that promote intergroup trust and harmony might also increase individuals' willingness to report discrimination': 'For example, organizations that promote diversity, recognize discrimination, and provide access to social support may create a safer environment for targets of prejudice to report experiences with discrimination' (B. Major & C.R. Kaiser, 'Perceiving and claiming discrimination', in L.B. Nielsen & R.L. Nelson (eds.), *Handbook of employment discrimination research,* Dordrecht: Springer, 2005, 296). See, however, also *infra* section 2.2.2.2.

25 S. Sturm, 'Law's role in addressing complex discrimination', in L.B. Nielsen & R.L. Nelson (eds.), *Handbook of employment discrimination research,* Dordrecht: Springer, 2005, 35–57.

26 Basically, one can identify two opposing camps in this regard (see L.B. Nielsen & R.L. Nelson, 'Scaling the pyramid: a sociolegal model of employment discrimination litigation', in L.B. Nielsen & R.L. Nelson (eds.), *Handbook of employment discrimination research: rights and realities,* Dordrecht: Springer, 2005, 6–8). The first camp is sceptical about the significance of discrimination as a source of inequality, concerning labour market and other societal outcomes. These researchers firstly point to the historical decline, in most Western societies, in (blatant or conscious) discriminatory attitudes across a variety of discrimination grounds (e.g. racist, sexist and homophobic attitudes), as well as pointing to similar declines in other indicators of discrimination (e.g. pay gaps). Secondly, researchers from this camp argue that it is possible to explain differential outcomes by means of non-discriminatory factors, such as differences in schooling, and differential preferences. See e.g. J. Donohue & P. Siegelman, 'The changing nature of employment discrimination litigation', *Stanford Law Review* 1991, *43*, 983–1033; J.J. Heckman, 'Detecting discrimination', *The Journal of Economic Perspectives* 1998, *12*, (2), 101–116; R. Nelson & W.P. Bridges, *Legalizing gender inequality,*

conclusions in any single direction, in this regard. This, in turn, also serves to make it hard to ascertain the macro-effects that discrimination law has (or could have) on disadvantaged groups.

This is not to say, however, that social sciences have not demonstrated *any* beneficial effects of discrimination law. Firstly, qualitative empirical research points to the fact that discrimination law is important since the *idea* of being protected from unlawful discrimination is valuable in itself for potential victims. For society as a whole, but especially for members of traditionally disadvantaged groups, non-discrimination law reaffirms principles of personhood and justice, adding to their confidence to participate more fully in society.[27]

Secondly, non-discrimination rights can also function as a transformative tool, which people can draw on as a symbolic resource to legitimate their claims and to gain leverage in everyday situations and negotiations.[28] Moreover, some research in social sciences also suggests that the presence of the legislation in itself, and its 'trickle-down effect', has a more general transformative capacity for culture as a whole, thereby contributing to declining historical trends in prejudice and discrimination.[29]

Finally, and more concretely, there are a few studies that suggest that anti-discrimination law correlates positively with how (some) minorities are effectively treated. For instance, research by Barron and Heble found the presence of discrimination law to have a significant positive correlation with

---

New York: Cambridge University Press, 1999. Researchers in the second camp instead see discrimination as (still) remaining a central cause and force of societal inequality. This camp does accept that historical trends in prejudice and discriminatory attitudes were declining up to a certain point, but believes that this decline is slowing down in our contemporary period. More importantly perhaps, the fundamental difference with the first camp consists in the fact that they believe the change in discriminatory public attitudes to be only superficial: overt and blatant forms of discrimination are claimed to have been replaced by more subtle forms. See e.g. R. Nelson & W.P. Bridges, *Legalizing gender inequality*, New York: Cambridge University Press, 1999; L. Bobo, 'Race and beliefs about affirmative action', in D.O. Sears, J. Sidanius & L. Bobo (eds.), *Racialized politics: the debate about racism in America*, Chicago: University of Chicago Press, 2000, 137–164; J. Sidanius, P. Singh, J.J. Hetts & C. Federico, 'It's not affirmative action, it's the blacks: the continuing relevance of race in American politics', in D.O. Sears, J. Sidanius & L. Bobo (eds.), *Racialized politics: the debate about racism in America*, Chicago: University of Chicago Press, 2000, 191–235.

27 J. Vrielink & V. Vandersteen, *Access to justice – a sociological study on cases of discrimination in the EU. National assessment report fieldwork research – Belgium*. Vienna: Fundamental Rights Agency, 2000; J. Vrielink, *Van haat gesproken?* Antwerp: Maklu, 2010; L.B. Nielsen & R.L. Nelson, 'Scaling the pyramid: a sociolegal model of employment discrimination litigation', in L.B. Nielsen & R.L. Nelson (eds.), *Handbook of employment discrimination research: rights and realities*, Dordrecht: Springer, 2005, 3–34.

28 C.R. Albiston, 'Mobilizing employment rights in the workplace', in L.B. Nielsen & R.L. Nelson (eds.), *Handbook of employment discrimination research: rights and realities*, Dordrecht: Springer, 2005, 301–323.

29 B. Van Klink, *De wet als symbool*. Deventer: W.E.J. Tjeenk Willink, 1998.

the way in which gays and lesbians are treated in employment situations.[30] The researchers performed comparative studies of localities in the US that offered protection against employment discrimination on the basis of sexual orientation, and those that do not. Their research revealed that public awareness of and support for sexual orientation laws is heightened in communities with (versus without) anti-discrimination legislation. Furthermore gay and lesbian job applicants experienced significantly less interpersonal discrimination in areas with (versus without) this protective legislation, even when statistically controlling for religious and political views.

2.2. UNINTENDED EFFECTS

The unintended consequences of discrimination law that are identified in social science research are relatively numerous (albeit often controversial). In the following I will discuss a number of them that are particularly relevant for (potential) victims and plaintiffs. More specifically, the focus will be on what I will refer to as 'shifting effects' (section 2.2.1), 'masking effects' (section 2.2.2), and 'harmful effects' (section 2.2.3) that discrimination law may sometimes have.

2.2.1. Shifting Discrimination

An effect that may occur under the influence of discrimination law is that discrimination is not so much eradicated or reduced, but that it 'shifts' instead. The most commonly described (and widely accepted) shifting effect of the introduction of discrimination law is for overt discrimination to become more covert, and hence harder to tackle by legal means.

After the initial introduction of discrimination legislation, instances of overt discrimination tend to decrease relatively quickly, with the norm gaining familiarity.[31] At the same time, however, more elusive strains of discrimination and bias emerge. Quite a lot of literature indicates, for instance, that employers have simply become more skilled at hiding their discriminatory animus, finessing discriminatory decisions so that they appear to be untainted by bias.[32] There are indications that other societal actors similarly learn to 'mask' their

30 L.G. Barron & M. Hebl, 'The force of law: the effects of sexual orientation antidiscrimination legislation on interpersonal discrimination in employment', *Psychology, Public Policy, and Law* 2013, 19 (2), 191–205.

31 T.K. Green, 'Discrimination in workplace dynamics', *Harv. C.R.-C.L. L. Rev.* 2003, *38*, 91–157.

32 J. Fink, 'Unintended consequences: how antidiscrimination litigation increases group bias in employer-defendants', *New Mexico Law Review* 2008, *38*, 333–372; S. Bisom-Rapp, 'Bulletproofing the workplace: symbol and substance in employment discrimination law practice', *Fla. St. University law review* 1999, (26), 959–1049; T.K. Green, 'Targeting workplace context: title VII as a tool for institutional reform', *Fordham L. Review* 2003, *71*, 659–724.

illegal conduct, developing mechanisms to make discriminatory decisions appear neutral.

Another, more controversial, shifting effect that is reported in some research is for changes in the *object* and *context* of discrimination to take place. In the employment context, for instance, the idea of discrimination law is for firms to increase their hiring of protected groups, or at least to decrease their discriminatory refusal to do so. Some researchers believe, however, that the opposite takes place, leading to employers becoming more reluctant to hire minorities. The reason for this is that employers know that, firstly, more lawsuits are brought, and greater financial compensation is awarded, for successful claims of discrimination in *firing* than for discriminatory refusals to *hire* people.[33] Moreover, discriminatory 'failure to hire' suits are harder to prove than discriminatory discharge suits, especially if there are multiple qualified candidates for a particular position.[34] As such, there is both a greater likelihood and a greater financial risk in an employer being successfully sued for an alleged discriminatory termination than for discriminatory refusals to hire particular candidates. Employers, it is argued, will therefore try to protect themselves from this risk, and one way to do so is to avoid hiring members of a protected class altogether.

Donohue and Siegelman predicted this effect as early as 1970. They claimed that the Civil Rights Act of 1964 had been successful in breaking down overt and flagrant discrimination in hiring, previously practised by many employers, but that this shift was likely to 'create a drag on the hiring of protected workers rather than the positive inducement it originally provided'.[35] Since employers will 'feel' firing-based costs due to discriminatory decisions only if they decide to hire protected individuals in the first place, those costs are seen to act as an implicit 'tax' on hiring.[36] In this sense, discrimination law is hypothesised to sometimes create a *disincentive* for employers to hire members of a protected class, rather than the *incentive* it is intended to constitute.

Although empirical data to substantiate (or refute) this hypothesis are scarce,[37] there is nevertheless some research available that suggests that –

---

33 P. Oyer & S. Shaefer, 'The unintended consequences of the '91 Civil Rights Act', *Regulation* 2003, (2), 45–46.

34 J. Fink, 'Unintended consequences: how antidiscrimination litigation increases group bias in employer-defendants', *New Mexico Law Review* 2008, *38*, 346.

35 J. Donohue & P. Siegelman, 'The changing nature of employment discrimination litigation', *Stanford Law Review* 1991, *43*, 1027. Compare, on a non-empirical basis i.a.: R.A. Posner, 'The efficiency and the efficacy of Title VII', *U. Pa. L. Rev.* 1987, 517–519; R.A. Epstein, *Forbidden grounds: the case against employment discrimination laws,* Harvard: Harvard University Press, 1992.

36 P. Oyer & S. Shaefer, 'The unintended consequences of the '91 Civil Rights Act', *Regulation* 2003, (2), 45–46; I. Ayres & P. Siegelman 'The Q-word as red herring: why disparate impact liability does not induce hiring quotas', *Tex. Law Review* 1996, (74), 1487–1526.

37 Jolls, for instance, observes that '[d]efinitive empirical evidence supporting the hiring-disincentive account has been difficult to come by' (C. Jolls, 'Antidiscrimination law's

correcting for other factors, and at least in some sectors of the economy[38] – the introduction of discrimination law can lead to a marginally *reduced* hiring of individuals belonging to disadvantaged groups.[39] Regarding dismissals, likewise, this same research has claimed that there has been an increase in individuals belonging to protected groups being dismissed as part of mass layoffs, since firms tend to face a greater risk of discrimination litigation when dismissing an individual worker than when dismissing a worker as part of a mass layoff. Moreover, individual-specific discharges underlie most discrimination suits, while class action suits concerning discrimination are rare.[40]

2.2.2. Discrimination Law as Masking Discrimination

Another unintended effect of discrimination law (or at least some forms thereof) to which some research points is that it can serve – paradoxically – to mask or cover up discrimination, rather than contributing to its elimination or reduction.

2.2.2.1. The 'Endogenisation' of Discrimination Law

Specifically on employment discrimination law, the work of Edelman and her colleagues is interesting. Edelman starts from the fact that discrimination law creates imperatives in organisations to achieve compliance with the law. Superficially, this seems like a positive development. However, due to what she terms the 'endogenisation' of discrimination, that compliance is often largely symbolic and not only fails to eliminate discrimination, but rather serves to obfuscate it, effectively 'bulletproofing' the organisation against discrimination claims as courts subsequently incorporate the organisational norms and practices into legal rules.[41]

Edelman refers to law regulating organisations as 'endogenous', on account of the fact that legal meaning and practice 'is formed in part through the actions of organizations and the models of organizational action that become

effects on implicit bias', in M. Gulate & M. Yelnosky (eds.), *Behavioral analyses of workplace discrimination*, Kluwer: Academic Publishers, 2007).

38 The findings of Oyer and Schaefer's research are, as regards hiring disincentives, limited to specific industries that, pre-1991, had employed few protected workers and had been building on this number; at the same time however it also led to protected workers becoming *more* concentrated in sections where they already had enjoyed strong representation (P. Oyer & S. Shaefer, 'The unintended consequences of the '91 Civil Rights Act', *Regulation* 2003, (2), 45–46).

39 *Ibid.*, 45–46.

40 J. Donohue & P. Siegelman, 'The changing nature of employment discrimination litigation', *Stanford Law Review* 1991, *43*, 983–1033; P. Oyer & S. Shaefer, 'The unintended consequences of the '91 Civil Rights Act', *Regulation* 2003, (2), 45–46.

41 L.B. Edelman, C. Uggen & H.S. Erlanger, 'The endogeneity of Legal regulation', *American Journal of Sociology* 1999, 406–454.

institutionalized in organizational fields'.[42] The legal ambiguity that is inherent in discrimination law leads organisations to create internal legal structures that are designed to symbolise attention to law. These structures lead to struggles over the meaning of law, with professionals and other officials seeking to implement law within their organisations. Because of their training, experience and interests, organisational actors thereby construct law in ways that are consistent with traditional managerial prerogatives and goals: the rights protection machinery becomes 'managerialised'. Through internal grievance procedures, for instance, organisations transform employee claims of rights violations into 'misunderstandings' that can be resolved without litigation.[43]

Edelman and her colleagues demonstrate that, as these and other constructions of discrimination law become institutionalised, they also strongly affect or determine how other social actors – including the judiciary – understand and interpret the meaning of the law, and of compliance with it. Their research finds that courts – themselves unsure about certain ambiguous aspects of discrimination law – 'tend to assign legal significance to certain employer policies in discrimination cases'.[44] Courts are shown to 'exhibit an increasing tendency to excuse employers from liability if they have adopted certain organisational forms, such as internal complaint mechanisms'. Thereby judicial and organisational practices in fact become mutually constituted ('endogenisation'):

'Rather than courts serving as a corrective to employing organizations when their policies stray from legal requirements, the courts' rulings on law have been influenced by the compliance structures that employers have developed within an organizational field.'[45]

So, although the development of internal non-discrimination procedures by employers may seem like a positive development, these can in fact 'serve to limit exposure to external legal scrutiny and gain further leverage in future disagreements with employees'.[46] Thereby employment non-discrimination rights are stripped of real impact, and the translation of formal discrimination law in organisational contexts paradoxically results in 'bulletproofing' these

42 L.B. Edelman, 'Legality and the endogeneity of law', in R.A. Kagina, M. Krygier & K.I. Winston (eds.), *Legality and community*, Lanham: Rowman and Littlefield, 2002, 201.

43 L.B. Edelman, H.S. Erlanger & J. Lande, 'Internal dispute resolution: the transformation of civil rights in the workplace', *Law and Society Review* 1993, *27*, 497–534.

44 L.B. Edelman, 'Law at work: the endogenous construction of civil rights', in L.B. Nielsen & R.L. Nelson (eds.), *Handbook of employment discrimination research: rights and realities*, Dordrecht: Springer, 2005, 337–352.

45 R.L. Nelson, E.C. Berrey & L.B. Nielsen, 'Divergent paths: conflicting conceptions of employment discrimination in law and the social sciences', *Annual Review of Law and Social Science* 2008, *4*, 103–122.

46 *Ibid.*

organisations against discrimination claims, rather than in remedying problems of discrimination.[47]

2.2.2.2. *Masking Morality*

More generally, there is some research that suggests that 'masking effects' can, paradoxically, also result from an overly moral(istic) focus on discrimination.[48] Attaching severe moral implications to discrimination and discrimination law may give rise to counterproductive results. This finding is in fact connected to the legitimising theories that were touched upon earlier in this chapter (*supra* section 1.1.1.2) – the just world belief in particular. The stronger the ideological and moral stigma that is attached to the equality and non-discrimination discourse, the more people will tend to resist the idea that they and their organisation discriminate. As such, a highly moralising non-discrimination discourse may serve to *mask*, rather then counter, discrimination, since it renders the problem unmentionable and invisible: no-one 'discriminates' and no-one is a 'racist' or a 'sexist', since that is regarded as the utmost evil, but this leads to the extant structures of inequality being left untouched.

A study by Van den Broeck,[49] for instance, suggests – for the case of racial and ethnic discrimination in the employment context – that everyday racism and potential situations of discrimination are rendered invisible, *especially* in those organisations that explicitly propound equality, diversity and non-discrimination as central moral values. Van den Broeck argues that the moral pressure and the resulting internalised wish and belief not to discriminate serve to maintain daily practices and structures of inequality.

2.2.3. *Harm*

Finally, discrimination law – like many legal interventions – can also have its own harmful effects on victims and plaintiffs. Such effects can be *direct*, due to the harmful effect that legal or institutional intervention sometimes has on plaintiffs (section 2.2.3.1). Some harmful effects on victims are also of a more *indirect* nature, due to the influence that discrimination law can have on other actors that in turn negatively impact victims of discrimination (section 2.2.3.2).

---

47 S. Sturm, 'Law's role in addressing complex discrimination. In L.B. Nielsen & R.L. Nelson (eds.), *Handbook of employment discrimination research: rights and realities,* Dordrecht: Springer, 2005, 35–57; S. Bisom-Rapp, 'Bulletproofing the workplace: symbol and substance in employment discrimination law practice', *Fla. St. University law review* 1999, *26*, 959–1049; L.B. Edelman, H.S. Erlanger & J. Lande, 'Internal dispute resolution: the transformation of civil rights in the workplace', *Law and Society Review* 1993, *27*, 497–534.

48 And/or from employing highly moralistic means to combat discrimination, such as a strong or even one-sided reliance on criminal sanctions.

49 L. Van den Broeck, *De ironie van gelijkheid. Over etnische diversiteit op de werkvloer.* S.l.: Kantharos, 2009.

2.2.3.1. *Direct Harm*

Some research indicates that (creating the possibility of filing) complaints concerning discrimination can inflict harm on those it is supposed to protect, even aside from issues of 'blaming the victim' and retaliation that were discussed previously (*supra* section 1.2).

A first type of harm has to do with the fact that most complaints that reach equality bodies or other competent institutions do not result in the case being taken to court, and many are – in the experience of the plaintiffs – also not (satisfactorily) dealt with extra-judicially due to limited manpower available to the institutions. Research suggests the impact of this to be highly negative among plaintiffs. Regularly plaintiffs report experiencing forms of 'secondary victimisation': after their experiences with discrimination, they feel 'doubly' denied and harmed if the complaint is not taken up by the equality body, or if the complaint fails to lead to a satisfactory outcome.[50] Similar types of harm occur if an equality body brings the case before a court but it results in an acquittal.

Finally, even plaintiffs in cases that came before a court and had a favourable outcome regularly report feelings of dissatisfaction, resentment or even harm, due to feeling ignored or 'unheard' in the legal proceedings, during which they felt they were insufficiently able to either tell their (side of the) story or to enter into dialogue with the opposing party.[51] More generally, people in discrimination cases regularly feel 'harmed' by being involved in legal proceeding (cf. *infra* section 2.2.3.2). Plaintiffs in research by Nielsen, Nelson and Lancaster, for instance, recounted how they found themselves 'in what seemed a maze of manipulative lawyers, judges in cahoots with employers, and unreasonable or mysterious rules that prevented them from ever telling their stories'.[52]

2.2.3.2. *Indirect Harm: Increasing Bias?*

Finally, some research even suggests that discrimination law, or at least particular modes of enforcement, may *increase* bias and the tendency to discriminate among those charged with discrimination, thereby – in turn – negatively impacting disadvantaged groups and individuals.

A study by Fink, for instance, claims the existence of a phenomenon termed 'litigation-induced group bias'.[53] Fink starts from the fact that social science

---

50 J. Vrielink, *Van haat gesproken?* Antwerp: Maklu, 2010; J. Vrielink & V. Vandersteen, *Access to justice – a sociological study on cases of discrimination in the EU. National assessment report fieldwork research – Belgium.* Vienna: Fundamental Rights Agency, 2011.

51 J. Vrielink, *Van haat gesproken?* Antwerp: Maklu, 2010; J. Fink, 'Unintended consequences: how antidiscrimination litigation increases group bias in employer-defendants', *New Mexico Law Review* 2008, *38*, 333–372.

52 E. Berrey, 'Sociology finds discrimination in the law', *Contexts* 2009, (1), 28–32.

53 Fink does emphasise that discrimination litigation is, of course, not the only or most significant cause of employer bias (J. Fink, 'Unintended consequences: how antidiscrimination litigation

research has long shown that litigation is 'a daunting and emotionally destructive process for all parties involved – plaintiffs, defendants, and witnesses alike'. Unsurprisingly then, the psychological and emotional response that defendants have towards plaintiffs turns out to 'often consist in strong frustration, hostility, and anger'.[54]

Whereas these effects tend to occur generally in litigation, Fink lists a number of reasons why they may be more pronounced in discrimination cases. This is the case, firstly, due to the strong moral and social stigma that is associated with discrimination claims, as compared to many other types of tort claims. This, Fink argues, leads to 'a heightened degree of defensiveness and resentment by the defendant'. Secondly, the financial costs of being a defendant in a discrimination suit are relatively high, since defendants – in light of the aforementioned stigma – pour significant resources into trying to refute allegations of discrimination. According to Fink, these high costs contribute to added resentment towards the plaintiff. Additionally, Fink lists several (social-) psychological tendencies that further complicate how defendants view plaintiffs in discrimination cases, referring for instance to the research by Kaiser and Miller[55] demonstrating that people who claim discrimination are perceived as 'troublemakers' even if the evidence clearly indicates the occurrence of discrimination (cf. *supra*).

Fink argues that the hostility that defendants experience in discrimination cases 'extends beyond the individual plaintiff, "spilling over" to other members of the protected class to which the plaintiff belongs'.[56] In other words, the litigation experience induces a bias against all those who share the plaintiff's protected characteristics.

To explain and substantiate this, Fink relies on social cognition research that shows that the mere introduction of so-called 'groupness'[57] into a situation – as allegations of discrimination inherently do – will exacerbate conflicts and generate various types of intergroup biases, such as assumptions of homogeneity of out-group members (i.e. the plaintiffs, in discrimination cases).[58] Fink also draws on research concerning experiences of personal

increases group bias in employer-defendants', *New Mexico Law Review* 2008, *38*, 336).

54 *Ibid.*, 334.

55 C.R. Kaiser & C.T. Miller, 'Reacting to impending discrimination: compensation for prejudice and attributions to discrimination', *Personality and social psychology bulletin* 2001, *27*, (10), 1357–1367.

56 J. Fink, 'Unintended consequences: how antidiscrimination litigation increases group bias in employer-defendants', *New Mexico Law Review* 2008, *38*, 334.

57 'Groupness' being understood as the psychological and social experience of feeling that one is in a group.

58 Fink refers, inter alia, to research by Linda Krieger: L.H. Krieger, 'Civil rights perestroika: intergroup relations after affirmative action', *Cal. L. Rev.* 1998, *86*, 1251–1333; L.H. Krieger, 'The content of our categories: a cognitive bias approach to discrimination and equal employment opportunity', *Stan. L. Rev.* 1995, *47*, (6), 1161–1248.

failure to explain transference of attitudes towards plaintiffs to the entire group to which the plaintiff belongs: lowered self-esteem that results from personal failure (such as being accused of discrimination) heightens individuals' sensitivity to group status and therefore tends to elicit extreme reactions to out-group members in general, while serving to protect the superiority of one's in-group.

Moreover, Fink claims that this increase in bias towards members of the plaintiff's protected class is not only of an unconscious and attitudinal nature, 'but instead has a concrete, negative impact for these individuals by reducing their prospect of getting hired'.[59]

3. CONCLUSION

All in all, the research described in this chapter paints a complicated picture of the effects and impact of discrimination law. While there is research which shows discrimination legislation to have a number of unequivocally positive effects, there seems reason for caution too, as other research suggests the legislation serves merely to shift or mask the phenomenon it purports to address, or that it may even have counterproductive effects.

In pointing to research on some of these unintended or counterproductive effects, I do not wish to suggest that these are the rule, or that they outweigh the benefits that discrimination law has, especially since many of the identified issues are not necessarily *inherent* effects of discrimination law. Instead, more often than not, they appear to be peculiar to specific measures and approaches, and would therefore seem to entail the possibility of solutions. In that regard, being conscious of the pitfalls may 'make a difference' in avoiding them.

---

[59] J. Fink, 'Unintended consequences: how antidiscrimination litigation increases group bias in employer-defendants', *New Mexico Law Review* 2008, *38*, 345.

FROM A 'RELATIVE' TO A 'RELATIONAL' EQUALITY: RETHINKING COMPARABILITY IN THE LIGHT OF RELATIONAL ACCOUNTS OF SOCIAL JUSTICE

Päivi Johanna Neuvonen

1. INTRODUCTION

Anti-discrimination law is often depicted as an important tool for implementing distributive policies in the name of social justice. In practice, however, the relationship between anti-discrimination law and the different ideals of distributive social justice is a complex one. One source of this complexity is that the traditional anti-discrimination model assumes that the alleged victim of discrimination is treated less favourably or is placed at a particular disadvantage *in comparison* with other persons. Protecting diversity is one of the central objectives of social policy in contemporary pluralistic societies. But the legal test for comparability seeks to determine whether two situations are relevantly similar for differential treatment to qualify as direct discrimination or relevantly different for similar treatment to qualify as indirect discrimination. This means that the comparability analysis may easily support a narrow view of what constitutes relevant subjectivity in discrimination law. The potential of anti-discrimination law and policies to contribute to the wider aims of social justice remains limited within a comparator-based approach to discrimination. One task of discrimination theory is therefore to consider what alternatives to the comparability analysis can be provided in discrimination law.

This chapter will rethink the requirement of comparability within a relational framework of egalitarian social justice. It will first explore how the idea of comparability is embedded in the case law of the Court of Justice of the EU (CJEU) and what critical responses it has fostered in anti-discrimination law scholarship (section 2). This analysis lays the foundation for the argument that the requirement of comparability often misinterprets the relational nature of social reality. The remaining sections of this chapter will develop a relational critique of comparability, first by suggesting that discrimination law should move from a 'relative' to a more 'relational' ideal of equality (section 3), and then by considering what implications this theoretical analysis might have for the different functions of comparability in EU anti-discrimination law (section 4). It will be concluded that placing more emphasis on the applicant's ability to relate as an equal with other members of society in deciding whether adverse treatment constitutes discrimination on one or several of the protected grounds can reshape our understanding of what constitutes relevant subjectivity under discrimination law, and thus reconcile the legal framework for combating discrimination with the wider objectives of social justice.

2. COMPARISONS IN THE LIGHT OF THE CASE LAW OF THE CJEU

The problems of formal equality, that is the principle of treating like cases alike, have been widely acknowledged.[1] Anti-discrimination law scholarship has instead focused on different concepts of substantive equality, many of which also promise to be in line with the wider goals of social policy.[2] However, as will be seen in this section, the legal test for discrimination is still often based on the requirement of a comparator both in the case of direct and indirect discrimination. This gap between the theoretical and practical approaches to equality and non-discrimination means that, although discrimination law might in theory seem able to advance social justice and provide a useful tool for social policy, in practice it depends on ideas and conceptions which make reaching these goals difficult. In order to better grasp this tension between practice and theory, this section will examine how the requirement of comparability is applied in EU anti-discrimination law. Similar questions could be discussed in relation to many other jurisdictions, including that of the European Court of Human Rights. This analysis demonstrates that, although comparability can take causal, justificatory, and hypothetical forms in the discrimination analysis, it nevertheless builds on a fundamentally 'relative' idea of equality.

The basic idea of comparability states that equal treatment is required in those cases which are relevantly alike and differential treatment is required in those cases which are relevantly unalike. The Court of Justice of the EU has affirmed this principle by stating that 'discrimination can arise only through the application of different rules to comparable situations or the application of

---

1 For more detail, see e.g. S. Fredman, *Discrimination Law*, Oxford University Press, 2011, 2nd ed.

2 For discussion on the tensions between the principle of equal treatment and the ideal of social transformation, see e.g. H. Collins, 'Discrimination, Equality and Social Inclusion', *The Modern Law Review* 2003 (66), 16, 17.

the same rule to different situations'.[3] In the case of direct discrimination, this means that 'one person is treated less favourably than another person who is in a comparable situation'.[4] In the case of indirect discrimination, seemingly neutral treatment would place one person with a protected characteristic 'at a particular disadvantage compared with other persons unless that provision, criterion or practice is objectively justified'.[5] The comparability analysis centres around the question 'which features of persons it takes to be relevantly alike or unlike' for the purposes of non-discrimination.[6] The claim for equal treatment is then based on the absence of objective differences other than the protected characteristic(s) between two situations, whereas a relevant difference between two situations can legitimate their differential treatment.

The establishment of a comparator is given a central role in the four EU equality directives.[7] In practice, the comparability analysis can play many different roles in identifying prohibited discrimination. The basic idea of comparability seeks to reveal whether persons or groups in a comparable situation have suffered the same negative effects as the applicant. If this question is answered positively, the necessary link between a protected ground and the adverse treatment in question will be missing. This role is often called 'causal' because it focuses on establishing a relevant connection between the protected ground/trait and adverse treatment. However, this is not the only task assigned to comparability in the discrimination analysis. While the 'primary role' of comparability is to establish less favourable treatment, it can also play

---

3 E.g. Case C-279/93 *Finanzamt Koln-Altstadt v Roland Schumacker* [1995] ECR I-225, para 30.

4 C-267/06 *Tadao Maruko v Versorgungsanstalt der deutschen Bühnen* [2008] ECR I-1757, para 66.

5 Ibid, para 66.

6 C. Knight, 'Describing Equality', *Law and Philosophy* 2009, (28) 327, 331.

7 These directives outline that direct discrimination occurs where one person is 'treated less favourably' on the basis of a protected ground than 'another is, has been or would be treated in a comparable situation'. See Article 2(a), Council Directive 2004/113/EC of 13 December 2004 implementing the principle of equal treatment between men and women in the access to and supply of goods and services [2004] OJ L 373/13; Article 2(1)(a), Directive 2006/54/EC of the European Parliament and of the Council of 5 July 2006 on the implementation of the principle of equal opportunities and equal treatment of men and women in matters of employment and occupation (recast) [2006] OJ L 204/23; Article 2(2)(a), Council Directive 2000/43/EC of 29 June 2000 implementing the principle of equal treatment between persons irrespective of their racial or ethnic origin [2000] OJ L 180/22; Article 2(2)(a), Council Directive 2000/78/EC of 27 November 2000 establishing a general framework for equal treatment in employment and occupation [2000] OJ L 303/16. See also Article 2(2)(a), Proposal for a Council Directive on implementing the principle of equal treatment between persons irrespective of religion or belief, disability, age or sexual orientation, COM (2008) 426 final. Indirect discrimination is defined as 'an apparently neutral criterion, provision, or practice' which would put persons holding a protected ground 'at a particular disadvantage compared with other persons', unless such practice can be objectively justified. See Article 2(b), Directive 2004/113; Article 2(1)(b), Directive 2006/54; Article 2(2)(b), Directive 2000/43; Article 2(2)(b), Directive 2000/78. See also Article 2(2)(b), COM (2008) 426 final.

a 'secondary evidential role' as a means of 'proving' discrimination.[8] This use of comparability is called 'justificatory' because it covers those situations in which the establishment of difference between the applicant and a comparator is accepted as an explanation for adverse treatment. Here the lack of comparability indicates that adverse treatment is based on the particular circumstances of the applicant, rather than on his/her protected characteristic.

The different 'roles' of comparability have been critically assessed by many commentators.[9] It has been pointed out that the lack of comparability is sometimes used as an 'escape' in those cases in which there is no other justification available.[10] In these situations, the quest for discrimination is rejected at the first stage of discrimination analysis.[11] Moreover, it has been noted that the CJEU often applies the test for comparability and the test for different treatment together.[12] Some argue on this basis that the comparability analysis is 'over-emphasised' in the discrimination analysis and that its 'evidentiary' functions could be replaced by directing more attention to the question 'why the discrimination has occurred'.[13] In order to better understand these different functions of comparability, it is helpful to have a closer look at the relevant case law. It will be seen below in this section how the Court engages with the comparability analysis both as a causal and a justificatory tool. These findings will then be examined in the light of the fact that sometimes it may be sufficient to indicate a hypothetical comparator in the absence of a real/actual comparator. The central question to this analysis is whether the use of a hypothetical comparator can overcome those problems that emerge from the traditional comparability analysis.

2.1. THE CAUSAL USE OF COMPARABILITY

Comparisons between men and women in the equal pay cases under what is now Article 157 TFEU constitute one area in which the controversies over

8 Eg G. Moon, 'Multiple Discrimination – Problems Compounded or Solutions Found?', *JUSTICE Journal* 2006 (3), 86, 92.

9 For instance, Aileen McColgan lists the following four 'roles' for a comparator in the discrimination analysis: comparisons can be used (1) to challenge the link between adverse treatment and the protected ground, (2) to provide a tool for assessing the reasons offered for adverse treatment, (3) to act as a justification for adverse treatment if no other 'justification defence' is permissible, and (4) to dismiss cases 'at an early stage' when the court applies an open-ended prohibition on discrimination. A. McColgan, 'Cracking the comparator problem: discrimination, 'equal' treatment and the role of comparisons' *European Human Rights Law Review* 2006 (6), 650, 656–59.

10 S. Prechal, 'Equality of Treatment, Non-Discrimination and Social Policy: Achievements in Three Themes', *Common Market Law Review* 2004 (41), 533, 545.

11 Ibid, 543.

12 Ibid, 543.

13 Moon (n 8) 92.

comparability have actualised in EU law.[14] This was the issue, for instance, in the *Allonby* case in which the applicant was a woman who previously worked as an hourly-paid part-time lecturer in an educational institution and, after having been made redundant, had continued to provide the same service to that institution through an educational undertaking which considered her to be a self-employed person. The central question in this case was whether she could use as a comparator for equal pay purposes a full-time male lecturer employed by the educational institution in question.[15] The Court's reference to the fact that 'there is no doubt that, if a comparison with Mr Johnson is to be made, the inequalities are numerous' illustrates how much is often at stake in the comparability analysis.[16] In this case, the Court nevertheless dismissed the applicant's claim on the basis that 'a man employed by the woman's previous employer' did not constitute a relevant comparator for 'the remuneration received for equal work or work of the same value'.[17]

Another area in which the issue of comparability has been frequently discussed concerns gender assignments. The Court has outlined that differential treatment can qualify as sex discrimination under EU law when a person who intends to undergo gender reassignment 'is treated unfavourably by comparison with persons of the sex to which he or she was deemed to belong before undergoing gender reassignment'.[18] This statement provides an example of the causal use of comparability in the context of sex discrimination. The *Richards* judgment includes a slightly different example of comparability in relation to gender assignments. This case concerned the right of a person who had already undergone male-to-female gender reassignment to a retirement pension at the same age as a person who was recognised as a woman under national law. Confirming comparability between the applicant who had undergone gender reassignment and other women led the Court to conclude that the principle of equal treatment for men and women in matters of social security can preclude national legislation which would place the applicant at a comparative disadvantage in this respect.[19] In this case, the comparability analysis also had a role in proving that discrimination had occurred.

Before the adoption of the Framework Employment Directive,[20] the Court's approach to comparability in the context of sexual orientation received much

---

14 Article 157, Consolidated versions of the Treaty on European Union and the Treaty on the Functioning of the European Union, OJ 2012 No. C326.

15 C-256/01 *Debra Allonby and Accrington & Rosendale College* [2004] ECR I-873, paras 25 and 42.

16 Ibid, para 36.

17 Ibid, para 50.

18 C-13/94 *P and S and Cornwall County Council* [1996] ECR I-2143, para 21.

19 C-423/04 *Sarah Margaret Richards v Secretary of State for Work and Pensions* [2006] ECR I-3585, para 38.

20 Council Directive 2000/78/EC of 27 November 2000 establishing a general framework for equal treatment in employment and occupation [2000] OJ L 303/16.

criticism. The *Grant* case concerned travel concessions granted to the employee's spouse or the person of the opposite sex with whom the employee had a stable relationship outside marriage. The Court had to answer the question whether the employer's refusal to grant these travel concessions to the person of the same sex with whom its employee had a stable relationship constituted sex discrimination under European Union law. As this case predated the adoption of the Framework Directive, the Court stated that it would be a task for the EU legislature to enact further norms on discrimination on the grounds of sexual orientation.[21] The Court also concluded that there was no direct sex discrimination in this case because the condition that the employee's partner must be a person of the opposite sex in order to qualify for travel concessions was applied to both sexes equally.[22] In other words, the Court compared the female applicant's situation to that of a male worker who was living with a person of the same sex, rather than to the situation of a female employee who was living with a person of the opposite sex. This approach has been criticised in relevant literature for using a disadvantaged group as a relevant pool for comparison.[23]

The later *Maruko* judgment discussed comparability in the case of sexual orientation in the light of the Framework Employment Directive. This case concerned the right of a surviving life partner to benefit from a widower's pension. The Court outlined in its judgment that EU anti-discrimination law can now preclude national legislation which prevents a registered life partner from receiving a survivor's benefit from the relevant pension scheme, although a married spouse would receive the benefit and national law treats life partnerships and marriages as 'comparable' in other contexts.[24] However, the Court of Justice emphasised that it is a task of the national court to decide whether a surviving life partner is in a comparable situation to a surviving spouse who is entitled to the benefit in question.[25]

In the recent *CHEZ* judgment, the Court also examined comparability in the context of ethnic origin. The applicant, who was of Bulgarian origin, was running a shop in a district where most inhabitants were of Roma origin. In that area, the CHEZ RB had installed electricity meters for consumers at a height of six or seven metres, whereas their height was less than two metres in those districts which were not so densely populated by Roma. The Court first noted that the important question was whether the practice in question would create a situation in which persons are 'the subject of "less favourable treatment" than other persons "in a comparable situation" on grounds relating in whole

21 Case C-249/96 *Lisa Jacqueline Grant v South-West Trains Ltd.* [1998] ECR I-621, para 36.
22 Ibid, para 27.
23 Eg E. Holzleithner, 'Mainstreaming Equality: Dis/Entangling Grounds of Discrimination', *Transnational Law & Contemporary Problems* 2005 (14), 927, 934–35.
24 C-267/06 *Tadao Maruko v Versorgungsanstalt der deutschen Bühnen* [2008] ECR I-1757, paras 73.
25 Ibid, para 73.

or in part to ethnic origin'.[26] In the Court's view, there was 'no doubt' that the mentioned practice created less favourable treatment in comparable situations.[27] This argument was based on the view that 'in principle, all final consumers of electricity who are supplied by the same distributor within an urban area must, irrespective of the district in which they reside, be regarded as being, in relation to that distributor, in a comparable situation so far as concerns the making available of an electricity meter intended to measure their consumption'.[28] As part of this reasoning, the Court also referred to its earlier finding that the establishment of comparability 'must be assessed in the light of all the elements which characterise them'.[29]

It is nevertheless controversial what elements the Court should actually take into account in assessing comparability in any given situation. In the *Lawrence* case, the Court expressed the view that, although the applicant and his/her comparator do not need to work for the same employer in equal pay cases, the differences in their pay conditions must be 'attributed to a single source'.[30] It has been noted that this approach considerably restricts the pool of relevant comparators.[31] Moreover, it may be difficult to predict in advance what material factors the Court chooses to use in establishing comparability or non-comparability. The Court's reasoning in the above-mentioned *Allonby* case also underlines the open-ended nature of comparability in so far as comparisons regarding the remuneration can only be made 'for equal work or work of the same value'.[32] This reference to the work of 'same value' shows that there is often a considerable amount of openness embedded even in the causal use of comparability.

The *Helmig* case provides another example of this unpredictability in the context of indirect sex discrimination. In this case, part-time female workers argued that they should receive the same overtime payment for hours worked in addition to their individual working hours as full-time workers received for hours worked after their normal working hours. In the Court's view, there would be unequal treatment between part-time and full-time workers 'whenever the overall pay of full-time employees is higher than that of part-time employees for the same number of hours'.[33] Thus, the Court took it for granted that the number

---

26 Case C-83/14 *CHEZ Razpredelenie Bulgaria AD v Komisia za zashtita ot diskriminatsia* EU:C:2015:480, para 70.

27 Ibid, para 86.

28 Ibid, para 90.

29 Ibid, para 89.

30 Case C-320/00 *A. G. Lawrence and Others v Regent Office Care Ltd, Commercial Catering Group and Mitie Secure Services Ltd* [2002] ECR I-7325, paras 17–18.

31 Prechal (n 10) 546.

32 C-256/01 *Debra Allonby and Accrington & Rosendale College* [2004] ECR I-903, paras 18 and 42.

33 Case C-399/92 *Stadt Lengerich v Angelika Helmig and Waltraud Schmidt v Deutsche Angestellten-Krankenkasse and Elke Herzog v Arbeiter-Samariter-Bund Landverband*

of hours worked would have an identical meaning to part-time and full-time workers. This approach has been referred to as a 'comparison trap' because it failed to recognise that the number of working hours may mean different things to part-time and full-time workers.[34] The Court has also held that a comparison between a group consisting predominantly of women and a group consisting predominantly of men who are paid by piece is valid only if 'the two groups each encompass all the workers who, taking into account of a set of factors such as the nature of the work, the training requirements and the working conditions, can be considered to be in a comparable situation… ensuring that the differences are due to purely fortuitous or short-term factors'.[35] This statement illustrates how the strict conditions for comparability can be used to block the causal link between adverse treatment and the protected ground.

In particular, the causal use of comparability leaves the Court with a lot of discretion when it is based on a general reasonableness analysis. In the *Gruber* case, the applicant, who had terminated her employment contract in order to take care of her children, argued that the reduction in her termination payment under national law constituted indirect discrimination against female workers.[36] The applicant suggested that a relevant comparison should be made between those workers who resign for maternity-related reasons and those workers who 'resign for important reasons', as the latter group receives a lower termination payment than the former group.[37] However, the Court adopted the view that the situation of those workers who resign in order to take care of their children was 'in substance and origin different' from the situation of those workers who resigned 'for an important reason related to working conditions in the undertaking or to the employer's conduct'.[38] It is not always self-evident when two situations are different 'in substance' and what should count as an 'important reason' in this context.

2.2. THE JUSTIFICATORY USE OF COMPARABILITY

The comparability analysis plays an important role in deciding whether a given situation falls within the scope of the protected grounds in the first place. However, things become more complex when comparisons are used not

Hamburg eV and Dagmar Lange v Bundesknappschaft Bochum and Angelika Kussfeld v Firma Detlef Bogdol GmbH and Ursula Ludewig v Kreis Segeberg [1994] ECR I-5727, para 26.

34 Prechal (n 10) 544.

35 Case C-400/93 *Specialarbejderforbundet i Danmark v Dansk Industri, formerly Industriens Arbejdsgivere, acting for Royal Copenhagen* A/S [1995] ECR I-1275, para 38.

36 Case C-249/97 *Gabriele Gruber v Silhouette International Schmied GmbH & Co. KG* [1999] ECR I-5295, para 15.

37 Ibid, para 29.

38 Ibid, paras 33–35.

just to decide whether there is a causal link with adverse treatment and the protected ground but also to consider whether discrimination has occurred and/or whether the treatment is question can be objectively justified. This situation is further complicated by the fact that the lack of comparability can play a justificatory role both explicitly and implicitly. The 'explicit' use of comparability refers to those parameters which are considered to be relevant when the court decides whether two situations are relevantly similar or different for the purposes of non-discrimination and equal treatment.[39] The 'implicit' use of comparability is in action when the right to non-discrimination and equal treatment is actualised 'if no sufficient reason exists for different treatment'.[40] Sometimes the Court explicitly returns to the issue of comparability when it discusses the possible justifications for differential treatment at the later stages of discrimination analysis. In other cases, the comparability analysis may be mixed with the reasonableness analysis more implicitly.

The *Brunnhofer* judgment illustrates the connection between comparability and objective reasons for the difference. In this case, the Court was asked whether the difference in the individual supplement to two employees who were classified in the same job category would constitute prohibited discrimination and whether it was based on objective reasons.[41] This analysis focused on the concepts of 'same work' and 'work to which equal value is attributed'.[42] According to the Court, the principle of equal treatment presupposes that 'the men and women to whom it applies are in identical or comparable situations' and that 'it must also be ascertained whether the employees concerned are performing the same work or work to which equal value may be attributed'.[43] The Court stated that the question of equal value in this context was 'entirely qualitative in character' and that being classified in the same job category did not alone indicate that two employees are performing work of equal value.[44] According to the Court, 'a number of factors' must be taken into account in deciding whether the applicant and the comparator are 'in fact' performing the same or comparable work.[45]

The Court returned to comparability when considering the burden of proof between the parties in regard to 'circumstances objectively justifying such a difference in treatment'.[46] The judgment held that a *prima facie* case of discrimination will only exist if the applicant can show both that 'the pay she

39 K.W. Simons, 'Equality as A Comparative Right', *Boston University Law Review* 1985 (65), 387, 424.

40 Ibid, 424.

41 Case C-381/99 *Susanna Brunnhofer v Bank der österreichischen Postsparkasse AG* [2001] ECR I-4961, para 26.

42 Ibid, para 25.

43 Ibid, para 39.

44 Ibid, paras 42 and 44.

45 Ibid, para 48.

46 Ibid, para 51.

receives from the employer is less than that of her chosen comparator' and that 'she does the same work or work of equal value comparable to that performed by him'.[47] Moreover, the issue of comparability was also addressed when the Court had to decide which legal criteria would indicate 'an objective justification for unequal treatment prima facie based on sex to be established'.[48] One valid way to justify the differential treatment was to show that two situations which initially were comparable were no longer comparable. The Court was clear in stating that 'the difference in pay between a woman and a man occupying the same job can be justified only by objective factors unrelated to any discrimination linked to the difference in sex'.[49] However, whether or not they are still 'occupying the same job' depends on the comparability analysis.

In the *Abdoulaye* judgment, male workers argued that the fact that female workers who were taking maternity leave were granted a lump-sum payment by the employer under the agreement on social benefits constituted sex discrimination under what is now Article 157 TFEU. This claim was based on the argument that the birth of a child should be considered 'a social event which concerns the whole family, including the father, and to deny him the same allowance amounts to unlawful discrimination'.[50] In this case, the Court nevertheless accepted the employer's view that female and male workers were 'in different situations' in regard to the benefit in question in so far as it was 'designed to offset the occupational disadvantages which arise to those workers as a result of their being away from work'.[51] But it is noteworthy that a reference to occupational disadvantages has not prevented comparability between male and female workers in other contexts. In the *Griesmar* case, the Court held that the situation of a male and a female civil servant is comparable in regard to the bringing up of children because a male civil servant 'who has assumed the task of bringing up his children has thereby been exposed to the same career-related disadvantages'.[52]

A similar tendency to use the lack of comparability as a material justification for differential treatment can also be traced in other contexts.[53] It has been argued that the questions concerning comparability should indeed be considered at the 'justification stage' because the burden of proof is then on the alleged

47 Ibid, para 58.
48 Ibid, paras 64 and 77.
49 Ibid, paras 79–80.
50 Case C-218/98 *Oumar Dabo Abdoulaye and Others v Régie nationale des usines Renault SA* [1999] ECR I-5723, para 7.
51 Ibid paras 20 and 22.
52 Case C-366/99 *Joseph Griesmar v Ministre de l'Economie, des Finances et de l'Industrie and Ministre de la Fonction publique, de la Réforme de l'Etat et de la Décentralisation* [2001] ECR I-9383, para 56.
53 In the context of taxation, see e.g. Case C-279/93 *Finanzamt Köln-Altstadt v Roland Schumacker* [1995] ECR I-225, para 37 and Case C-107/94 *P. H. Asscher v Staatssecretaris van Financiën* [1996] ECR I-3089, paras 42 and 48 – 49.

discriminator.[54] This would reduce the risk of the Court using the requirement of comparability as an 'easy dismissal' of the discrimination claim and thus as an excuse to avoid a more substantive analysis of the discrimination claim.[55] But the way in which the Court uses comparability to prove discrimination has also been described as 'methodologically puzzling'.[56] In academic commentary, it has been suggested that these issues could be addressed by adopting a more inclusive approach to what constitutes a relevant comparator, using more hypothetical comparators, and/or developing alternative methodologies to comparability analysis.[57] Section 2.3 will move on to consider whether the use of hypothetical comparators provides an adequate solution to the problem of comparability in EU anti-discrimination law.

2.3. THE USE OF A HYPOTHETICAL COMPARATOR

In the early *MacCarthys* judgment, the Court outlined that the establishment of a relevant comparator could not be limited by 'a requirement of contemporaneity'.[58] This meant that the applicant and her male comparator were not required to simultaneously do 'equal work for the same employer' in a case concerning equal pay between men and women.[59] However, in *MacCarthys*, the Court still rejected the use of a 'hypothetical comparator', stating that it would only observe 'concrete appraisals of the work actually performed by employees of different sex within the same establishment or service'.[60] This situation changed with the adoption of the current EU equality directives. All four directives now accept the use of hypothetical comparators in proving discrimination. In other words, it is possible to claim that the victim of discrimination is treated less favourably than another person *would be* treated in a comparable situation.[61] The important question in discrimination theory is whether the acceptance of hypothetical comparators can alleviate the methodological problems that relate to the causal and justificatory use of comparability analysis, as discussed above in Sections 2.1 and 2.2.

Accepting a hypothetical comparator indicates that it is adequate to establish the 'probability of "his" or "her" better treatment'.[62] This means that the

54 McColgan (9) 677.
55 Ibid, 651.
56 Prechal (n 10) 543.
57 Eg S. Goldberg, 'Discrimination By Comparison', *Yale Law Journal* 2010–11 (120), 728, 805–807.
58 Case 129/79 *Macarthys Ltd v Wendy Smith* [1980] ECR 1275, para 11.
59 Ibid, para 13.
60 Ibid, para 15.
61 Eg L. Waddington and M. Bell, 'More Equal than Others: Distinguishing European Union Equality Directives', *Common Market Law Review* 2001 (38), 587, 592.
62 Holzleithner (n 23) 934.

Court can legitimately consider 'what would happen to someone in the same circumstances as the complainant but lacking their particular characteristics'.[63] It has been noted that, in order to be effective, a hypothetical comparator would need to reflect relevant 'intra-group differences'.[64] The use of hypothetical comparators is therefore likely to be more useful in proving single-ground discrimination than multiple or intersectional discrimination.[65] Adding more elements to the comparability analysis in the case of multiple discrimination can arguably be 'theoretical and difficult'.[66] The requirement of comparability is accordingly criticised by scholars who question the 'grounds-based approach' to discrimination because it only protects those individuals who can identify themselves with 'a pre-determined protected group' and ignores intersectional discrimination that follows from the 'complexity' of social identities.[67] The potential of hypothetical comparators to reform the discrimination analysis arguably remains limited in so far as the Court holds that the alleged discrimination must originate from 'a single source'.[68]

Thus, even the use of a hypothetical comparator may provide an inadequate solution in the case of intersectional discrimination. If all the victims of adverse treatment are not in exactly the same situation in terms of their work performance, there is also a risk of the employer using what has been called 'counterfeit comparators'.[69] Those persons who are 'poorly performing' might be used as comparators to demonstrate that the members of a disadvantaged group were not discriminated against when they were dismissed because other people also lost their jobs.[70] Another concern with regard to comparability analysis is that, if the employers only dismiss some members of a protected group, they might defend themselves by pointing out that others who also hold the protected characteristics did not suffer any adverse treatment.[71] Moreover, in so far as access to equality depends on actual or hypothetical comparability, the 'less privileged' will have access to equality only in so far as they can 'prove sameness' with the 'more privileged'.[72] It can be concluded on the basis of these remarks that all forms of comparability have their own problems.

Many scholars now explore what alternative methodologies to the comparator-based models can be provided in establishing prohibited discrimination. It has, for instance, been suggested that the courts should simply

63 Moon (n 8) 91.
64 V. Chege, 'The European Union Anti-Discrimination Directives and European Equality Law: The Case of Multi-dimensional Discrimination', *ERA Forum* 2012 (13), 275, 288.
65 Ibid, 288.
66 Moon (n 8) 99.
67 A. McColgan, 'Reconfiguring Discrimination Law', *Public Law* 2007, 74, 75 and 77.
68 Prechal (n 10) 546.
69 Chege (n 64) 287.
70 Ibid ,287.
71 Goldberg (n 64) 809.
72 McColgan (n 9) 656.

consider 'why the claimant was treated as she was'.[73] The so-called 'but for' test could also be used to prove that adverse treatment constitutes prohibited discrimination. Here the important question is whether 'the defendant would have treated the claimant so but for the protected ground'.[74] In regard to maternity-related benefits, the Court has already stated that women taking maternity leave 'are in a special position which requires them to be afforded special protection, but which is not comparable either with that of a man or with that of a woman actually at work'.[75] It is also noteworthy that all four equality directives now include provisions concerning harassment.[76] The concept of harassment does not depend on the establishment of a comparator pool but focuses on the 'purpose' or 'effect' of adverse treatment in terms of 'human dignity'. The idea of human dignity is nevertheless open to various different interpretations.[77] Arguably, a more developed 'substantive approach' is needed to support 'a comparator-free approach'.[78] The relational account of equality in the next section can be seen as one attempt to develop a more 'substantive' understanding of prohibited discrimination.

3. A 'RELATIONAL' CRITIQUE OF COMPARABILITY: THE DISCRIMINATION ANALYSIS IN THE LIGHT OF RELATIONAL ACCOUNTS OF EGALITARIAN SOCIAL JUSTICE

Comparability provides one answer to the question what a just distribution means in the context of anti-discrimination law and policies. The requirement of comparability as 'likeness between claimant and existing beneficiaries' can be seen a means of negotiating 'what a statute's underlying distributive

73 Moon (n 8) 92.

74 E.g. M. Connolly, 'Discriminatory Motive And the But For Test: The Proper Approach to Direct Discrimination in Britain and the United States', *International Journal of Discrimination and the Law* 2007 (9), 37, 39. But Connolly qualifies this approach by suggesting that the legitimate question under this test is 'would the defendant have treated him so, but for the protected ground?', rather than 'would the claimant have received unfavourable treatment, but for the protected ground?'. Ibid 40.

75 Case C-342/93 *Joan Gillespie and others v Northern Health and Social Services Boards, Department of Health and Social Services, Eastern Health and Social Services Board and Southern Health and Social Services Board* [1996] ECR I-475, para 17. See also the earlier *Dekker* case for a similar approach. See also eg Case C-177/88 *Elisabeth Johanna Pacifica Dekker v Stichting Vormingscentrum voor Jong Volwassenen (VJV-Centrum) Plus* [1990] ECR I-3941.

76 Article 2(c), Directive 2004/113; Article 2(1)(c), Directive 2006/54; Article 3, Directive 2000/43; Article 3, Directive 2000/78. See also Article 3 of COM(2008) 426 final.

77 Chege (n 64) 287.

78 Ibid, 280.

principle is'.[79] But making comparisons requires a 'standard' which is often provided by those who are powerful or privileged in society. It has been noted that, as part of the comparability analysis, 'difference' becomes a reference to 'the less favoured' and loses its meaning 'as a quality of the relationship between persons'.[80] Moreover, the 'undimensionality' that follows from the comparability analysis may neglect the 'complexly situated nature' of those who claim adverse treatment.[81] Thus, if discrimination law is regarded as a tool for social engineering, it seems all the more important to critically evaluate the requirement of comparability.

It has been suggested that discrimination law is at a turning point both 'methodologically' and 'conceptually'.[82] The main reason for this 'crisis' is that the 'comparator methodology' is in conflict with the so-called second generation theories of identity discrimination.[83] However, in so far as the explicit and implicit requirements of comparability are not altogether abandoned by those institutions which enact and apply discrimination law, it is important to consider what factors, other than likeness vs. difference, could constitute relevant comparability. One way to answer this question is to distinguish between the 'relative' and 'relational' conceptions of equality. The term 'relative' considers something 'in relation or in proportion to something else', whereas the term 'relational' refers to 'the way in which two or more people or things are connected'.[84] Equality can accordingly be understood both as 'as a comparison' and 'as a way of structuring human relationships'.[85] It will be seen below in this section that the relational approach to equality shifts the focus of discrimination analysis from whether the victim of adverse treatment is in a similar or different position to a comparator to how the treatment in question affects his/her relational subject-position.

The argument for a more relational account of equality draws on the way in which the importance of just and equal relationships is described within the democratic account of egalitarian social justice, as developed by such scholars as Elizabeth Anderson and Samuel Scheffler. The principles of social justice can be egalitarian or non-egalitarian. What is particular to the egalitarian accounts of justice is that they focus on the question of how some people are treated in relation to others.[86] However, philosophical egalitarians hold different

---

79 D. Réaume, 'Dignity, Equality, and Comparison', in D. Hellman and S. Moreau (eds.), *Philosophical Foundations of Discrimination Law*, Oxford, Oxford University Press, 2013.

80 McColgan (n 67) who refers to M. Minow, 'Justice Engendered', *Harvard Law Review* 1987 (101), 10.

81 McColgan (n 67) 79.

82 Goldberg (n 57) 728.

83 Ibid, 728.

84 For these definitions, see The Oxford Dictionaries, http://www.oxforddictionaries.com.

85 S. Berns, 'Towards A Theory of Relational Equality', *UNSW Law Journal* 1993 (16), 394, 396.

86 Eg J. Gardner, 'Discrimination as Injustice', *Oxford Journal of Legal Studies* 1996 (16), 353, 355.

views on what equality should mean in this context. One of the main debates in contemporary philosophical egalitarianism is whether equality should be understood as 'an equal distribution of non-relational goods among individuals' or as 'a kind of social relation between persons'.[87] This debate concerning the nature of egalitarian justice is relevant to the analysis of comparability because it highlights the question 'what equality means for the way we relate to each other'.[88] This view is articulated in Elizabeth Anderson's article 'What is the Point of Equality', which suggests that mainstream egalitarianism 'fails the most fundamental test any egalitarian theory must meet: that is its principles express equal respect and concern for all citizens'.[89] From this starting point she argues that the aim of egalitarian justice is 'to end oppression which by definition is socially imposed' and 'to create a community in which people stand in relations of equality to others'.[90]

What is important is that the relational account of egalitarian social justice views 'unequal relationships' as 'a potential problem of justice in its own right'.[91] The critical edge of relational accounts of egalitarian social justice is directed towards the so-called responsibility-sensitive theories of distributive equality.[92] But the argument of equality as a 'normative ideal of human relations'[93] can also provide an alternative to the current 'relative' understanding of equality in discrimination law. Above all, the relational account of egalitarian social justice demonstrates that more attention should be directed at how the distributive principles are related to just and equal social relationships.[94] It is clear that

87 Eg E. Anderson, 'The Fundamental Disagreement between Luck Egalitarians and Relational Egalitarians', *Canadian Journal of Philosophy* 2012 (36), 1, 1. This controversy can also been described as uncertainty over whether inequalities are unjust because they are 'accidental', i.e. based on 'brute luck' or 'circumstances' or whether they are unjust by reflecting 'social hierarchies', 'domination' and 'oppression'. Ibid, 2.

88 C. Lake, *Equality and Responsibility*, Oxford, Oxford University Press, 2001, 87.

89 E. Anderson, 'What is the Point of Equality', *Ethics* 1999 (109), 287, 289. Anderson holds that equality is opposed to the undemocratic distribution of power that leads to oppression and hierarchies of social status. E. Anderson, *The Imperative of Integration*, Princeton, Princeton University Press, 2010, 21.

90 E. Anderson, 'What Is the Point of Equality', *l.c.*, 298.

91 C. Schemmel, 'Distributive and relational equality', *Politics, Philosophy & Economics* 2011 (11), 123, 125. This approach claims that the way in which people are treated is relevant to social justice as 'independent of, or at least not reducible to, the distributive effects of such treatment'. Ibid 125.

92 Most contemporary versions of liberal egalitarianism are concerned with neutralising the effect of what is called 'brute luck'. In brief, the liberal egalitarian ideal of equal opportunities promises to distinguish between unchosen circumstances for which people cannot be considered to be responsible and genuine choices for which people should bear full responsibility. For further discussion, see eg R. Dworkin, *Sovereign Virtue: The Theory and Practice of Equality*, Harvard, Harvard University Press, 2000.

93 S. Scheffler, *Equality and Tradition: Questions of Value in Moral and Political Philosophy*, Oxford, Oxford University Press, 2007, 234.

94 Ibid, 228. For Scheffler, this means that 'differing contingencies of individuals' situations' must be abstracted in so far as they 'claim equal rights as citizens' but that the 'interpretation

distributive principles may be 'instrumental to securing such relationships, follow from them, or even be constitutive of them'.[95] The central question for rethinking comparability from a relational perspective is therefore whether, and if so how, discrimination law can adopt distributive principles which value 'equal social relationships' more than the initial comparability. This emphasis on equal relationships finds an expression in the statement that equality is not only the 'concept that tells us that different treatment of people does matter' but it is also the 'concept that forces us to consider how society treats people in relationship to one another'.[96]

To sum up, the question of what distributive goals discrimination law can and should have is closely connected to the more general question of what social justice means in the context of discrimination law. The relational account of egalitarian social justice defends the idea that 'particular social and political relationships' are needed 'by justice on grounds of self-respect'.[97] This approach is important because it can provide an alternative to the 'relative' account of distribution in discrimination law. In particular, the 'relational' account of equality can modify the requirement of comparability, whether explicit, implicit, actual or hypothetical, by underlining that discrimination law plays a central role in regulating just and equal social relationships within society. The next section will complete the relational critique of comparability by considering how a relational understanding of equality could be used to revise the legal test for discrimination. It will be suggested that comparability is no longer defined solely by virtue of likeness but also by virtue of the right to equal social relations as protected in discrimination law.

4. TOWARDS A MORE RELATIONAL TEST FOR DISCRIMINATION?

The traditional anti-discrimination model focuses on the actual or hypothetical similarity or difference between two situations in deciding whether adverse treatment falls within the scope of one or several of the protected grounds (causal role) and whether discriminatory treatment is based on objective differences between two situations (justificatory role). The relational anti-discrimination model would focus on the differences in the applicant's ability to relate as an equal member of society and the role of adverse treatment in constraining this

---

and application of those rights will often depend on features of their individual circumstances'. Ibid 191–92.

95 Anderson (n 90) 314.

96 E. Chemirensky, 'In Defense of Equality: A Reply to Professor Westen', *Michigan Law Review* 1983 (81), 575, 585.

97 C. Schemmel, 'Why Relational Egalitarians Should Care About Distributions', *Social Theory and Practice* 2011 (37), 365, 366.

ability. Under this account, a person or group may suffer from discrimination if their ability to enter into just and equal societal relations with other members of society is diminished due to adverse trait-based treatment.[98] This explanation still leaves open the substantive question of what exactly it means to relate as an equal within society and/or enter into just and equal societal relations with other member of society. This is where anti-discrimination law and policies can benefit from a further dialogue with different accounts of egalitarian and non-egalitarian social justice.

Discrimination law can be described as 'a policy regulating inter-personal relationships'.[99] It has been noted that the 'interpersonal relations' of mutual recognition will often occur within different 'social structures' and 'institutional arrangements'.[100] Discrimination law can form one such 'institutionalized model' that regulates social interactions which maintain the subject's 'relation-to-self'[101] and to others. From a relational perspective, 'being treated as an equal' means that one is able to relate as an equal to other members of society. Shifting the focus of discrimination analysis to the 'equality of relationships' could therefore modify the legal test for discrimination as follows:

(1) *Causal use of comparability*: The relational approach does not necessarily remove the element of comparison from the discrimination analysis, but it changes the focus of relevant comparisons. The relational anti-discrimination model focuses on the question of how the applicant is able to relate in comparison to others. A relevant comparator is someone who can relate as an equal. This confirms that a comparator can also be the applicant him/herself 'but for' the adverse (trait-based) treatment.

(2) *Justificatory use of comparability*: The lack of comparability is often used as a justification for adverse treatment. In these situations, a relational perspective can provide a balancing factor within the reasonableness assessment. It may follow from this that those individual factors and circumstances that are argued to constitute an 'objective difference' may lose their relevance because the trait-based treatment in question would diminish the applicant's ability to relate as an equal.

(3) *Hypothetical comparability*: The relational approach to the discrimination analysis can also be understood as a revised version of hypothetical comparability. As noted above, a relevant hypothetical comparison can be

98 This principle can also explain discrimination when the list of protected grounds is open-ended. In these situations, the focus would be on whether the adverse treatment on the basis of the ground in question has negative effects on the person's ability to relate as an equal.

99 E.g. E. Muir, 'The Transformative Function of EU Equality Law', *European Review of Private Law* 2013 (5 & 6), 1231, 1231 and 1234.

100 H. Lopes and T. Calapez, 'The Relational Dimension of Identity – Theoretical and Empirical Exploration', *Review of Social Economy* 2012 (LXX), 81, 101.

101 A. Honneth, *The I and We: Studies in the Theory of Recognition*, Polity Press, 2012 206.

made in relation to how the applicant him/herself could relate with other members of society in the absence of adverse trait-based treatment.

(4) *Beyond discrimination*: The 'equality of relationships' principle can also provide more substance to what 'human dignity' means in the context of harassment and other prohibited forms of degrading treatment.

This chapter has suggested that protecting the ability to 'relate as an equal' can provide a more substantive distributive goal for anti-discrimination law and policies. The aim of this critical discussion was not to abandon comparisons but, as Susan Goldberg puts it, to view comparability analysis as 'one among a set of many imperfect methodological choices for seeing discrimination'.[102] The key to the relational test for discrimination is that having one or several of the protected grounds must not cause any loss in the ability to relate as an equal with other members of society. This approach can therefore be seen as an example of 'contextual' analysis of what constitutes discrimination.[103] It is clear that the court must still be able to prove that it is tackling discrimination instead of other forms of adverse treatment. A contextual approach to discrimination may open the door for more diverse discrimination claims, but it does not give a 'free pass' to them.[104] It is therefore important to further consider what it means to relate as an equal within society and how this depends on the chosen ideal of social justice.

An alternative approach would be to argue that anti-discrimination law and policies has no a priori distributive role and/or that other methods of policy making are more apt for social transformation. It has rightly been observed that 'one problem with anti-discrimination laws is that they insist upon the granting of relative rights, whereas some social ills (including even the structural disadvantage of group of individuals) may better be tackled by granting of absolute rights'.[105] This chapter nevertheless adopted a view that anti-discrimination law can play an important role in creating, shaping, and maintaining those social relationships in which social inclusion is actualised. From this starting point, the relational account of equality can provide a more inclusive approach to when adverse treatment constitutes prohibited discrimination without granting an absolute right to equal treatment. Moreover, the relational account of equality can also make the discrimination analysis more susceptible to societal power-relations in so far as the constitution of relevant subjectivity under discrimination law is concerned. It follows from this that anti-discrimination law and policies can provide one, but clearly not the only, tool for realising the democratic ideal of egalitarian social justice.

---

102 Goldberg (n 57) 809.

103 Ibid, 803.

104 Ibid, 811.

105 B. De Witte, 'From a "Common Principle of Equality" to "European Antidiscrimination Law"', *American Behavioral Scientist* 2010 (53), 1715, 1725.

5. CONCLUSION

This chapter considered how rethinking equality in more relational terms could reconcile anti-discrimination law with the wider objectives of social justice. It first explained how comparability as one of the key concepts of discrimination law is a dynamic legal tool which takes both explicit and implicit forms. The case law of the Court of Justice of the EU was used to demonstrate that the issue of 'similarity vs. difference' often lies at the heart of the discrimination analysis and the legal right to non-discrimination and equal treatment is dependent on demonstrating either actual or hypothetical comparability between two situations. The chapter first argued that the potential of discrimination law to advance social justice is hindered by the narrow and assimilationist view of subjectivity that arises from the requirement of comparability. It then moved on to examine how a more relational conception of equality could offer a new perspective on the current tension between discrimination law and social policy

The distinction between the 'relative' and 'relational' account of equality underpinned the analysis of comparability in the last two sections of the chapter. The requirement of comparability is rooted in the 'relative' concept of equality which fails to adequately take into account the relational nature of social reality. A brief insight into the democratic ideal of egalitarian social justice supported the argument about the 'relational' concept of equality, which can be used to rethink the requirement of comparability and which will therefore have more potential to accommodate the aims of social policy within anti-discrimination law, including social inclusion and diversity. Finally, the chapter briefly discussed what practical implications this shift from a 'relative' to a 'relational' account of equality would have for the discrimination analysis. It concluded that a revised substantive test for discrimination will need to address the question of how discrimination law as a social institution enables and inhibits just and equal relationships between individuals and social groups.

www.ingramcontent.com/pod-product-compliance
Ingram Content Group UK Ltd.
Pitfield, Milton Keynes, MK11 3LW, UK
UKHW051922100926
8556IPUK00021B/1333